D0757917

IRONY AND AUTHORITY IN ROMANTIC POETRY

Irony and Authority in Romantic Poetry

David Simpson

First published 1979 by
THE MACMILLAN PRESS LTD
London and Basingstoke
Associated companies in Delhi
Dublin Hong Kong Johannesburg Lagos
Melbourne New York Singapore Tokyo

Printed in Great Britain by

BILLING AND SONS LTD
Guildford, Worcester and London

British Library Cataloguing in Publication Data

Simpson, David
  Irony and authority in Romantic
  poetry
  1. English poetry – 19th century –
  History and Criticism 2. Romanticism
  I. Title
  821'.7'09   PR590

  ISBN 0–333–25910–6

For Charles, Christiane, and
Richard Simpson

Contents

Illustrations

The illustrations 'The Little Boy Lost' and 'The Little Boy Found' on pp. 50 and 51 are reproduced from the W copy of *Songs of Innocence and Experience* with the permission of the Provost and Fellows of King's College, Cambridge.

Preface

This book is about Romantic poetry, and in particular those features of it which relate to what we have come to call 'hermeneutics'. I hope that those already familiar with the arguments around this term will permit me to say something about my sense of its place here; such readers, in fact, might well prefer to read my final chapter first, reversing a sequence of presentation which they may recognise as pseudo-inductive. For the 'hermeneutic circle' operates on the paradox of past and present, part and whole, whereby each is seen only through the other. We 'read' a text, it suggests—and this 'text' can be an event in history—but the *order* which that text will compose is already latent within us as some kind of preconception. Because we only see this order as it is experienced, we can never see it from a critical distance, never comment upon it as an 'object'; thus we cannot ever achieve a theoretical command over its 'origins', which are posited simultaneously in past *and* present. The very idea of an origin, it must be noted, implies investment in the model of cause and effect (i.e. a historical sequence), a model which can only be applied to the experience of simultaneity by disrupting it with a conscious imposition of priorities. There is a very important modern critical argument around this issue, but my purpose here is, paradoxically, to try to demonstrate its own 'origins', or at least presence, within Romantic aesthetics. I believe that the Romantics were aware of exactly the problems we now discuss under the heading of 'hermeneutics' and that they used the paradoxes implicit in them to fashion a discourse based on transference, repetition, and the 'double bind'.

Romanticism, according to this argument, conceived and exploited and perhaps suffered the radical instability of the 'self', the fragility of the autonomous ego; and this instability seems both to have been inherited as a philosophical proposition and at the same time to have been presented as an ethical imperative, part of the polemic against authority, over self as over others. Causality is replaced by simultaneity as 'history' is threatened by hermeneutics;

and this simultaneity ultimately, I believe, came to be extended
from author to reader as a demand for moral self-determination. For
causality is ultimately a myth of authority, as Blake well knew; and to
adhere to a myth of causality at the same time as admitting that its
depths are impossible to fathom is a myth of despair.

But simultaneity had problems of its own, both at the level of
experience and at the level of talking about experience. If it is known
as and *only* as it is acted or performed, how do we relate it to other
parts and aspects of experience which give it a context? And, as a
problem for poetic communication, how do we talk 'about' it, given
that there seems to be no privileged language in which to do so? These
are the problems which I shall spend most of my time talking about,
and it will doubtless seem that I am presenting a rather negative
version of Romanticism. In fact, positive and negative are inseparable, and often present themselves as movements about a 'zero' point
of synthesis which is only ever tentatively occupied. Kant introduced
the necessity of the synthesis of concept and intuition largely to
combat materialism, and Hegel found that he had to move the
balance back again to rescue empirical experience from the contempt
of the idealists. I think that the 'negative' side of the Romantic
equation has not had its fair share of recognition. We may be missing
something of importance if we move straight to the epiphanies which
it may yet provide without the working through of that negativity.
Blake is preoccupied with the imagery of pain, for there is no coming
together without taking apart.

This preoccupation with the 'hermeneutic' aspects of Romantic
aesthetics generates, of course, a peculiar paradox. How can I make a
case for the historical origins or presence of this syndrome without
falling into the traps which the syndrome itself sets up for me? How
can I 'discover' the historical incidence of a problem within which, if
we take it in good faith, I must still be trapped? There is no logical
answer to this problem; as far as I can see, it is a true paradox. But
there is some prospect of relief from it in the evidence itself, the
'words' which the poets wrote down. Of course, I may be pre-
selecting them in certain motivated ways as I decide what does and
does not constitute 'evidence'. But if the problem stands, then it
stands for us all, and it will be up to every reader to test out his
suspicions of (or agreement with) this pre-selection against his own
'readings'. This can only be done by the *act* of reading; and this itself is
the moment of transference, in finer tones or otherwise, which the
poets also employ.

E. D. Hirsch Jnr., most recently in *The Aims of Interpretation*, has argued forcefully against what he sees as the alternatives of despair and anarchistic joyance which result from a complete and literal acceptance of the paradox of the 'hermeneutic circle'. He believes that such an acceptance threatens the whole foundation of humanistic culture, education, and institutional life. But these three things need not go together. It seems to me, for example, that the Romantics were very concerned with the first two, in their own ways, and very suspicious of the third. We can have culture and education based on continually asking fundamental questions, and some kinds of institutional forms can be seen to inhibit this kind of questioning by pretending to have found the answers already. Thus, when Hirsch asks us to break the circle by having faith in the possibility of reconstructing 'authorial meaning' (p. 8), I can only answer that that is exactly what I think I am doing. I think that I am respecting the 'original meanings' of these poets when I find them to be discouraging or qualifying this very quest. Instead, we are urgently pressured to find meaning for ourselves, in a region where we can perhaps perform or experience a conviction of shared intention but can never 'describe' it. An extreme version of this isolation is the relationship of the Kierkegaardian believer to his God; another version is the relationship of love as it appears in Blake. Romanticism does not always deny the social contract, although it always questions it; and it always re-establishes what it accepts.

The argument is, then, that Romantic poetry is organised to make us confront the question of authority, especially as it pertains to the contract between author and reader. This must simultaneously question what critics have tended to rely on as the 'historical' method, just as it questions my own claim to be historical. How, for example, is the reader of 1798 to be distinguished from the reader of 1978? The answer is another question: 'which reader of 1798, and for which reader of 1978?' I think that this is a serious question. We cannot assume that in passively receiving and speaking forth a historical past we are doing something more secure than simply reifying it. The message I receive from these poets is that they were very uneasy about the availability of this very habit; a habit which may look like self-effacement but which cannot properly be so until it has passed through self-recognition. Again, we are back to a moment of choice.

But perhaps this is a tedious way of explaining why I have not given carefully constructed accounts of the reaction to the French Revolution, or a properly documented consideration of the reviews and the reviewers. Let me stress that I do not think these things unimportant; it is simply that one can only write one book at a time. It may well be, for example, that the rather esoteric explorations of self-focussing revolutions which these writers offer have much to do with the repressive legislation and draconian censorship introduced during the Revolutionary and Napoleonic Wars. The ethical reservations which they project about their own tendencies towards authority, combined with the high sense of urgency about passing on those reservations, may after all be part of a sophisticated self-protection, producing a version of 'revolution' which is permissible precisely because personal, because unorganised in the social sense. In this context we would wish to examine the peculiar concept of immanent and gradually ameliorating 'truth' as it is presented in Godwin and Schiller. I hope that what follows may stimulate others to explore this and other such questions.

I must, however, explain briefly what I mean by 'irony' in what follows. I do not mean that if a writer says 'X' we are to understand that he means 'Y'; this would be the stable notion of irony, irony as definitive statement, which does not seem to me to have much place in Romanticism. The situation as I see it is that, if a writer says 'X', then we question the meaning of what he says both as we receive it into our own codes and canons of significance and as it relates to the context of the rest of his utterances, their moods and voices. This double focus is likely to produce a paradox of the hermeneutic sort; how are we to be sure where one begins and the other ends? This is Romantic irony.

The question of influences is not one to be taken lightly by any student of the Romantics, and if I am able to assert that there are no conscious plagiarisms in what follows, then I must at the same time admit to the conviction that there are a great many assimilations from what Shelley called the 'spirit of the age'. I sense much common interest between my own work and that of Geoffrey Hartman and Paul de Man, though this was largely discovered in retrospect. From Harold Bloom I have borrowed the term 'misprision' and have given it, as if in homage to his own theory as expressed in *Poetry and Repression: Revisionism from Blake to Stevens* (pp. 1–27), a new twist of meaning, attributing it not to the poet in his tradition but to one side of the Wordsworthian mind in the act of perception itself, and in its relation to a prior creation. For I believe that Wordsworth still had an investment in the idea of the 'noumenal' core of phenomena, in 'things in themselves', and that this generated an anxiety about misrepresentation. Thus, when I describe the Romantic idea of perception as fundamentally 'phenomenalist', I mean to include the qualification suggested by Michael G. Cooke, *The Romantic Will* (p. 234 n. 1), that the world may include 'a distinct and perhaps definitive organization in every sense precedent to man, and strictly tending to co-opt him'. This does to my mind speak for an anxiety felt by Wordsworth, and it points to an explanation for the necessity of interference (to preclude passivity) as well as of the guilt which tended to follow such interference (now seen as over-activity). There will undoubtedly be those who do not care for this version of Wordsworth, and such readers could not do better than to consult Albert O. Wlecke, *Wordsworth and the Sublime*, a book which I discovered after finishing my own, and which offers conclusions exactly opposite to mine. Wlecke argues that the 'sublime' represents for Wordsworth a transcendental fusion of the intentional act and the intended object, producing a positive state of selflessness in which all ethical discomfort is redundant. My own perspective, for the poems which I discuss, is that Wordsworth always retains a lingering faith in the 'ego' he would thus be losing, and in its corollary the 'pure' object; that he is committed to dualism even as he celebrates coadunation. I think that this was Blake's reading of Wordsworth.

I have preserved misspellings and oddities of punctuation in all passages quoted; most obviously so in Keats's prose. Because I have cited and referred to rather a large number of sources, I have in general used only short titles for citations. Full details are given in the bibliography. Further, I have sometimes noted the work of other critics where it has only a peripheral or even antithetical bearing on my own, in order that those readers who might wish to follow up a point or a debate can do so. Documentation of certain parts of what follows might be thought to be too full; again, this is because I imagine that different readers will want to follow up different things, and I have tried to assist this process as fully as possible.

Finally there are debts to be acknowledged. Arthur Sale's articulate disbelief and friendly opposition was an invaluable stimulus for thinking about Keats. Donald Mackinnon gave me much encouragement at an early stage of research, along with a good deal of his time; and John Beer has responded patiently, carefully, and generously to a host of small inquiries along the way. Robert Gleckner was kind enough to send me an offprint of one of his papers, and the editor of *Studies in Romanticism* has allowed me to re-employ in revised form parts of an earlier paper on Keats. Dan Brown and Frank Kermode lent me a room to write in at an important time. I must also thank Mr and Mrs Eugene Power and the Master and Fellows of Magdalene College, Cambridge, for a very important year spent at the University of Michigan. Theodore Redpath, William Walsh, and the anonymous reader for the Macmillan Press have all made valuable suggestions for amendment and inclusion; and Margaret Clayton read a specimen chapter and provided further ideas and advice. Peter Croft has been extremely helpful in allowing access to the Blake material in the library of King's College, and in organising photography. John Barrell, who saw this work through its doctoral career, proved to be a model of 'authority' in offering no interference and demanding no attendance, at the same time as being scrupulously attentive and responsive when I have needed his help. I would have been much slower in coming to an understanding of the Romantics had not John Wright refused to answer certain questions; this is one of the greatest debts of all. Finally, friends have given more than they can know, or would accept any credit for; Kathy Wheeler, Bruce Keeling, Maureen Corcoran, Irma Liberty, David Kohn, Brian Davis, and many others. See you in Jerusalem.

D.E.S.
King's College
Cambridge
May 1978

1 The Urn Overwrought

ODE ON A GRECIAN URN

I

Thou still unravished bride of quietness,
Thou foster-child of silence and slow time,
Silvan historian, who canst thus express
A flowery tale more sweetly than our rhyme!
What leaf-fringed legend haunts about thy shape   5
Of deities or mortals, or of both,
In Tempe or the dales of Arcady?
What men or gods are these? What maidens loth?
What mad pursuit? What struggle to escape?
What pipes and timbrels? What wild ecstasy?   10

II

Heard melodies are sweet, but those unheard
Are sweeter; therefore, ye soft pipes, play on;
Not to the sensual ear, but, more endeared,
Pipe to the spirit ditties of no tone.
Fair youth beneath the trees, thou canst not leave   15
Thy song, nor ever can those trees be bare;
Bold lover, never, never canst thou kiss,
Though winning near the goal—yet do not grieve:
She cannot fade, though thou hast not thy bliss,
For ever wilt thou love, and she be fair!   20

III

Ah, happy, happy boughs, that cannot shed
Your leaves, nor ever bid the spring adieu;

And, happy melodist, unwearièd,
For ever piping songs for ever new!
More happy love, more happy, happy love!   25
For ever warm and still to be enjoyed,—
For ever panting, and for ever young—
All breathing human passion far above,
That leaves a heart high-sorrowful and cloyed,
A burning forehead, and a parching tongue.   30

IV

Who are these coming to the sacrifice?
To what green altar, O mysterious priest,
Lead'st thou that heifer lowing at the skies,
And all her silken flanks with garlands dressed?
What little town by river or sea shore,   35
Or mountain-built with peaceful citadel,
Is emptied of this folk, this pious morn?
And, little town, thy streets for evermore
Will silent be; and not a soul to tell
Why thou art desolate can e'er return.   40

V

O Attic shape! Fair attitude! With brede
Of marble men and maidens overwrought,
With forest branches and the trodden weed—
Thou, silent form, dost tease us out of thought
As doth eternity. Cold pastoral!   45
When old age shall this generation waste,
Thou shalt remain, in midst of other woe
Than ours, a friend to man, to whom thou say'st,
'Beauty is truth, truth beauty'—that is all
Ye know on earth, and all ye need to know.   50

LA BELLE DAME SANS MERCI
(the first version)

I

Oh, what can ail thee, knight-at-arms,
Alone and palely loitering?
The sedge has withered from the lake,
And no birds sing!

II

Oh, what can ail thee, knight-at-arms,   5
So haggard and so woe-begone?
The squirrel's granary is full,
And the harvest's done.

III

I see a lily on thy brow,
With anguish moist and fever-dew,   10
And on thy cheek a fading rose
Fast withereth too.

IV

I met a lady in the meads
Full beautiful, a fairy's child,
Her hair was long, her foot was light,   15
And her eyes were wild.

V

I made a garland for her head,
And bracelets too, and fragrant zone;
She looked at me as she did love,
And made sweet moan.   20

VI

I set her on my pacing steed,
And nothing else saw all day long;
For sidelong would she bend, and sing
A fairy's song.

VII

She found me roots of relish sweet,   25
And honey wild, and manna dew;
And sure in language strange she said,
'I love thee true'.

VIII

She took me to her elfin grot,
And there she wept, and sighed full sore,   30
And there I shut her wild wild eyes
With kisses four.

IX

And there she lullèd me asleep,
And there I dreamed—Ah! woe betide!—
The latest dream I ever dreamed   35
On the cold hill side.

X

I saw pale kings, and princes too,
Pale warriors, death-pale were they all;
They cried—'La belle Dame sans merci
Hath thee in thrall!'   40

XI

I saw their starved lips in the gloam
With horrid warning gapèd wide,
And I awoke, and found me here
On the cold hill side.

XII

And this is why I sojourn here,   45
Alone and palely loitering,
Though the sedge is withered from the lake,
And no birds sing.

LA BELLE DAME SANS MERCI
(the '*Indicator*' version)

I

Ah, what can ail thee, wretched wight,
Alone and palely loitering;
The sedge is withered from the lake,
And no birds sing.

II

Ah, what can ail thee, wretched wight,   5
So haggard and so woe-begone?
The squirrel's granary is full,
And the harvest's done.

III

I see a lily on thy brow,
With anguish moist and fever dew;   10
And on thy cheek a fading rose
Fast withereth too.

IV

I met a Lady in the meads
Full beautiful, a fairy's child;
Her hair was long, her foot was light,   15
And her eyes were wild.

V

I set her on my pacing steed,
And nothing else saw all day long;
For sideways would she lean, and sing
A fairy's song.   20

VI

I made a garland for her head,
And bracelets too, and fragrant zone;
She looked at me as she did love,
And made sweet moan.

VII

She found me roots of relish sweet,   25
And honey wild, and manna dew;
And sure in language strange she said,
I love thee true.

VIII

She took me to her elfin grot,
And there she gazed and sighèd deep,   30
And there I shut her wild sad eyes—
So kissed to sleep.

IX

And there we slumbered on the moss,
And there I dreamed—ah, woe betide—
The latest dream I ever dreamed   35
On the cold hill side.

X

I saw pale kings, and princes too,
Pale warriors, death-pale were they all;
Who cried—'La belle Dame sans mercy
Hath thee in thrall!'   40

XI

I saw their starved lips in the gloom
With horrid warning gapèd wide,
And I awoke, and found me here
On the cold hill side.

XII

And this is why I sojourn here   45
Alone and palely loitering
Though the sedge is withered from the lake,
And no birds sing.

My initial approach will seem somewhat oblique, moving as it does
through a poem which many have written about, Keats's 'Ode on a
Grecian Urn', and passing on to one which very few critics have taken
seriously, 'La Belle Dame Sans Merci'. I shall try to suggest that these
popular and esoteric voices can be viewed together in a more
meaningful way than the mere ulterior fusion of images, the 'sedge
shaded urn',[1] would indicate, and that in this synoptic approach there
lies a clue to one of the hitherto 'unwritten' areas of the history of
Romanticism.

The distinction is paradoxical to begin with, for the 'popularity' of
the first poem has not exhausted its meaning, nor succeeded in
positioning it as anything more than a notorious enigma within the
exegetical tradition. The experience of the critic before the poem
seems to have been very much that of the poem's narrator before the
urn itself; puzzlement, insecure insight, and thwarted philosophical
ambition. I hope that what follows will offer some justification of this
instability, or at least some explanation of the terms of the confusion.
At the same time, it will seem that the comparative unpopularity of
the second poem, and in particular of the yet further distanced second
version of that poem, might be the consequence of a purposeful
blindness, a determined sidestepping, a withering from the edge of a
problem whose terms are inevitably disturbing to the mind in its
normative state, wherein it is disposed to preserve a stable personal
identity.[2] What is overtly dramatised in this poem offers, I think,
some clues toward finding a 'meaning' for the 'Ode', some
contributions to that precise delineation of its ironies and paradoxes
which has never yet been achieved—and possibly never will be—but
which remains, in a repetition of its narrator's own drama, the

unspoken goal of all critical ravishing, even when it accepts indeterminacy as its own basic premise.

I hope it will not seem necessary to resurrect the entire body of material which has grown from and around the 'Ode on a Grecian Urn'.[3] As a starting point, it may be said that criticism, perhaps as a consequence of its own historical needs as much as of any imperative towards ultimate truths, seems to be moving to a position whereby the poem is interpreted through the hypothesis of a 'speaker' or 'dramatic' persona, who is held at a distance from the 'poet' whom we conceive to be behind the whole artifact.[4] I have suggested elsewhere that this controlling persona, whom we shall call the 'poet', can be seen to exercise a parodic or ironic overview, placing in a critical light the attempts of the speaker to cull meaning and moral guidance from the silent object before him.[5] As such, the poet would seem to provide that level of heightened self-consciousness and stable positioning which we now tend to call 'metalanguage' or 'metacommentary'.[6] The process of recognising this overview implicitly involves the reading mind in a confrontation with and refinement of its own intentions and ambitions. It is the violent fluctuation between the speaker's various responses to the urn—from the opening curiosity, through an almost pompous benediction ('therefore, ye soft pipes, play on') and apparent empathy (stanza III), to outraged dismissal ('Cold pastoral!')—which warns us that this perspective might not be wholly endorsed by the poet behind him; perhaps we are not to empathise with this hectic rise and fall of the pleasure thermometer without some retraction of good faith. The extravagance and preciosity of the puns seems another pointer, for example the 'leaf-fringed legend' (5) and the 'brede' (41). Could there be a double reading of 'flowery tale' (4), with the poet reading 'florid' where the speaker intends 'floral', in a superimposition of metacomment upon comment?[7] And what about the lurching assonances of '. . . sensual ear . . . endeared' (13) and 'O Attic shape! Fair attitude!' (41)?[8] Does not the 'trodden weed' (43) have something of the resounding thump of Cowper's 'constant flail', the swaggering, even ironic precision of standard eighteenth-century poetic diction? Enough to suggest, perhaps, that 'overwrought' (42) points to another convergence of comment and metacomment, wherein the speaker as well as the figures on the urn are over-excited, over-crafted, as Keats described himself becoming 'overwrought' in the composition of 'Endymion' (Letters, I, 146).

The third stanza must be the crux in any decision about the

viability of a consciously distanced 'speaker' for the poem. The polarities have already been expressed in the two most suggestive accounts of the 'Ode', those of Brooks and Wasserman. Where Wasserman wants to locate the repetition of 'happy' in the context of eighteenth-century philology as a serious expression of the 'summum bonum' (*The Finer Tone*, pp. 22—3), thus reading the stanza as the height of empathic abandon wherein 'the subject is engaging in the life of the predicate' (p. 31), Brooks finds in it the highest development of irony and paradox in the entire poem. He sees the protagonist as giving way to 'a tendency to linger over the scene sentimentally' (*The Well-Wrought Urn*, p. 145).[9] Perhaps both these possibilities can be seen together, from the perspectives of speaker and poet respectively, within the model of a 'double consciousness'.

There is some evidence, indeed, that the very genre of the ode might have been regarded by Keats as exactly the medium for this sort of fragmentation of personal identity. Hugh Blair's *Lectures on Rhetoric and Belles Lettres*, an inordinately popular work in the later part of the eighteenth century, speaks of the ode as the most ancient poetic form, close to music:

> Hence, that neglect of regularity, those digressions, and that disorder which it is supposed to admit; and which, indeed, most Lyric Poets have not failed sufficiently to exemplify in their practice (III, 138).

He goes on:

> . . . the Poet, when he begins to write an Ode, if he has any real warmth of genius, is apt to deliver himself up to it, without controul or restraint . . . He gets up into the clouds; becomes so abrupt in his transitions; so eccentric and irregular in his motions, and of course so obscure, that we essay in vain to follow him, or to partake of his raptures (190).

Coleridge has some harsh words to address to the writers of a certain class of odes, when he writes of 'the madness prepense of pseudo-poesy, or the startling *hysteric* of weakness over-exerting itself, which bursts on the unprepared reader in sundry odes and apostrophes to abstract terms.'[10] I find it hard to subscribe to the myth of Keats as the purveyor of 'aesthetic' experience at the expense of conscious control, although I am content to see the two side by side. If the comments of Blair and Coleridge represent a climate of critical opinion of which Keats was aware, then I would want to argue a case for his exploiting this licence and turning it against itself, and against any incautious reader who might meekly invest in the credibility of the speaker's voice.

The speaker's perspective is to be seen as limited, then, I think. Such a view goes some way towards explaining the imagery of sexual violation which opens the poem. The gesture of appropriation which the speaker seeks to enact is very much one of ravishing, as the intentional faculty, that centre-piece of the phenomenalist's vocabulary, is shown as an aggressor, an ungenerous digestor of free standing things in the world. This is a crime, indeed, against the wise passiveness of 'negative capability', wherein one exercises an unstrenuous participation in the lives of urns and sparrows.[11] Such a view also seems to involve us in a privileged alliance with the poet as the overseer and the provider of metacommentary, in that he is established within the fictional strategy as endorsing the message of the urn itself, and its rebuke of the speaker. To put things this way, of course, involves us in the thorny question of how the last lines are to be read. My interpretation demands the priority of one reading over others, at least at the present stage of the argument, but I wish to allow for a secondary measure of indeterminacy, for reasons which will later be made clear. The prior reading is that the message of the urn comes within the verdict of the poet's voice, which begins five lines from the end of the poem; and I must emphasise that this poet/speaker division is for the moment strictly a descriptive convenience, so that we could as well attribute the change of tone to the speaker at a higher level of self-consciousness.[12] Because poet and urn are in accord here, it does not much matter whether the entire last two lines, or just the aphorism itself, are 'spoken' by the urn; the poet is speaking 'for' the urn. That is to say, in the one case, the 'Ye' (50) would refer to mankind at large, and to the speaker in particular, and in the other it would denote the urn itself; though of course we must recognise the differentiation from the 'thou' of ll. 47–8, which to my mind makes the first reading the obvious one. But since the sufficiency of the urn's message is endorsed by the poet and held up as an example to mankind, the two readings can be held together, and I would argue that the hint of indeterminacy which is incorporated into these lines can be seen as part of their 'meaning'. The 'Ye' can denote both mankind (the speaker) and the urn at the level of 'sense', despite the oddity of an urn being able to 'know' and the differentiation from the 'thou' at the level of grammar; for the poet seems to be speaking for both urn and audience, and the act of knowing can only be a mediated synthesis of perceiver and perceived, as we shall see. There seems little doubt, however, that the aphorism is validated by being set against the fury and the mire of the speaker's ambitions, the 'irritable reaching after fact & reason' (*Letters*, I, 193). As we disdain poetry which has 'a palpable design upon us', so we resent the speaker for his designs upon the urn, his refusal to remain 'great & unobtrusive' (*ibid.*, 224).[13]

I shall now try to introduce a turn in the argument, one which will serve, if commentary be permitted such moments, to overturn the overt urn. The strategy described above clearly depends upon a certainty that the urn 'exists', that it is there in all its stillness and eternity as a viable alternative to the frantic interest of the speaker. It is now generally accepted by scholars and critics, however, that there was no specific 'urn' behind the poem. Far from being a specific museum piece, Keats's urn seems to have been a composite creation, made up out of a synthesis of various classical objects which he had seen and admired.[14] It looks, then, as if Keats deliberately created the fiction of a 'real' urn in order to distance his poetic persona from the speaker; to provide, in other words, the fixed level of metacommentary which enables the speaker's behaviour to be seen in a critical, ironic light, and which further achieves an element of closure in the experience of reading the poem. It will already be apparent that critics have always sensed this closure to be of dubious integrity—hence the squabbles over who says what to whom—and indeed it is the very emphasis which these lines seem to demand which causes so much anxiety. The case has been well put by Barbara Herrnstein Smith in *The Poetics of Closure: a Study of How Poems End* (p. 195):

> . . . if Keats had deliberately set himself to construct the most securely closed poem ever written, he could hardly have bettered them. They are all there: verbal repetitions, monosyllabic diction, metrical regularity, formal parallelism, unqualified absolutes, closural allusions, and the oracular assertion of an utter and ultimate verity. And yet it is an open question whether or not these lines offer a poetically legitimate or effective resolution to the thematic structure of the entire ode.

In terms of our argument, it would seem that Keats, in providing a strong closure where a weaker one—or none at all— would suffice, is forcing a rift, trying to upset the 'single state' of any reader who might tend to enact a synthesis of the various contraries within the poem as part of the process of reading. For such a reader, this synthesis would be a precondition of intelligibility; he would be looking for a voice which could speak for a coherent personality, one into which he could comfortably read himself. Without placing the argument on the level of conscious intentionalities, however, it is worth asking whether there might not be some clues to be gathered from Keats's invention of a 'real' urn. This invention speaks for a predicament exactly opposite to that of the speaker. Whereas the speaker is forced to recognise that the world will not respond to his desires and designs, Keats has already gone through the business of creating that world: this urn. His famous maxim, that 'every mental pursuit takes its reality and worth from the ardour of the pursuer' (*Letters*, I, 242), while seeming to contradict the implicit critical presentation of the speaker, who is nothing if not ardent, is at the same time applicable to the poet's prior invention of the 'real' urn.

I shall now try to apply this information to the end of the poem. It will be apparent from what has already been said that the overdetermined closure itself contains a suppressed cyclic imperative, demanding re-reading and reconstruction in the attempt to justify the pseudo-finality of those lines. Wasserman seems to sense just this when he says that 'the drama seems to have taken us on a perilous journey only to return us to the point from which we started' (*The Finer Tone*, p. 47). Going back to the beginning, we find that the opening lines offer not two but at least three paraphrastic options. First, there is the sense of 'still and unravished'; secondly, there is the a priori reading 'as yet unravished, but I, in this reading, hope to achieve just that'; and thirdly, there is the a posteriori reading which is a retrospective summary of our experience of the whole poem, available in the memory or on a second or subsequent reading, which indicates that the most recent attempt at violation has failed. The first two options are available to a single reading, in the context of a 'closed' form, but the third only arises when we respond to the cyclic imperative.[15] The ambiguity which is first apparent promises us an isolated incident of fictional experience, wherein we are implicitly treating the poem as an 'object', thus repeating exactly the behaviour of the speaker even before we have recognised it. The third option commits us to a process in time, where no false objectification of meaning is possible, and 'being' comes to consist only in a continual becoming.

It could be argued that our dissatisfaction with the 'closure' of the poem duplicates exactly the drama which Keats has covered over in himself by hypostatising a real urn. This invented reality seems to function as a wish-fulfilment, enabling Keats to create an ironic distance between the 'poet' who utters the last lines and the speaker of the rest of the poem. The speaker's impatience with the intractable quiddity of the urn begins to look like dramatic self-justification on Keats's part, as the drama which must have gone into creating the urn is reflected back, in an inverted manner, on to the speaker. The urn appears as everything which the speaker is not, in a sort of negative justification of its identity. As soon as the 'real' urn is displaced, however, we can see that the creative predicament is really closer to that of the speaker than to that of the 'poet'; it is one where meaning does only come with the ardour of the pursuer, as things which are no-things take on life in the active imagination of the beholder.[16] The efforts of the speaker thus become a repetition of the artist's pursuit. The two personae come together, and what is being interrogated is nothing less than the creative process itself, providing Keats with a 'product' which he can then use to reflect back upon his own striving. Perhaps this recognition of Keats's own struggle is hinted at by John Jones, in his *John Keats's Dream of Truth*, when he says that the poet 'wants to *write* a Grecian Urn' (p. 220); it is certainly touched upon by Spitzer when he suggests that the uncertainty of the final punctuations reveals 'the hesitations of the poet in regard to the relationship of the aphorism to the rest of the legend' (p. 222). Keats in his public voice said very little about this poem, and gave no hint that the urn might have been anything other than a 'single' one. It is as if some profound and even unconscious honesty is making him refuse himself, and his readers, the relief of an absolute closure, at the very moment of suggesting one. If we see the two personae coming together at this level, then we can readmit Walter Evert's reading (see note 13 above), excluded earlier in the cause of expository clarity, as at least a possibility among the other possibilities.[17]

What is here preserved as a structural principle is close to the literally expressed scepticism of the preface to 'Endymion', which describes that poem as 'denoting a feverish attempt, rather than a deed accomplished' (*Poems*, p. 119). The great 'Ode' seems to do both things; it contains the attempt within the deed, and brings the two together. This oscillation, I think, remained with Keats for the rest of his life. He could write in good faith that 'the sense of Beauty overcomes every other consideration, or rather obliterates all consideration' (*Letters*, I, 194), but this applies to 'a great poet', which he was, thankfully, never sure that he was. Writing to Fanny Brawne towards the end of his life, he speaks as a voice within a voice:

'If I should die,' said I to myself, 'I have left no immortal work behind me—nothing to make my friends proud of my memory—but I have lov'd the principle of beauty in all things, and if I had had time I would have made myself remember'd.' (*Letters*, II, 263)

I take this voice very seriously, borne out as it is in the structure of the poem, in the similarity-within-difference of the two personae. The urn is made real because real things bring with them a sense of certainty, a spurring up into action, as opposed to imaginary things which, like imaginary grievances, 'nail a man down for a sufferer, as on a cross' (*ibid.*, 181). Yet the famous notion of 'negative capability' has to do with 'remaining content with half knowledge' (*Letters*, I, 194), and this is what speaker and poet must both learn. The speaker learns by the poet's rebuke, and the poet learns through the intransigent mystery of his 'own' creation, and its refusal to allow him to escape with the illusion of an achieved metacommentary. It is the drama which the voice of the 'poet' seems to cover over—thereby in fact revealing it—which I find to be yet more starkly expressed in the poem I shall now turn to, 'La Belle Dame Sans Merci'.

I shall concentrate to begin with on the problem of establishing the personae in the poem. Perhaps the most natural assumption would be that the first three stanzas are spoken by the questioner, with the rest of the poem representing the reply of the 'wretched wight'; this is Wasserman's reading (*The Finer Tone*, p. 78). This seems a reasonable beginning, since the poem begins interrogatively, and the fourth stanza arrives as the most obviously 'meaningful' way of filling the gap, answering the question. Our first reading, if I may hypostatise such an event as a mode of explanation, leads us through the poem on this assumption, though within it we are at once aware that the protagonist is unsure of the exact status of his vision /experience, and of his capacity to induce or receive it again. At the end, he is either rendered inert and unable to move from the spot by some external force, or he is waiting in the hope that something will occur to resolve his doubts. We do not know whether this passivity is the result of compulsion or conscious decision, but it does seem that the context provides no indication that his problem is about to be solved through any agency in the ordinary natural world; the sedge is withered and there is no birdsong. Whereas the speaker of the other poem is frustrated by the refusal of the object to respond to his ambitious curiosity, the 'wretched wight' is not even sure that he has an object; and in this he is close to the position which we have argued as that of Keats himself, after the urn has been dislodged from its self-evident 'reality'. Along with the disappearance of overtly real stimuli, we lose the almost witty positioning of the speaker by the poet, or—as the distinction is slightly different in this case—of one persona by the other.[18] Further, the overdetermination of closure is less developed. The last stanza does seem to be presented as a conclusion ('And this is why I sojourn here'), but the cyclic imperative is clear in the exact repetition of the opening lines, and in the complete absence of determinate explanation preceding the demonstrative clause. The dream, for example, seems to have told us who the lady 'is', but there is no ontological certainty involved in this particular proper name, announced as it is in an ambiguous foreign language and referring us back only to the enigma of the poem's title—a repetition for the reader of the protagonist's own problem of cognition.

I have suggested an initial division of the stanzas between two speakers, in the ratio of 3:9. At the same time, however, the parallelisms between the opening lines of the stanzas seem to suggest a division in the ratio of 2:4:2:1:2:1. Stanzas III to VI all begin with 'I' clauses, thus introducing a pattern which seems to bridge the gap which we have wished to introduce between stanzas III and IV.[19] This parallelism points to a suspension which is both epistemological and ontological. It refuses to reinforce or make clear the boundaries between one self and another, and at the same time removes any sure means of establishing relationships between subject and object, inner and outer.[20] Even if this particular implication goes by comfortably enough on a first reading, its centrality is emphasised by the incidence of other such suspensions at other points in the poem where there might seem to be a possibility of clear distinctions being made. Keats's use of the word 'met' (13), for example, may well touch upon the Middle English form of the verb 'to dream'.[21] The poem does belong most ostensibly to the genre of the mediaeval ballad (which itself often places its subjects in ambiguous relationships with the world around them), and Keats was notorious for the distillation of elements of his reading into his own creative activity. If this be admitted, then we can recognise a suspension. The obvious reading, with the sense of to 'encounter', assumes a clear self/other distinction, but the second, latent reading works against this, by locating the event within the dream experience, that ambiguous realm where the question of the precise mediation of subject and object is always problematic, perhaps even necessarily unanswerable.

Again, the primary meaning of 'sans merci' in the title is, one must assume, 'without pity'. This is the common meaning in Old French, which sometimes shares the English spelling,[22] as the scribe of the

'*Indicator*' version may be surreptitiously recognising in his apparent slip of the pen. At the same time, however, there was the standard colloquial usage of 'merci' as 'thanks'.[23] The two meanings once again imply antithetical relationships between the wight and the lady, who can be seen either as the 'doer', the agent (reading 'mercy' or 'pity'), or as the 'done to', the recipient (reading 'thanks' or 'gratitude'). This ambivalence fits better into the '*Indicator*' version than into the earlier one. As Matthey has observed, the later version involves the wight more actively, and makes the lady 'no longer a sort of "lamia"' (p. 179). That is to say, there is more of a sharing of responsibility and consequently more blurring of determinate identities.

Reliance upon the causal model is one of the most deeply rooted features of habitual experience. I shall discuss later the scepticism which eighteenth-century thinkers extended to the whole apparatus of cause and effect as any part of a valid philosophical method. For the moment, it is enough to see it being questioned in the poem. Where the problem in the 'Ode on a Grecian Urn' seems to consist chiefly in deciding who says what to whom, our second poem both repeats this (the speaker's relationship to the wight) and introduces a variation, asking us who *does* what to whom (the wight's relation to the lady). Thus there seems to be a repetition within the poem, as the dubious connection between wight and lady recurs again in the relation of speaker and wight — an ambiguity which may be more central to the 'meaning' precisely because it is less immediately apparent.[24]

Equally indeterminate is the nature of the temporal sequence. As readers, our progress is in the present; that is to say, as the 'wretched wight' (assuming that it is him) recounts the events which for him are in the past, we are reading them, empathically and for the first time, as a present experience in step with the evolution of its details. The two double readings of stanzas VI and VII are important here. 'She looked at me as she did love' (23) implies, in the context of an immediate reading, 'she looked at me while she was loving', and the 'sure' (27) in the next stanza contributes to the sense of certainty and affirmation coming from being 'on the spot'. In the retrospective reading, however, which is that of the speaker who is relating these incidents, these certainties are unsettled. The 'as' comes to be read as an elided version of 'as if', and 'sure' is delivered with a knitting of the brows, in the sense of 'surely she did, didn't she?' These two perspectives seem to dramatise the experience of reading the poem at the dictates of the cyclic imperative. Once again, as in the opening lines of the 'Ode on a Grecian Urn', we see how the recognition of time, including the temporality of the reading experience itself, can be absorbed within the scope of the ambiguities. The self-evident status of the events on the first reading is found to be complicated on the second; the first speaker, or questioner, and with him the reader, ends up by being committed to the same problem as besets the second speaker, the wight. Thus the syntactic parallelism of the third and fourth stanzas reinforces the wider movement of the poem as it refuses to answer any questions, and refuses itself as an 'object' of attention. Neither questioner, wight, nor reader are given anything which would allow them to separate out a selfhood from which events could be categorised and ordered. As the wight tells the story of his own beguiling, so the questioner is also beguiled into active participation, placed in thrall; and with him goes the reader, whose proxy he is.[25] All three personae therefore come together in a search for meaning which is endless and compulsively repeated. Questioner and reader, who approach with the implicit feeling of coming willingly into a landscape of readily available meanings, find themselves trapped by the wight who, in the very act of describing what has happened to him, is repeating, for his own hearers and in an ever expanding circle of inclusion, the casting of the spell under which he is himself languishing.[26] The search for significance forces us to abandon the unspoken concept of 'meaning' within which we approach the poem; it is the simple, separate person, the single state of man which lies behind the posture of the 'open mind', which is denied us. Sympathy and sociability are not embraced as reasoned choices out of a generous series of options; they are demanded by an inexorable logic and forced upon us as soon as we determine to begin a serious interrogation of the poem.

The syntactic insurrection need not even stop at the point we have reached so far. Once the first crack in the edifice is apparent, the fabric of normative meaning begins to fall apart entirely. It may be irrelevant to ponder whether 'ah, woe betide' (34) is to be read as an exclamatory interjection or as a qualification of the line which follows it, but more serious questions can be asked. The second halves of each of the first two stanzas, for example, could as well be parts of an answer as parts of a question or statements of context. Their relationship to the events of the poem is suggestive but ultimately indeterminate. Stanza III could be spoken by the wight to the questioner; as indeed it is, implicitly, once the mechanism of transference is perceived. Does the figure on the horse, or walking beside it (stanza V), see nothing else but the lady, the horse, or nothing else at all? The 'latest dream' (35) is both the most recent and the most untimely; and if untimely, does this imply that it came too late to warn him, or, conversely, too soon for him to want to be robbed of his state of bliss? Further, what exactly is the connection between 'La Belle Dame' and the 'fairy's child' (14)? Everything seems to imply that they are identical, but at least one critic (Matthey, p. 180) has seen them as separate personalities, and we do indeed have only Hume's category of 'contiguity' to go by. It is possible, for example, that the lady of the dream is a mythological figure casting a judgement upon a 'real' event.

I can now explain why it is that the second version of the poem seems to me the authoritative one. Firstly, it moves further towards the complete suspension of determinate causal, temporal, and ontological relationships. Slight revisions are enough to achieve this. 'So kissed to sleep' (32) removes the literalism of the earlier line, and suspends the subject-predicate relationship. Poised between an individual and a collective pronoun, between 'I' and 'we', it is hard to decide who is doing what to whom. The description 'we slumbered' (33) implies a shared activity, and is itself located between pairs of stanzas beginning 'She . . . She . . . ' and 'I . . . I . . . ' The 'wild sad eyes' (31) also make the lady seem less overtly aggressive than in the earlier version.

Secondly, the '*Indicator*' poem is a paring down, a reduction to essential details, of a drama which is in the first version coloured and deflected by an adherence to the language of the mediaeval ballad. The general preference for the 'archaic' version, indeed, could be taken to speak for the eagerness with which we tend to opt for contextual explanations as an alternative to facing up to intrinsic structural difficulties; we read the poem as part of, rather than in spite of, a received genre. Thus I would read Keats's famous comment on the significance of 'kisses four', where he contends that

> I was obliged to choose an even number that both eyes might have fair play: and to speak truly I think two a piece quite sufficient—Suppose I had said seven; there would have been three and a half a piece—a very awkward affair—and well got out of on my side (*Letters*, II, 97)

as a parodic anticipation of the literalism of the hypothetical reader. His pointing to this line immediately after copying out the first draft may well indicate that he was aware of the sorts of details which such readers would demand to have explained. The hint of symbolic overtones, and all their distracting functions, completely disappears in the revision.[27]

One can point to important analogues in Romantic poetry of this 'paring down' process. For example, there is 'Christabel'. Hazlitt's review of the poem is a model of how to put the right observations to wrong, or at least ungenerous, use. Thus he finds fault with what could be seen to be Coleridge's very virtue, that 'he comes to no conclusion',[28] citing as evidence the line first written in after l. 252, 'Hideous, deformed, and pale of hue' (*Poetical Works* p. 224 gives a slightly different wording). This line qualifies the visitor as a negative presence, and thereby makes it easier for the reader to orient himself within the bounds of an available meaning; it makes, as Hazlitt says, 'common sense' (p. 146) of the poem. Common sense, however, does not seem to be what Coleridge has in mind. In leaving out this lurid detail, he has suspended judgement on the lady's status, forced us into a more careful approach. Hazlitt as good as admits this when he says, taking us right back to the argument for the Keats poem, that 'Christabel' 'is more like a dream than a reality. The mind, in reading it, is spell-bound' (p. 146).

A much more important example is, of course, 'The Rime of the Ancient Mariner'; that is, the process whereby it becomes so after starting life as 'The Rime of the Ancyent Marinere'. The archaic diction largely disappears, and, from 1802 onwards, so does the 'argument' which prefaces the poem, working as it does to promote a sense of fixity and established signification. The marginal glosses, first published in *Sibylline Leaves* in 1817, can be seen as an ironic response on Coleridge's part to the controversy which the poem had generated. I shall be discussing this later; for the moment it is enough to suggest that the verse embodies meanings which the glosses do not explain and, conversely, that the glosses suggest implications and consequences which do not seem to be in the verse. Read in this way, these marginal comments are far from sealing off the events of the poem within a 'metacommentary'; on the contrary, they put us on our guard and alert us to the problems and responsibilities of readership. Keats certainly seems to have had this poem in mind when he conceived 'La Belle Dame Sans Merci'. Not only does it deal with exactly the same mechanism of beguilement and transference, in that the wedding guest, and the reader with him, are gathered beneath the old sailor's spell (and, perhaps, his endless search for its meaning?), but it contains some specific anticipations of the imagery and vocabulary of Keats's poem. The seamen suffer from parched lips while standing 'agape' (*Poetical Works*, p. 192), and 'agape' was Keats's first attempt at 'gaped wide' (*Letters*, II, 96). Coleridge's mariners look up 'sideways' (p. 195), the sails sigh 'like sedge' (p. 199), and there is exactly the same double reading of 'sure' (p. 198) as Keats will use— and will use again in 'The Fall of Hyperion' (*Poems*, pp. 669–70).[29]

From this point, the reference points become bewilderingly manifold. What we have seen at work in the 'spontaneous' business of writing poetry can be situated, I shall try to suggest, in the wider context of the models of knowledge production and possibility which characterise the late eighteenth and early nineteenth centuries. To say this is immediately to involve oneself in difficult methodological questions which cannot be sidestepped, yet which seem to preclude in their very formulation any opportunity we might have for solving them. If I assert that this is a repetition of the events of the poems we have been examining, and that they in turn take their context from a wider historical situation, then I must beg the question of how that situation relates to our own, and ask at what precise point of conjunction between the two the 'construction' I am describing might originate. In this sense the 'reading' of history can seem as inabsolute as the speaker's attempt to pin down the urn and as circular as the wight-questioner-reader's experience of his beautiful lady. This was a problem for the Romantics in their analysis of the moment of perception, as it is for us in the reconstruction of their history. We can never be sure of the degree to which we are the generous transcribers of fact, and of how far we remain the architects of personally and socially determined patterns. The awareness of the unconscious has only compounded this problem, for its very theorisation presupposes a reservoir of inarticulable determining influences within and around the conscious mind; the 'will' or the ethical faculty can thus only tentatively define one 'self' out of an indefinite number of possibles. We do not possess the fixed self-availability necessary to construct a past from a stable 'moment' in our own time, so that the prospect of an articulable mediation between then and now becomes even more remote. At this point the possibility of a total narcissism becomes most threatening; we hallucinate the image of a 'belle dame' before us and outside us. But the important point about Keats's poem, as I have said, is that the protagonist does not know *anything* determinate about the self-other relation. His 'relief', if there is any relief, comes in the narration and the passing on of the experience, and his appeal is therefore rhetorical, contingent, like that of the ancient mariner, upon the eye and the mind of his audience. This is exactly the position

I have put forward in arguing, as I have done in the Preface to this book, that the case must be judged with reference to the evidence adduced along the way. I hope that this will be seen as a more serious gesture than a mere demand for attention. Romantic poets do not describe and imitate as much as they stimulate, and this stimulation must, it seems to me, bear upon the position of the critical reader as he tries to take account of his own context.

To summarise, we do not have the *simple* state of subjectivity necessary to allow us to project that simplicity back into history. I think that the Romantics were very anxious to disturb the illusion of such simplicity—for Blake the reified unity of the ego—even as they understood the inevitability of its recurring presence in the cycle of self-formation. Hence these tears. Michel Foucault has aptly described this predicament as it relates to the project of defining a culture or a historical situation:

> It is obvious that the archive of a society, a culture, or a civilization cannot be described exhaustively; or even, no doubt, the archive of a whole period. On the other hand, it is not possible for us to describe our own archive, since it is from within these rules that we speak, since it is that which gives to what we can say—and to itself, the object of our discourse—its modes of appearance, its forms of existence and coexistence, its system of accumulation, historicity, and disappearance. The archive cannot be described in its totality; and in its presence it is unavoidable.[30]

We do not have a cognitive grasp on the things which make us what we are (for us the usual metaphors involve socio-economic and psychological determinants) precisely because we have already defined these things as undiscoverable. We cannot proceed in ignorance of the hermeneutic circle, but we cannot solve the questions it raises. I shall try to argue that the poets themselves thought and created within the shadow of this problem, and that their awareness of it led them to fashion artifacts wherein the issue is repeated and transferred, in a finer tone, rather than definitively solved. In so doing, I shall leave a few half-open doors indicating possible solutions along the way—those, I hope, apparent to the Romantics themselves—but the major intention will be to demonstrate this transference and repetition, along with the erosion of 'metacommentary' which is part of it. In Romantic poetry one continually finds the metacomment distinguished and distanced from the primary level of response—as with the speakers of Keats's poems—only to be reabsorbed and undercut by a higher level of self-consciousness.

This is the point at which I must offer a further formulation of what I mean by 'irony'. The movement which has been described as that between comment and metacomment could be taken to define the strategy of irony as it is most commonly understood. This involves fixity and stability, the provision of a point of view from which we can deliver a judgement. The movement from metacomment back into comment, which we have also described, can then be seen to involve another level of irony—the irony of irony. This second stage is the one where I would go about defining a specifically 'Romantic' irony, and this is what is meant when the term is used in what follows. It is perhaps worth pointing out that the most recent and thoroughgoing attempt in English to discuss irony as a principle of literary structure, that of Wayne Booth, refuses clearly and precisely to deal with this irony of irony. The issue is first taken up in *The Rhetoric of Fiction*, first published in 1961, and becomes more and more apparent in his subsequent work. It is in *A Rhetoric of Irony* that we find the most explicit account of the terms of his case:

> . . . pursued to the end, an ironic temper can dissolve everything, in an infinite chain of solvents. It is not irony but the desire to understand irony that brings such a chain to a stop. And that is why a rhetoric of irony is required if we are not to be caught, as many men of our time have claimed to be caught, in an infinite regress of negations. And it is why I devote the following chapters to 'learning where to stop' (p. 59, footnote).[31]

There is a great deal of sense and integrity to this polemic, and learning where to stop was not an entirely unfamiliar exercise for the Romantics themselves. But too much is missed along the way if we start out by embracing the first principles of a crusade to save culture and literature. I would not agree, for example, that what Booth calls 'unstable irony' has a 'dulling effect', nor that 'a spate of uninterpretable ironies has the same effect as providing no experience in irony at all' (p. 227). We may take the scope and intensity of Booth's case to indicate how much of a living issue this argument remains. As an example of the other side of the case, one might take Beda Allemann, whose essay 'Ironie als literarisches Prinzip', in *Ironie und Dichtung*, reveals, as one might expect from a German critic, a warmer response to the paradigm established by Friedrich Schlegel:

> Literary irony is the more ironic, the more it is able to renounce the signs of irony—without losing its clarity. This fact entails the consequence that

an adequate, purely formal definition of irony cannot be given for literature. Where the signals are missing, where indeed the inadequacy of the signals is precisely the precondition of the highest degree of irony, then we must necessarily give up hopes of a purely formal analysis, for the entirely negative signal can no longer be differentiated (p. 20).[32]

What Allemann here describes as a literary phenomenon can be applied, I shall try to argue, to the Romantic concept of experience; that 'experience' which poetry purports to describe or re-enact. It can be seen to depend upon the exact situation which so worries Booth, the absence of the stable, locating overview which would fix the status of the first-level response, the 'comment', within a definitive context which can then spur us up into action. The end of this argument is necessarily implicit in its beginning, but the withered sedge and the absence of birdsong take on a surprising variety of forms.

2 Kindling the Torch

> . . . the Writer wishes, in the following Essays, to convey not in-
> struction merely, but fundamental instruction; not so much to show my
> Reader this or that fact, as to kindle his own torch for him, and leave it
> to himself to chuse the particular objects, which he might wish to
> examine by its light . . . The primary facts essential to the intelligibility
> of my principles I can prove to others only as far as I can prevail on
> them to retire *into themselves* and make their own minds the objects of
> their stedfast attention.
>
> Coleridge, *The Friend*

I

In the discussion which follows, I shall inevitably find myself trying to
pitch the argument back to an anterior point, one where the search for
meaning and selfhood seems to promise some success. This anteriority is a sort of fiction in itself, and I do not mean to imply a fixed
historical development. Most of the poems to be discussed were
written before 1820, but many of them seem to come down to the
same convoluted paradigm, the same compulsory sojourn. Rather, it
is a descriptive moment, an attempt to hold off the conclusion in
order to build up a context and to show the range of options it offers;
but at the same time we shall find ourselves constantly laying and
unlaying the same bricks, in a process marked by repetition rather
than clearly defined progress.

The first mechanism to be considered is the deconstruction of
habitual consciousness; a clearing of the ground, a creation of empty
space which might potentially be filled with something of greater
integrity than what is displaced. But this is necessarily going to bring
up, at this very moment, the question of the nature of the
reoccupation, which often involves the same slippage and the same
corrective gestures, repeated over and over again. Only in the
consciousness of this persisting paradox can interpretation proceed
without destroying itself before the shrine of a projected objectivity.

The range of options, the making of choices, is embodied in a series of strategies which I shall refer to collectively as 'the heuristic method'. The phrase paraphrases almost perfectly: serving to or encouraging the desire to discover, through a process of trial and error, or selection and substitution; the playing of past assumptions (habitual experience) against new limits of meaning; forcing the pupil (reader) to use the given materials in the service of self-discovery; the method used in making decisions when the supply of information is limited, when all the possibilities cannot be fully explored (how well this suits the theory of mind wherein what is most important is most indescribable). [1]

The emphasis upon self-finding and self-creation, with the consequent disestablishment of the text as an authority and the stressing of its function as a heuristic stimulus, occurs all over Romantic aesthetics. The ideal reader, for Wordsworth, would 'decide by his own feelings genuinely, and not by reflection upon what will probably be the judgement of others'. [2] He will not look to predetermined standards of competence and normalcy, but to his own creative response. The task of the poet then becomes one of arousing the 'co-operating *power* in the mind of the Reader' (*Prose*, III, 81), which will involve stimulating the reflexive activity in which 'each man is a memory to himself'. [3] This alone can redeem a discourse which, despite Wordsworth's persistent and notorious assertions of a kind of clarity, must remain difficult and even insignificant, appealing to 'few and scattered hearers' (*ibid.*, 83), and must fail to register at all among those who 'do not *read* books' but 'merely snatch a glance at them that they may talk about them'. [4] For Wordsworth, then, the reader must meet the poet half way, to the same degree that the poet himself must engage with nature. What is, as we shall see, the source of an indeterminate epistemological relationship between the poet and the world, becomes an aesthetical prerequisite in the relationship of the poem to the reader.

Few writers have explored the mechanisms of indirect communication more deeply than Coleridge, and we are perhaps only just beginning to provide the context within which his notoriously 'fragmentary' output can be seen to be connected by definite methodological principles. [5] The presentation of the fragment, the artifact or argument which is in some sense deliberately incomplete, can be seen as one way of providing a reader with the materials of self-construction. [6] If meaning is to appear, we have to become what we behold; 'we must *be* it in order to *know* it'. [7] Quoting Plotinus, Coleridge says:

For in order to direct the view aright, it behoves that the beholder should have made himself congenerous and similar to the object beheld. Never could the eye have beheld the sun, had not its own essence been soliform (*Biographia*, I, 80).

The writer's task is thus to provide a medium equivalent to the 'natural sun' which 'calls up the breeze to chase away the usurping vapours of the night-season, and thus converts the air itself into the minister of its own purification' (*Biographia*, II, 215). The precondition of Christian belief is the precondition of the achievement of all worthwhile knowledge; nothing will be gained as long as 'we attempt to master by the reflex acts of the Understanding what we can only *know* by the act of *becoming*' (*ibid.*, 216). Everything must be designed 'to enable the spectator to judge in the same spirit in which the Artist produced, or ought to have produced' (*ibid.*, 222). The model is nothing less than that of the redemptive act of Christ himself; He is become as we are, that we may become as He is.[8] The effort is not wholly on the part of the reader, by any means. The writer must work hard to introduce that disguised guiding hand which will be able to suggest the desired meaning without setting the reader's will in opposition. Coleridge was well aware of the dialectics of communication, and the need to insinuate, rather than announce, the meaning he might wish to pass on:

A man will borrow a part from his opponent the more easily, if he feels himself justified in continuing to reject a part. While there yet remain important points in which he can still feel himself in the right, in which he still finds firm footing for continued resistance, he will gradually adopt those opinions, which were the least remote from his own convictions, as not less congruous with his own theory than with that which he reprobates. In like manner with a kind of instinctive prudence, he will abandon by little and little his weakest posts, till at length he seems to forget that they had ever belonged to him, or affects to consider them at most as accidental and 'petty annexments', the removal of which leaves the citadel unhurt and unendangered (*Biographia*, II, 29).[9]

The risk involved, as Coleridge was so often to find, is that of total misunderstanding, a risk taken by any writer who has something to say yet is compelled to an indirect way of saying it. Shelley also recognised just this:

But this practice of entire sincerity towards other men would avail to no good end, if they were incapable of practising it towards their own minds. In fact, truth cannot be communicated until it is perceived. The interests therefore of truth required that an orator should so far as possible produce in his hearers that state of mind in which alone his exhortations could fairly be contemplated and examined.[10]

The poet's task, like the orator's, is to turn secondary communication into primary perception, and to unsettle the habits of mind which are accustomed to find meaning only in the secondary activity. Shelley's own efforts in this direction were not always, as I shall suggest, as overt as the notorious relationship of Laon and Cythna, calculated as it was 'to startle the reader from the trance of ordinary life'.[11]

This is not to say, of course, that all the poets of the earlier eighteenth century were authoritarians in this sense, nor to propose that the Romantics were the first to pay attention to such problems. But it can be said that the Romantic writer confronts the business of communication in a new and more urgent way, in that he is preoccupied with the potential gap, not only between his own 'meaning' (as he is aware of it) and his means of expression, but also between the resultant 'text' and its reader. The obligation which the poet feels to recognise the integrity of that reader even as he suspects it is one of the paradoxes attendant upon this crisis in the idea of authority; another such paradox is the tendency towards a more covert but equally extensive authoritarianism in the writer who replaces statement by insinuation. Various poets cope with these problems in different ways, as we shall see. Blake, for example, seems to me to incorporate into his methods a more thoroughgoing critique of his own assumptions than does, say, Coleridge, whose version of Christianity seems to provide him with a fabric of truths which are not questioned, though their modes of operation are crucially heuristic; but even this is truer of the prose than of the poetry.

For the moment, however, these paradoxes may be left aside, while the basic evidence is being presented. I have space only to indicate, rather than document, the scope and importance of the shift from implicitly authoritative to explicitly heuristic methods in types of discourse other than the poetic. The young Hegel, in an essay of 1798—9, has this to say of the required attitude to the reception of the Scriptures:

> Nowhere more than in the communication of the divine is it necessary for the recipient to grasp the communication with the depths of his own spirit. Nowhere is it less possible to learn, to assimilate passively, because everything expressed about the divine in the language of reflection is *eo ipso* contradictory; and the passive spiritless assimilation of such an

expression not only leaves the deeper spirit empty but also distracts the intellect which assimilates it and for which it is a contradiction. This always objective language hence attains sense and weight only in the spirit of the reader and to an extent which differs with the degree in which the relationships of life and the opposition of life and death have come into his consciousness.[12]

In other words, completed meaning is dependent upon the inner, active faculties, and without them there is only paradox and contradiction. Even when meaning is achieved, it will vary subjectively, according to experience. In political theory, we find Godwin stressing the need for a self-deduced recognition of the social contract, imposed not by arbitrary authority but by reason;[13] and in philosophical method generally there is a new emphasis upon providing the enquirer with the tools of his task, in the *a priori* sense, rather than with the mere results of other, completed enquiries. The discipline of 'criticism', as Kant understands it, 'does not consider the question objectively, but in relation to the foundation of the knowledge upon which the question is based'.[14] The grand design of the first great *Kritik* can be seen to be that of a propaedeutic, a clearing of the ground, a deconstruction; it is, as Coleridge said of Plato, essentially 'predisciplinary'.[15] Not that it appears to have been seen that way by many of its readers; for Hegel, writing in the introduction to the *Science of Logic* (1812–16), felt the need to complain about precisely the fashionable willingness to receive Kant's results without undergoing once more the *production* of those results. Serious philosophy must therefore start once more from Kant, ignoring his followers:

> But what with Kant is a result, forms the immediate starting-point in this philosophizing, so that the preceding exposition from which that result issued and which is a philosophical cognition, is cut away beforehand. The Kantian philosophy thus serves as a cushion for intellectual indolence which soothes itself with the conviction that everything is already proved and settled. Consequently for genuine knowledge, for a specific content of thought which is not to be found in such barren and arid complacency, one must turn to that preceding exposition.[16]

This is exactly the sort of inertia which Hegel sees it as his own task to overcome:

> . . . for the logic of the *Notion*, a completely ready-made and solidified, one may say, ossified material is already to hand, and the problem is to

render this material fluid and to re-kindle the spontaneity of the Notion in such dead matter.[17]

Both Kant and Hegel, then, can be taken to insist upon a fundamentally heuristic method, though there are significant differences of emphasis within the methods; Hegel, for example, is anxious to re-establish the truth value of empirical perceptions and to reunite the 'divided' faculty of pure reason (see *Science of Logic*, pp. 45–6). They share also, I think, the refusal of absolute closure and of an invulnerable 'metacomment'. The Kantian 'practical reason' is not an organic *outgrowth* of the problems of pure reason (except in the troublesome sense that it presumes a common psychological mechanism in all minds), but a solution of them based upon an absolute sortal distinction between the nature of the problems and the nature of the solution; the latter is not, in this sense, 'connected' to the former, as it cannot possibly be if it is to remain invulnerable. Thus, in our chosen sense of the word, it is not a 'metacomment', because its necessity is not ultimately, I would argue, contained within, or at the periphery of, the set of primary problems. Conversely, it is a stepping out, a refutation by dismissal, by a chosen alternative related only negatively to the internal dissensions of pure speculative reason. Hegel never allows for this 'leap' outside the model of the ongoing mediation of subject and object, for the commitment to actual experience involves a continued, uninterrupted working through of the method as the task of living. There is no way 'out', there is only a carrying on, just as there is a continual reading of 'La Belle Dame Sans Merci'. Whereas with Kant the dualism is maintained by an (in the empirical sense) unbridgeable gap between pure and practical reason (unless, as I have hinted, we share the assumption that the one will 'heal' the failure of the other in *all* minds), Hegel's holism is such by virtue of including all experience, and is thus impossible to halt as it aggregates through continuing time.[18]

In the context of English aesthetical and philosophical theory, it is certainly not adquate to suggest that the emphasis upon a heuristic method was unanimously endorsed. Dugald Stewart approved the strategy of what Burke described as setting 'the reader himself in the track of invention',[19] but there was a significant and familiar reluctance to approve the difficulties and obscurities—one might say, the 'labour'—implicit in such a method as a proper vehicle for artistic communication. Gerard can sanction 'moderate difficulty, such as exercises the mind without fatiguing it', commending those mean-

ings which are 'comprehended only on attention'; but he objects, as
does Thomas Brown, to that 'great obscurity' which demands
abnormal effort for its comprehension.[20] Hazlitt too showed himself
impatient of those styles which kept their meaning hidden, 'serving
merely as an index, or clue to direct us in the search of it' (*Works* I,
125). Thus it is not surprising that he should be intolerant of a writer
such as Coleridge, whom he saw as 'determined to set out from no
premises, and to arrive at no conclusion', and who dared to commit
himself to print without having 'made up his own mind on any of the
subjects of which he professes to treat' (*Works*, VII, 116; XVI, 101).
Hazlitt might have looked to one of Keats's voices for support, the one
which says that beauty in poetry 'should never be half way therby
making the reader breathless instead of content' (*Letters*, I, 238). But
Keats goes on to confess that 'it is easier to think what Poetry should
be than to write it' and, some two months later, to argue the necessity
of the proving on the pulses; 'We read fine—things but never feel them
to thee full until we have gone the same steps as the Author' (*ibid.*,
279). This going over, as Keats well knew, could involve a great deal
of 'pains and trouble', perhaps even full time enrolment in the school
of suffering.

II

So much for the general importance of the heuristic method in its
general context as a theoretical formulation. I shall now pass on to
more specific implications within the strategy of deconstruction,
which is the first moment of any method which might seek to create
something of greater integrity than what it replaces, involving the
taking to pieces of what we 'are' when we undertake the poetic
experience. This taking to pieces was for Shelley the prime task of
philosophy:

> Philosophy, impatient as it may be to build, has much work yet
> remaining, as pioneer for the overgrowth of ages. It makes one step
> towards this object; it destroys error, and the roots of error. It leaves, what
> it is too often the duty of the reformer in political and ethical questions to
> leave, a vacancy. It reduces the mind to that freedom in which it would
> have acted, but for the misuse of words and signs, the instruments of its
> own creation (*Complete Works*, VI, 195).

This function is marked, in the period we have come to call the
'Romantic', by a shift of metaphors. Michel Foucault, in *The Birth of*

the Clinic: An Archaeology of Medical Perception, has pointed out (p. 65)

> . . . the two great mythical experiences on which the philosophy of the
> eighteenth century had wished to base its beginning: the foreign spectator
> in an unknown country, and the man born blind restored to light.

I would agree with this. The metaphor of the traveller, informed by
numerous popular accounts of exotic travels and anthropological
oddities, is indeed prominent in philosophical discourse, often in the
cause of demonstrating cultural relativity, and the Molyneux
problem was without doubt the central riddle in the discussions of the
theory of vision.[21] With Romanticism, there is a change of emphasis,
and the dominant metaphor comes to be that of childhood—no
longer the setting of a subjectivity which is in some sense at least pre-
established against the modifications demanded by a new environment or faculty, but rather the deconstruction of that very subjectivity into a state of pure potentiality, beginning again. Blake
wrote to Butts, in 1802:

> I would not send you a Drawing or a Picture till I had again reconsidered
> my notions of Art & had put myself back as if I was a learner . . .[22]

The moment of emptiness, of infinite possibility, is a vital one in
Schiller's idea of the aesthetic education, being the point at which
man reads himself out of his cultural limitations:

> In order to exchange passivity for autonomy (Selbsttätigkeit), a passive
> determination for an active one, man must therefore be momentarily *free
> of all determination whatsoever*, and pass through a state of pure de-
> terminability. He must consequently, in a certain sense, return to that
> negative state of complete absence of determination in which he found
> himself before anything at all had made an impression upon his senses
> (*Aesthetic Education*, p. 141).[23]

All this is but a metaphor, as Schiller himself realised:

> The naive is *childlikeness where it is no longer expected*, and precisely on this
> account cannot be ascribed to actual childhood in the most rigorous sense
> (*Naive and Sentimental Poetry*, p. 90).

As Blake put it, 'Neither Youth nor Childhood is Folly or Incapacity
Some Children are Fools & so are some Old Men' (Erd. 677, K. 794).
There is no determinate definition of, or signification attached to,
childhood, since children only exist for the adult mind as 'not adult',
negative entities representing the antithesis of what the adult sees in
himself. In Kantian parlance, children are not knowable as 'things in

themselves' but rather as phenomena; implicitly, what they 'are' is as much a consequence of the beholder's eye as of any declared ontological fixity. The image of childhood discomforts us, to quote Blake again, because it reproaches us 'with the errors of acquired folly' (Erd. 589, K. 87). We look back at what Coleridge called 'the seeming identity of body and minds in infants' (On Poesy or Art', in *Biographia*, II, 263) as a causal fantasy projected beyond the disunity experienced all too often in adult life. Infancy for Shelley was a time when

> We less habitually distinguished all that we saw and felt, from ourselves. They seemed as it were to constitute one mass. There are some persons who, in this respect, are always children (*Complete Works*, VI, 195).

Locke's account of childhood, denying as it does the existence of innate ideas and a pre-established personality,[24] is contributing precisely to this intentional location of the child, which exists as it is constructed by the adult. It comes to be in itself what the adult thinks it is, for this is the only model of behaviour it can respond to. Far from reducing the child to insignificance, Locke's argument thus stresses the crucial responsibility of the adult; because the child brings nothing into the world with him except the capacity to receive ideas, any errors on the part of the adult or educator have an absolute and tyrannical significance:

> There is nothing more ordinary, than that *Children* should receive into their Minds Propositions (especially about Matters of Religion) from their Parents, Nurses, or those about them: which being insinuated into their unwary, as well as unbiass'd Understandings, and fastened by degrees, are at last (equally, whether true or false) riveted there by long Custom and Education beyond all possibility of being pull'd out again (Bk. IV, ch. XX, 9).

The wayward development of the child thus becomes a mirror of the corruption and inadequacy of the adult's world and values; a guilt-inducing image, and therefore at the same time an imperative towards self-clarification and reorganisation. It is worth noting that the apparently opposing views of the integrity of childhood held by the Lockean and the traditional Neoplatonic conventions can be seen, in this context, to come down to the same thing. For Locke, to put it crudely, the child is essentially unformed before birth, except for certain pre-natal sensory experiences, and brings with it into life simply the potential for experience. From the Neoplatonic point of view, the moment of birth is the passage out of an undifferentiated pre-existence, a world in which, as Coleridge put it:

> . . . Some have said
> We liv'd ere yet this *fleshly* robe we wore (*Letters*, I, 261)[25]

The moment of the 'fall' is usually positioned within this tradition at some point between birth and the development of linguistic capacity, and this brings the image very closely into line with Locke's usage, wherein the condition of infinite possibility at birth very quickly lapses into fixed forms and rigid personality structures, dominated by the habituating force of the association of ideas. Locke is far more subtle and ambivalent than were many of those who read him,[26] and far closer to the 'Romantic' mind than we might expect from his reputation. Like those who subscribe to the myth of pre-existence, he places the burden of responsibility firmly upon the adult and his potentially (and probably) fallen world.

This positioning of the child in terms of the adult consciousness makes him an 'ironist', a persona whose exact status in himself is indeterminable, and therefore unassailable, and whose function consists in this negativity, this emptiness, the disruption of institutions and personalities outside himself through being perceived by them as their 'other'. In the words of Novalis

> A child is far cleverer and wiser than an adult—the child must necessarily be an *ironical* child.[27]

Schiller's *On Naive and Sentimental Poetry* offers more evidence of this same function:

> The child's act . . . puts the world to shame, and this our hearts also confess by the satisfaction they derive from such an act (p. 93).

The child is a demystifying force, exercising 'natural sincerity' (p. 99) and thereby unsettling the habitual values founded in artificial manners and conventions. In this he is exactly the proxy of the poet, who 'revokes everything in himself that recalls an artificial world (künstliche Welt)', thus restoring 'nature within himself to her original simplicity' (pp. 141–2).[28]

But the child, or, properly speaking, the image of the child as the adult conceives him, is not an 'ironist' in the simplest, determinate sense. He is himself denied the level of metacommentary, the stable identity which would enable him to replace in any absolute way the authority which he challenges; this makes him a 'Romantic ironist'.

Wordsworth saw in Cambridge a microcosm of the corrupt social system which would reappear on a grander scale in London, a world marked by

> . . . Decency and Custom starving Truth;
> And blind Authority, beating with his Staff
> The Child that might have led him . . .
>
> (*The Prelude*, III, 639-41)

but his notion of what childhood might represent in itself was much more complicated. The child functions in this passage as a negative qualifier, something outside the adult world; but when the adult himself begins to struggle to identify his own childhood, to try to relate it causally to the person he has become, then the problems begin:

> . . . he cannot recall past time; he cannot begin his journey afresh; he cannot untwist the links by which, in no undelightful harmony, images and sentiments are wedded in his mind. Granted that the sacred light of childhood is and must be for him no more than a remembrance. He may, notwithstanding, be remanded to nature . . .[29]

Wordsworth was well aware that the anterior stages of our own personalities are only ever available as overinscribed with the refractive distortions of adult self-consciousness. We have seen Keats making an urn out of a selection of classical objects and pretending that it is 'real', but at the same time incorporating a slight faltering of tone as a surreptitious confession of the true nature of the case. It is the same movement of assertion and retraction that we can follow, on a much more extended scale, throughout *The Prelude* in its discussion of the poet's childhood. As the positivity of the urn is offered as a negative qualifier—it takes its life and identity from being something other than the speaker—so for Wordsworth the most affirmative version of childhood is its status as 'not adult':

> No outcast he, bewilder'd and depress'd;
> Along his infant veins are interfus'd
> The gravitation and the filial bond
> Of nature, that connect him with the world (II, 261-4).

This idea of the sympathetically interdetermining relation between child and world functions partly as a contrast to the modern child, whom Wordsworth sees being raised as 'no Child, /But a dwarf Man' (V, 294-5), and also, more inwardly, as a fantasy or gesture of faith built around the mystery and irrecoverability of the poet's own childhood, which has only been seen to be meaningful after it has passed by; the significance of what has happened to the narrator of the poem only begins to be apparent, and then only by glimpses and in an incomplete, perpetually threatened way, after being fitted into a context provided by more recent experiences which can soften and surround the confusion, and often the pain, of immediacy. The identity of the 'boy' who blew his hootings to the silent owls (V. 389f.) provided a puzzle for editors and biographers until the publication of Manuscript JJ (see *The Prelude*, p. 639) identified him as Wordsworth himself, a fact taken for granted by many readers, even when they come upon the reference to his death. The movement whereby the autobiographical situation is concealed beneath a third person pronoun is very significant in the context of other poems which suggest the absolute irrecoverability of past experience.[30] 'The Brothers', for example, can be read as an account of the attempt to re-enact or re-establish a situation which has existed in the past, but which death and time have rendered irrevocably unrepeatable. It is tempting to see Wordsworth himself imaged in the figure of Leonard standing over his brother's grave. The opportunity or desire to recover the past have come only when such recovery is absolutely impossible. This is why the fundamental structure of *The Prelude* seems to be one of repetition, for the object of desire, the stable identification or regaining of a prior moment of time, is one which is by its very definition impossible to achieve. The reader who is inducted into the experience of the poem in its fullest sense finds himself in a position very close to that of the protagonist of 'La Belle Dame Sans Merci', compelled to a silent sojourn punctuated from time to time by a brief flash of 'meaning'—the tautological coherence which comes from being inside the experience at the moment when it is happening—which he then feels the need, or the obligation, to experience again.[31] The moments of synthesis when imagination transforms the materials of memory into immediate experience are followed by long periods of doubt and alienation:

> . . . so wide appears
> The vacancy between me and those days,
> Which yet have such self-presence in my mind
> That, sometimes, when I think of them, I seem
> Two consciousnesses, conscious of myself
> And of some other Being (II, 28–33).

This alternation of positive and negative moments—and notice how it is carried through in Wordsworth's syntax, where the omission of the comma necessary to make l. 30 simply parenthetical serves to force it into a causal connection with the description of division which follows, thus synthesising certainty and doubt—is seen by Shelley as the precise nature of the creative part of the mind:

> . . . this arises from within, like the colour of a flower which fades and changes as it is developed, and the conscious portions of our natures are unprophetic either of its approach or its departure . . . The toil and the delay recommended by critics, can be justly interpreted to mean no more than a careful observation of the inspired moments, and an artificial connection of the spaces between their suggestions by the intertexture of conventional expressions (*Complete Works*, VII, 135–6).

The toil and delay is the poet's own, of course, the moment that he begins to function as the commentator upon his own imaginative experience. With Wordsworth, we find time and time again that the moments of insight prescribe implicitly their own insufficiency, that they come too late to be applied to the situations which most deserve them, and have prompted them in the first place. Take, for example, that most written-upon poem. 'A Slumber Did My Spirit Seal'.

> A slumber did my spirit seal;
> I had no human fears:
> She seemed a thing that could not feel
> The touch of earthly years.
>
> No motion has she now, no force;
> She neither hears nor sees;
> Rolled round in earth's diurnal course,
> With rocks, and stones, and trees.[32]

The ambiguities in this poem are too well known to call for lengthy demonstration here, and what I have to say will by no means satisfy all readings. But let us note the parallels to 'La Belle Dame Sans Merci'. If we read the 'slumber' as a literal state of sleep, and what follows as a dream, then it is by no means clear whether the second stanza, despite the change in tense, is enunciated as part of that dream or as the recognition which follows waking up. Does the second stanza represent a frightening vision which the speaker will escape as he wakes up in the silent space following the end of the poem, or is it the account of the situation into which he wakes up, a tortured present dominated by the absence of the 'she'? We cannot even be sure whether the 'she' is alive or dead at the moment when the poem begins; the first stanza could be either a vision of a person already dead, or an intimation of the death of someone now living. These eight lines thus anticipate the uncertainties I have already described in the Keats poem, but here I shall offer one particular reading—though one which does not exclude others—as a way of pointing to an aspect of Wordsworth's consciousness which will be important to my general argument. The ambiguities, indeed, can be related to the indeterminacy of the autobiographical analogues to this poem, for it may be related to any of several points in the poet's own life. Coleridge wrote to Poole, in the context of the death of his own child, opining that the poem was perhaps inspired by a meditation on the possible death of his sister (*Letters*, I, 479). But the fixing of the 'she', within one reading at least, within the context of the narrator's own guilt, seems to beg reference to Annette, and also to Annette's child (this association in the poet's mind of mother and child, both of whom are 'excluded', may help to explain the peculiar positioning of 'Lucy' as between a child and a lover). It is possible to read the poem positively, of course; the taking up of a life into the natural ebb and flow of rocks and trees can seem to be a sublimation. But the other reading comes to seem more convincing, and satisfies more of the details of the lyric, though the ambiguity can be related to a division in Wordsworth's own consciousness. The poet, or narrator, has recognised too late the limitations of his former attitude to the 'she'. Having seen her as 'a thing', he has been guilty of a horrifying reification of a human life into mere materiality, and his metaphorical materialism, wherein he regarded her as a thing, has been turned into literal truth by the fact of death. The bitter paradox is that it is only the taking away of life which educates the speaker and makes him aware of his own limitations, so that he is now cut off from being able to make amends. Because the reference is to another person, the tone called forth is one involving guilt; but the essential feature of the poem, an enlightenment or insight coming too late to be exercised where it most belongs, is very close to Wordsworth's confrontation with his own childhood. It is as if the notorious—and, I shall later argue, inevitable—Wordsworthian intentionality, the habit of centering everything on the self, invades even his most painful examinations of otherness.

Another poem which seems to me to invite comparison here, in its study of time and anteriority, is 'The Two April Mornings' (*Poetical Works*, IV, 69–71). The events seem to interpret themselves until we come to Matthew's lines:

> I looked at her, and looked again:
> And did not wish her mine! (l. 55—6)

Conventionally enough, this can be taken to imply that no-one can replace the daughter he has lost. But the emphasis which the line demands seems to denote a strange tone of self-reproach, and this begins to be meaningful when we read back into the poem, to find that Matthew, on visiting his daughter's grave,

> loved her more,
> For so it seemed, than till that day
> I e'er had loved before (l. 38—40)

Matthew too, it is implied, has gone through the same moment of recognition of his own prior shortcomings as has the narrator of 'A Slumber Did My Spirit Seal'; he too bears with him the sense that he has misappropriated the meaning of a life which has subsequently been taken from him. Part of the reason why he does not wish to involve himself in any recognition of the second girl may well be the fear that once again he will fail in the nature of his response, as he feels he has failed his own child.[33] Even if we would not wish to insist on a reading which I admit is by no means explicit, and which perhaps reads too much self-castigation into Matthew, I think we must recognise the ambiguity of his utterances. Presented as they are in 'direct' speech (which is yet reported), unglossed either by Matthew himself or by the narrator, they preserve their mystery; neither narrator nor reader can be sure of what Matthew really had in mind, and he has taken his secret with him to the grave. It may even have been that he was himself unsure of why he said what he did, and that this occasioned his remembrance, posing a problem which is then passed on to narrator and reader. In being passed on, it is further compounded. Whereas the narrator would have had the tone of Matthew's remarks to help him to construe them, we do not; we have only the implication of tonality. Further, we have to cope also with the tonality of the narrator himself. Thus read, the poem becomes an exercise in displaced origins.

The subtlety of the presentation of anteriority in this poem is worth noting; it is a model example of the structure of recession. We are introduced to the narrator and Matthew, presented within what seems to be the simplest sort of reported speech. The old man is then led to recall a day 'Full thirty years behind' (l. 24); but what he is reminded of is itself a recollection, an experience at the graveside which took its force from his memories of Emma when she was alive. We return out of this doubly distanced event into what promises to be the same historical time as began the poem, only to find ourselves, and the events in which we have imaginatively participated, pushed yet further apart with the information that the whole poem is a recollection of the narrator's, Matthew himself being now in the grave. This is exactly the strategy which has been described as belonging to 'The Eve of St Agnes', though here it has a different function. It is not so much the reader as the narrator who seems exposed at the end. His own memory is a muted repetition of Matthew's recollections, and though there is no overt criticism implied in this, it is hard not to come away with at least a slight sense of uneasiness at the passing of time, and the slight, albeit very slight, intimation of a fault. The mechanism is one of transference. The pain which Matthew feels at the memory of his own younger years is described, while nothing like this is described for the narrator; but Matthew stands to the narrator in the same relation as the girl did to Matthew. Even at the most innocent level, a memory of the past is not a simply affirmative or enjoyable experience.

The more affirmative side of the paradox of childhood must be mentioned, that whereby the 'metaphorical' status of infancy is conceived of as its very virtue; it has no meaning from within, but only achieves significance when viewed from the adult perspective, so that we gain more from the presence of the retrospective fiction of childhood than we ever gained from the condition itself. The important fact is in the becoming, or the striving to become, not in the being. As Kierkegaard puts it:

> But as for the adult it is the most impossible thing of all to become a little child (simply understood), so too for a little child (simply understood) it is the most impossible thing of all to become *as* a child, precisely for the reason that he *is* a child.[34]

One of the finest examples of childhood working as a device of deconstruction and leaving the adult with the desire to become '*as* a child' is 'Anecdote For Fathers' (*Poetical Works*, I, 241-3).[35] The narrator's diction seems to me to be coloured by a specifically adult consciousness, in a way which seems implicitly 'dramatic'. Although Wordsworth only ever described 'The Thorn' as belonging to this mode of presentation, many of the *Lyrical Ballads* resolve themselves into dramatic situations.[36] 'We Are Seven', for example, which is explained in the Preface of 1800 as demonstrating 'the perplexity and

obscurity which in childhood attend our notions of death, or rather
our utter inability to admit that notion' (*Prose*, I, 126), appears much
more genuinely dialectical than this statement would imply, being
presented in dialogue form. The interchange between child and adult
shows that neither will give way to the other, each wishing to
preserve the integrity of his or her own discourse. The child does not
recognise that of the adult, and the adult recognises that of the child
only by a strange, distanced condescension. In 'Anecdote For Fathers'
there is a pompous and patronising aspect to the adult's meditations,
as he sees the child 'cast in beauty's mould' (l. 3), and 'graceful in his
rustic dress' (l. 26). This is combined with his monopoly of the
thoughts expressed; 'My thoughts . . . (l. 9) I thought . . . (l. 10)'
(the 1798 version also reads 'My' for 'Our' in l. 11), and with his
sentimental and rather spurious indulgence in a superficial happiness
which he sees as excluding all pain; pain is exactly what the child will
teach him. As the giveaway word, if we need one, the adult's mood is
one of 'idleness' (l. 28). It is this mood which leads him to the
vicarious comparison between his two homes, which itself turns into
a determination to establish a hierarchy of preference between them.
This movement from inclusion to exclusion, from seeing together to
pushing apart, seems to enact exactly the tyrannical function of reason
in its more familiar role in the Romantic vocabulary.[37] Noticeable
also is the explicit physical coercion, almost approaching violence, as
the adult grasps the child by the arm and insists on an opinion; there
are two successive references to this in successive stanzas (three in the
earlier version). The taking by the arm is but a muted version of the
violence which Harry Gill exerts upon Goody Blake:

> And fiercely by the arm he took her,
> And by the arm he held her fast,
> And fiercely by the arm he shook her,
> And cried, 'I've caught you then at last!' (*Poetical Works*, IV, 175)

and it is the analogue of the psychological pressure which the adult is
applying. The child is being forced to participate in a discourse which
he does not understand and which does not come naturally to him. He
panics, and seizes on the first thing which he sees as a 'reason' for a
decision given only to gratify the adult's aggression.[38] It is the logical
disruption which the child's reply brings about which forces the
adult—and, implicitly, the reader—into a recognition of what has
been happening, and only then, I think, do the more subtle hints of
adult tyranny earlier in the poem begin to be apparent. The *non*

sequitur forces a re-reading and a reassessment. The adult lapse is really irrecoverable within the poem, for it is only in the last stanza, after the child has demonstrated the enormity of his own love, or terror (and I don't think we can tell which it is), by sacrificing the integrity of his own way of seeing the world, that we see any expression of love or affection from the older person. But Wordsworth has left us in a state of shock which could be conducive to a new vision of things. The poem effects a deconstruction, and ends at the point where a reconstruction might be seen to be a possibility, a point where we have learned, in Shelley's words, that our whole life has been 'an education of error' (*Complete Works*, VI, 195). In terms of our argument about metacommentary, we are left with the challenge to provide it, rather than with the thing itself.[39] And the same goes for the child. We do not know what he '*is*', so much as what he is not, and the lesson we have learnt is a self-directed one. The final assimilation, qualified as it is with the intimation of love, is at the same time gently tinged with an inevitable hint of adult egocentricity. It is the adult who achieves 'meaning', and the child who is there to provide it, and who risks 'vanishing' as he does so—no more than a hint, but a hint nevertheless, which can take its place in a large group of Wordsworthian poems dealing with the intentionality of consciousness and the appropriation of meaning. I shall return to this.

For the moment, however, it seems fairer to say that 'Anecdote For Fathers' does provide the heuristic imperative, both in the discovery of the poem's sense and in the habits one might wish to exercise as a consequence of reading it, in a largely or predominantly positive prospectus. The child, whatever he may be in himself, has an energising effect on the adult who is woken from the state of mere reason. For the narrator of *The Prelude*, however, the image of childhood is very often associated with mystery and loss, as it is, implicitly, for the poet of 'To A Butterfly' (*Poetical Works*, I, 226), where this most fleeting and evanescent species is made the bearer of the connection with a lost infancy. The further the narrator moves from his beginnings, the more able he ought to become to fit them into some sort of pattern. But this brings with it the increasing risk of decay in the memory; and, paradoxically, at those moments when the imagination is most successful in revitalising past events, the effect is very often one of disturbing chaos or disorientation. In every adumbration of his past, the narrator is moving yet further from it, committed to historical time in the very production of the poem. Imagination and memory erode each other, to the same degree as they provide for each other. The one offers immediacy and chaos, the other stability and deadness; there seems to be no moment which can hold both stability and immediacy.

I have already thrown out some hints about the Wordsworthian paradoxes implicit in Hegel's *The Phenomenology of Mind*;[40] it is worth pointing out that his *Science of Logic* contains a philosophical formulation of the problem of beginnings which can be read as a very close parallel to the poetic treatment of the same theme in *The Prelude*. Hegel is very careful never to allow his reader to posit a determinate beginning at the beginning, either in the ego or outside it (see pp. 75–8), for the reification of either mind or nature would result in materialistic fixity, a model within which our desires must always fall short of our capacities, since what is desired will remain eternally other. More simply, for the less strenuous mind, the provision of determinate beginnings is a short cut precluding the need for heuristic participation and construction. For Hegel, all abstraction from the business of this construction is delusive, and this extends even to that most conventional of all devices of 'metacomment', the chapter heading and section division:

> . . . I would point out that the divisions and headings of the books, sections and chapters given in this work as well as the explanations associated with them, are made to facilitate a preliminary survey and strictly are only of *historical* value. They do not belong to the content and body of the science but are compilations of an external reflection which has already run through the whole of the exposition and consequently knows and indicates in advance the sequence of its moments before these are brought forward by the subject matter itself (pp. 54–5).

The resting points and moments of determinacy which are provided by the conventions of narrative separation are not, then, to be allowed to us in this sense within a proper reading. There is no beginning outside of or prior to construction and activity:

> . . . there is nothing, nothing in heaven or in nature or mind or anywhere else which does not equally contain both immediacy and mediation, so that these two determinations reveal themselves to be *unseparated* and inseparable and the opposition between them to be a nullity (p. 68).[41]

Translated into the vocabulary of *The Prelude*, this means that there can be no present which is not mediated through the context of a past, and no past which is not reciprocally constructed out of a present. Moreover, such 'constructed' moments in the past can themselves be but moments immediately open to complication by reflection upon their own beginnings and anteriorities. Wordsworth recognises the constructed nature of the past for the mind:

> Of these and other kindred notices
> I cannot say what portion is in truth
> The naked recollection of that time,
> And what may rather have been call'd to life
> By after meditation (III, 644–8).

At his most confident moments in the discussions of imagination, Wordsworth could be taken to imply, like Hegel, that only as long as the process of reconstruction and relocation is carried on is there any viable reality at all; the alternative is deadness, fixity. The famous metaphor of the traveller in the cave (VIII, 711f.) describes how the eye first beholds a vision of shifting forms and shapes, one which 'instantly unsettles and recedes' (718), but which eventually settles itself into a determinate perspective and a fixed form:

> Till every effort, every motion gone,
> The scene before him lies in perfect view,
> Exposed and lifeless, as a written book (725–7).

This must then be reactivated into 'a new quickening' (729), and the implication is that this can only happen on the second look, and consequent upon some sort of active meditation on the part of the beholder. Wordsworth does not allow himself to be drawn into epistemological definitions of how or why this might happen, but this second glance is differentiated from the first experience of the cavern in that it produces images of order where before was only chaos; every nuance produces 'some type /Or picture of the world' (736–7). This intentionalising of perception, though it produces its own problems in other contexts, seems nevertheless to be the precondition of any meaning whatsoever, and it relies on an anterior vision which is by definition irrecoverable, and on this occasion, apparently, not even desired. The passage seems to me to stand as a close parallel and instance of the more famous account of reconstructed experience, wherein poetry is deemed to take its origin from

> . . . emotion recollected in tranquillity: the emotion is contemplated till by a species of reaction the tranquillity gradually disappears, and an emotion, similar to that which was before the subject of contemplation, is gradually produced, and does itself actually exist in the mind (*Prose*, I, 148).

This deferring of signification has at least two functions, I think.

Firstly, it softens the force of 'present' experiences, which can be so disrupting and overwhelming as to be incommunicable and uncomfortable, except as modified by the memory; a memory which, moreover, at its most efficient and imaginative, can seem to re-enact prior experiences in their fullest intensities—open boats and low breathings, for example. Secondly, it promises that a 'present' which seems, for whatever reason, absolutely meaningless *as* it is experienced, may yet accede to some meaning as it is structured by the retrospective consciousness. Events may then be

> . . . not vain
> Nor profitless, if haply they impress'd
> Collateral objects and appearances,
> Albeit lifeless then, and doom'd to sleep
> Until maturer seasons called them forth
> To impregnate and to elevate the mind (I, 619–24).[42]

Wordsworth and Hegel also share the running together or identification of ends and beginnings, as the whole process of exposition is seen to be nothing more than an investigation of the nature and possibility for a beginning. Thus it is

> that progress in philosophy is rather a retrogression and a grounding or establishing by means of which we first obtain the result that what we began with is not something merely arbitrarily assumed but is in fact the *truth*, and also the *primary truth* . . . The essential requirement for the science of logic is not so much that the beginning be a pure immediacy, but rather that the whole of the science be within itself a circle in which the first is also the last and the last is also the first (*Science of Logic*, pp. 70– 1).[43]

Hegel goes on:

> It also follows that because that which forms the beginning is still undeveloped, devoid of content, it is not truly known in the beginning; it is the science of logic in its whole compass which first constitutes the completed knowledge of it with its developed content and first truly grounds that knowledge (p. 72).

In Wordsworthian parlance, childhood is nothing 'meaningful' as it is experienced by the child, but only as it is recovered, to whatever degree, by the adult. We can start anywhere. For Hegel, the beginning is simply pure being; not nothing, but a pure, empty being which contains in it the capacity to become something (pp. 72– 3). In the same style, Kierkegaard will argue, in *Philosophical Fragments*, that the on-the-spot disciple of the historical Christ may actually have been at a disadvantage compared with those of us who have come since, because the historical presence of Christ could only have compounded the ambiguities which were an essential part of his persona. But Hegel is much more consistently confident than Wordsworth in making a virtue of the necessity of reconstructing the beginning. In a passage in the *Science of Logic* which can be read together with the implicit identification of regress and progress in *The Prelude*, he has this to say:

> . . . each step of the *advance* in the process of further determination, while getting further away from the indeterminate beginning is also *getting back nearer* to it, and that therefore, what at first sight may appear to be different, the retrogressive grounding of the beginning, and the *progressive further determining* of it, coincide and are the same (p. 841).

Since we cannot anticipate a properly founded beginning at the start, we may allow ourselves to commence with 'simple universality'. But the viability of this posture depends upon our ability to construct ourselves out of and beyond it. Wordsworth is well aware that, in general terms, 'to the place which had perplex'd us first/We must descend' (VI, 514–5), but he knew also that the re-finding could be nothing more than a reactivation of the initial perplexity, wherein

> . . . each most obvious and particular thought,
> Not in a mystical and idle sense,
> But in the words of reason deeply weigh'd,
> Hath no beginning (II, 234–7).

Retrospective experience has its own mysteries; 'We see but darkly/Even when we look behind us' (III, 492–3). When the narrator says that he will allow one portion of his tale to remain

> Where it lies hidden in its endless home
> Among the depths of time (V, 197–8)

the interesting word is 'endless'; the search for it has no conclusion. In a passage in Book XI, Wordsworth makes what seems the microcosmic repetition of Kant's move from speculative to practical reason:

> Oh! mystery of Man, from what a depth
> Proceed thy honours! I am lost, but see
> In simple childhood something of the base
> On which thy greatness stands, but this I feel,
> That from thyself it is that thou must give,
> Else never canst receive. The days gone by
> Come back upon me from the dawn almost

> Of life: the hiding-places of my power
> Seem open; I approach, and then they close;
> I see by glimpses now . . . (329–38).

That is to say, given the impossibility of solving the problem of how the personality might have been constituted in terms of causality or the reception of sense (or other) data, we must look for a basis in the self as it is put out into the world, be it an act of will or an act of giving.[44] But this option in turn is swallowed up in a renewed account of vanishing meaning, and the aspiration to give

> While yet we may, as far as words can give,
> A substance and a life to what I feel:
> I would enshrine the spirit of the past
> For future restoration (340–3)

suggests that the real conclusion of the meditation is once more to throw one's hopes for the achieving of significance forward into a hypothetical future. With the impending end of the poem, this can only mean, as it so often means, a transference of the problem to the consciousness of the attentive reader. We are all 'wretched wights' at this point.[45]

Wordsworth, then, is in a position something like that of the old men and women seen by the narrator of Shelley's 'The Triumph of Life', who

> . . . follow in the dance, with limbs decayed,
> Seeking to reach the light which leaves them still
> Farther behind and deeper in the shade (*Poetical Works*, p. 511).

The beginning is moving further and further ahead into an unattainable future, as the life process itself winds down through time. Burke had argued, in his treatise on the sublime, that

> . . . a light now appearing, and now leaving us, and so off and on, is even more terrible than total darkness; and a sort of uncertain sounds are, when the necessary dispositions concur, more alarming than a total silence (*Philosophical Enquiry*, p. 84).

I doubt that Wordsworth would have endorsed this more than occasionally; but he was aware of the dialectic, and of the sometimes total gap between the apparency and adequacy of experience as it is at the time and as it is as remembered or reconstructed.

I want now to examine one more version of the image of childhood, that represented in Blake's *Songs of Innocence*. Firstly, I should make my presuppositions clear, in saying that I tend to read at least some of these poems as being spoken by dramatically presented narrators, adult voices which may be trying to describe, or thinking that they are describing, the state of innocence, but which are implicitly conditioned by the perspectives of experience. As evidence for this, one might offer not just a reading of the poems but the observation that *Songs of Innocence* was first published as a separate volume.[46] Moreover, the combined volume, which appeared later, is announced as 'Shewing the two Contrary States of the Human Soul',[47] but says nothing about each half only showing one of these states. Contraries for Blake were the source of progression, and it seems most likely that he would have included the dialectic of progress within the perspective of innocence itself. Fixity is not a Blakean virtue; he has provided himself with a medium which, both in its production and in its reception, demands perpetual rein-terpretation and recreation. The designs of the illuminated plates were not simply reordered from one edition to the next, but also recoloured. Although the tones seem to have become gradually darker and deeper as the years went by, there does not seem to have been any determinate relationship intended between colour and signification, any more than there is such a relationship between text and design, or between different parts of the design.[48] Blake is deliberately keeping in motion the question of 'meaning', stirring up the standing waters, and refusing to accede to any stable concept of completion. The true 'state of the text' is the whole history and production of the text, not simply before it reaches the printed page, but in the mind and eye of the reader who comes to it, and who will see in it different things at different times. This inclusion of context is an essential part of Blake's artifact, just as, I would argue, the 'poem' called 'Ode on a Grecian Urn' has six versions of the last lines, and as 'La Belle Dame Sans Merci' exists in two states, so that we can fruitfully search for meaning in the gaps between them.

Blake, like Hegel, abrogates beginnings, more purposefully and willingly than does Wordsworth.[49] In this context, it is worth taking a hard look at the presentation of childhood in *Songs of Innocence*. The first poems I shall discuss are 'The Little Boy lost' and 'The Little Boy found' (*Songs*, 13–14). Critics have tended to read them as expressive of the need to regard God as a human phenomenon, and any discomfort we may feel tends to be ascribed to the inhibitive levels of adult sophistication with which we are burdened, and which we must slough off in order to apprehend the poems.[50] Without discounting any of this outright—for discounting is a dangerous thing with Blake—I want to suggest that another reading is possible. Joseph H. Wicksteed, in his *Blake's Innocence and Experience* (p. 105), has said that 'the double poem seems clearly religious in intention, and contrasts the false light with the true'. Taking up the point about true and false lights from a less orthodox perspective, one might well ask which is which. Is the child being saved or damned in being led out of the mire? He begins by metaphorically projecting a father image which is not there at all; do we see him as saddened or relieved by the disappearance or distancing of the vapour? When we read 'no father was there', are we to conclude that there was no father at any time, or that there is a father who simply was not there at that time? What is the exact relationship of 'God ever nigh' to the 'father in white', expressed as it is in vague analogical language? The boy starts by looking for a father who is not there, and ends up finding one. Overtly, and certainly from the perspective of an adult or narrator who is satisfied with himself and believes in all the advantages of his condition, the poems are about the comforting return to security; if this persona be questioned, however, other readings begin to suggest themselves. Could not the 'wand'ring light' as well represent the difficult yet potentially expanding presence of uncommitted imagination, which becomes condensed, as much through the child's own fear as through adult repression, into finite, fixed form as a composite figure of authority, God-father? Perhaps I am being over-ingenious, but an argument can be made. The title of the first poem is decorated with tiny figures and animals, including that of the piper who is found throughout the book. David Erdman, in his *The Illuminated Blake*, p. 54, announces that 'this is not our friendly piper . . . but a wood sprite luring infants into swamps'. How do we know this? These figures are noticeably absent from the second of the two poems, the finding. So too are the angels which frame the text of the first poem, and the two other figures which Erdman reads as 'surrogates for mother and father anticipating the next page'. Why should we assume, as Erdman does, that the single figure in the margin of the second poem 'extends a welcoming arm' (p. 55)? This argument interprets the figure as related to the awaiting mother (though, as Keynes has noticed, the adult holding the child's hand itself seems female); it could as well be taken to be the embodiment of the 'wand'ring light', straining towards the child which is being taken from it, and from the social and imaginative world represented in the lively forms framing the text of the earlier plate.[51]

Let me say again that I am not insisting that this interpretation is the only one, or the 'right' one; only that it can be made to work. A passage from 'Auguries of Innocence', for example, might be taken to support the Swedenborgian reading:

> God Appears & God is Light
> To those poor Souls who dwell in Night
> But does a Human Form Display
> To those who Dwell in Realms of day (Erd. 484, K. 434)

But this in turn depends upon a fixed view of the relation of day to night, as well as on an assumption that Blake is using the image in the same way. For these poems are a challenge, a questioning of how we regard the relationship of adult and child. In being led out of the mire, the child is also being led out of the plate; what is shown laterally in the side to side movement of the first design (leaving us outside, as observers) is seen head-on in the second. The movement is towards us, in what almost seems to be a frontal confrontation with the reader and his world, a begging of the question. To move out of the plate is, implicitly, to be led out of innocence; or, more accurately, to be led away from the chance of regaining it, through experience. Lateral progress through the book, which would be, in the most stringent sense, 'reading', is replaced by extraction *from* the book, which is interference, intentionality. I believe that Blake recognised adult sophistication and provided for it; made it, in fact, the means of our salvation. To try to opt outright for a naiveté which one imagines to be typical of childhood may be the most insidious form of repression, as well as a misunderstanding of how the image of childhood may be functioning.

There appears to be but one step between innocence and experience, as the frontispieces to the two books seem to remind us. The piper of innocence, left foot forward (*Songs*, 2), seems to have taken only one step into experience (*Songs*, 28); the pulsation of an artery, perhaps. But the landscape has changed, he no longer has his pipe, and the child (or *a* child) who was before in free attendance around his head is now clamped firmly upon it, in an aggressive St Christopher posture.[52] It is as if the adult is trying to reclaim the child who has already disappeared in the first 'Introduction' poem (*Songs*, 4) with the passage from inspiration to composition, spontaneity to formal communication. I believe that this process of finding and losing goes on throughout the volume, and that innocence is not the state in which we begin our speculations, but the one which we must

The Little Boy found

The little boy lost in the lonely fen,
Led by the wand'ring light,
Began to cry, but God ever nigh,
Appeard like his father in white.

He kissed the child & by the hand led
And to his mother brought,
Who in sorrow pale, thro' the lonely dale
Her little boy weeping sought.

try to find again, through them. This may be one meaning to be attached to the tiny figure who appears, or takes shape, as bound to the tree in the title plate (*Songs*, 3); is this innocence imprisoned? Or Blake himself, straining to interrupt the conventional learning process, under adult supervision, going on in front of him?[53] If so, then innocence for the two children pictured has already been lost; or, in terms of a more forward looking directive, has yet to be discovered. All of which can be taken, I think, as placing the relation of the two 'Little Boy' poems in a more complicated light. In 'Milton', we find this account of Milton's passage out of Eternity and back into mortal life:

> . . . and those in immortality gave forth their Emanations
> Like Females of sweet beauty, to guard round him & to feed
> His lips with food of Eden in his cold and dim repose!
> But to himself he seemd a wanderer lost in dreary night.
>
> (Erd. 108, K. 496).

Milton's passage is a necessary one; might it not be that the little boy must also go through the experience of thinking himself lost in the dreary night?[54]

In the context of these options, I would like to discuss another poem about childhood, 'Infant Joy' (*Songs*, 25).

> I have no name
> I am but two days old—
> What shall I call thee?
> I happy am
> Joy is my name,—
> Sweet joy befall thee!
>
> Pretty joy!
> Sweet joy but two days old.
> Sweet joy I call thee:
> Thou dost smile.
> I sing the while
> Sweet joy befall thee.

This poem is usually described as a celebration of maternal love, a loving dialogue between adult and infant.[55] Even those who have noted that the adult (for, once more, there is no definite statement that it is the mother) puts words into the infant's mouth, or interprets its gestures verbally, have tended to imply that this is a positive and entirely generous process.[56] But it need not be read in this way alone. We can separate out the persona which speaks the poem from the organisational intelligence behind the whole artifact. The child is at the pre-linguistic stage, he does not 'speak', but he is 'spoken'. This might not seem so important, were it not for the fact that the compulsion toward differentiation is exactly what the adult projects, at the same time as it is being ironically undermined in the enunciation of his or her own monologue.[57] The speaker turns (that is, paraphrases the infant into turning) the description of a state—'I happy am'—into a proper noun—'Joy is my name'—society's gesture of appropriation and admission, and, of course, of signification. What is presented superficially as a benediction seems to have a sinister undertone in the containing of 'fall' within 'befall', a fall which the infant is committed to in being unable to prevent himself being spoken by the adult, thus gratifying the adult curiosity.[58] The infant's 'smile', which is turned into determinate meaning by the adult's singing, takes on a most melancholy implication in the context of this sort of reading, as a smile of resignation before an inevitable fate. Coleridge had asked himself, 'The first smile—what kind of *reason* it displays' (N 330), and this appears to have been a familiar question. Thus Thomas Reid:

> A few days after they are born, sometimes a few hours, we see them smile in their sleep. But what they smile at is not easy to guess; for they do not smile at anything they see, when awake, for some months after they are born.[59]

Blake has many eloquent descriptions of the fate of the new born child in the world around it, where all too often

> The father forms a whip to rouze the sluggish senses to act
> And scourges off all youthful fancies from the new-born man
> (Erd. 282, K. 110)

and where the child is then forced to become 'an Infant horror' (Erd. 239, K. 727).[60] In this larger context, as well as in that provided by an exclusive reading of the poem itself, it is hard to preserve the 'pseudo-innocent' celebratory version of the events described. We can question the design, moreover, in the same way as we have questioned that of the 'Little Boy' poems. Because our culture deems that birth is a joyous occasion, the flower containing the group of figures is usually deemed to be opening, with the limp flower yet to open. But this latter flower could as well have gone through its cycle already, and the open flower could be in the process of closing. Similarly, the dark skies which frame the design in its later states could either be closing in or dispersing, according as one sees the flower as active or passive. And who is the third figure, not in any way defined by the text?[61] Once again, I must stress that I do not mean to imply that my reading is the authoritative one, and it is not simply modesty which makes me say so. For we can pass on beyond it, to a higher level of consciousness and self-consciousness. The benediction again comes to seem positive, and the smile again holds a degree of promise, when we recall or realise that the fall is a necessary fall, and that there is no innocence except as it is discovered and constructed. Thel's terrified refusal to enter existence produced fixity and sterility; the alternative is a conscious embracing of experience in order that something beyond it shall be made possible. This is what is involved in the gesture of Milton, and in that of Jesus in 'Jerusalem', who asks the sceptical Albion:

> Wouldest thou love one who never died
> For thee or ever die for one who had not died for thee
> And if God dieth not for Man & giveth not himself
> Eternally for Man Man could not exist! for Man is Love:
> As God is Love: every kindness to another is a little Death
> In the Divine Image nor can Man exist but by Brotherhood
>
> (Erd. 253, K. 743).

'The Lamb' argues the identity of child, lamb, and God; and if the above passage speaks for the grand design inherent in entering the world, then the expression of love on the adult's part can indeed be redeemed from the darker purposes of my exposition; but only, I think, by working through it and realising its possibilities.[62] Through successive levels of self-consciousness, we are, and are not, Infant Joy, and infant joy, as the fall into definition is redeemed in the discovery of ultimate brotherhood, and sisterhood; identity.

It may be, then, that there is a way out of the silent sojourn held out to us here, and it is significant that both Wordsworth, in 'Anecdote for Fathers', and Blake, intimate that the approach involved is one of love. Things are not always this simple, however. The level of complexity which is *almost* able to be stored in the memory when it stems from a short lyric is almost impossible to quantify in this way when seen in the context of the larger works, and the prophetic books in particular. This means that all reading tends to be deconstruction and reconstruction, where meaning must be perpetually established and re-established.[63] This giving way to the selflessness of change and process is, as Milton tells Satan, the only way in which the awakened consciousness can preclude its own passage into fixity and authoritarian identity:

> Thy purpose & the purpose of thy Priests & of thy Churches
> Is to impress on men the fear of death; to teach
> Trembling & fear, terror, constriction; abject selfishness
> Mine is to teach Men to despise death & to go on
> In fearless majesty annihilating Self, laughing to scorn
> Thy Laws & terrors, shaking down thy Synagogues as webs
> (Erd. 138, K. 530).[64]

Coleridge metaphorically expressed the need for this continual refounding in the image of childhood, as in his definition of 'genius':

> To carry on the feelings of childhood into the powers of manhood; to combine the child's sense of wonder and novelty with the appearances, which every day for perhaps forty years had rendered familiar . . . (*Biographia*, I, 59).[65]

But one implication of the cyclic imperative in Romantic literature is that the mind closes again as soon as it has opened. Thus there is no point in trying to arouse a pre-established 'innocence' which is not even there. Instead, the task of the communicator must be to tease his reader into questioning the values of experience *by means of* his exercising them. I have argued that Blake, whether or not he is writing poems 'for' children, is certainly writing for adults who might wish to become 'as' children—that is, adults who embody in childhood the denial of their own habitual consciousnesses. Coleridge too allowed and planned for a certain prior corruption in his readership:

> Though I might find numerous precedents, I shall not desire the reader to strip his mind of all prejudices, or to keep all prior systems out of view during his examination of the present. For in truth, such requests appear to me not much unlike the advice given to hypochondriacal patients in Dr. Buchan's domestic medicine; videlicet, to preserve themselves uniformly tranquil and in good spirits. Till I had discovered the art of destroying the memory *a parte post*, without injury to its future operations, and without detriment to the judgement, I should suppress the request as premature; and therefore, however much I may *wish* to be read with an unprejudiced mind, I do not presume to state it as a necessary condition (*ibid.*, p. 162).

We have seen the announcement of the task of deconstruction in the context of a general theoretical questioning of authority, and discussed also its embodiment in the metaphor of childhood, of beginnings. I have tried to touch also on some of the complications and difficulties of such an undertaking, both from within and without. Not the least of these is laziness or impatience, or simple defensiveness, on the part of the reader. In terms of Coleridge's own distinction between thought and attention, it is much easier to deal with 'the order and connection of Thoughts and Images, each of which is in itself already and familiarly known', than to participate in 'the voluntary production in our own minds of those states of consciousness, to which, as to his fundamental facts, the Writer has referred us' (*The Friend*, I, 16). I shall now pass on to an account of the way in which this attachment to what is familiarly known— which is in fact a cloud of unknowing—was challenged through the use of language as a self-conscious and obtrusive medium demanding interpretation rather than reception; a medium which takes us by the arm and shakes us into activity, rather than one which vanishes in reverence for the prior clarity of the message it embodies.

3 Language Within Language

And on the sand would I make signs to range
These woofs, as they were woven, of my thought;
Clear, elemental shapes, whose smallest change
A subtler language within language wrought:
The key of truths which once were dimly taught
In old Crotona

Shelley, *The Revolt of Islam*

I

I have been arguing so far for the presence of a paradigm of deconstruction in the image of childhood, and have further suggested that the use of this image precludes its being used to provide closure or metacomment. That is to say, the adult recognises the apparent impossibility of becoming a child and therefore also recognises the implicitly partial or incomplete status of his representation of the child. The imperative towards self-correction which the image of the child provides is thus always tinged with an insecurity, as the 'essence' of childhood remains at an unregainable and mysterious distance. Wordsworth's 'To A Highland Girl' (*Poetical Works*, III, 73–5), for example, beautifully dramatises the urgencies of identification which beset the adult as he beholds a beautiful childhood:

> Thou art to me but as a wave
> Of the wild sea; and I would have
> Some claim upon thee, if I could,
> Though but of common neighbourhood.
> What joy to hear thee, and to see!
> Thy elder Brother I would be,
> Thy Father—anything to thee! (ll. 55–61)

The failure of complete identification produces an urgent desire for some metonymic proximity; and both father and brother, be it noted,

57

are implicitly authoritarian roles, however benevolently the narrator may conceive of them. This, as we would expect, gives way to a quieter resignation as the poet realises that he must rely upon his memory to preserve the living function of the image. Significantly, the poet 'frees' both the girl and the place from the potentially inhibiting effects of his 'colonial' imagination:

> I feel this place was made for her;
> To give new pleasure like the past,
> Continued long as life shall last. (ll. 69— 71)

Refusing to release the image, as Wordsworth releases it here, back into the medium of the living reality in which it subsists, would be an act of authority, signalled by the paternal metaphor. Romantic aesthetics was, I believe, very much concerned to provide for this release, and thus to keep alive the epistemology of interchange between selves and other selves. In this context it might be expected that the status of language, containing as it does the potential for both fixity and suggestion, would be an important conscious issue for the writers of the period.

This was indeed the case. Of course, poetic expression has always tended to operate disjunctively in the context of whatever norms we might establish for any moment in the history of language; but in the Romantic period, the disjunction became much more conscious in that it was implicitly related to theoretical arguments which can be seen to depend upon the crisis in authority as it questions the viability of pre-established and received meanings.

For the 'standard' eighteenth-century mind, if we may hypostatise such a thing, language was felt to be the medium which kept at bay a world which in essence was chaotic and disruptive.[1] Locke had determined, in his important distinction between nominal and real essences (*Essay*, Bk. III, ch. VIf.), that the orthodoxy of his followers should be nominalist or conceptualist rather than realist. The nominalist argument maintains that, roughly speaking, language *is* meaning, that it provides the only prospect of coherence in a world which would otherwise be a taxonomical chaos, an infinite pro-liferation of indescribables.[2] We describe and categorise objects by language alone, and without it we have no articulable hold on experience. The fantasy of a 'natural' language, either of gesture or of a posited determinate relation between objects or phenomena and sounds, was not entirely unvoiced, but in general it may be said that language is related to the mind rather than to the world; or at least, to some mediated representative construct between mind and world. Coleridge puts the nominalist case very clearly in a letter of 1826:

> For (as I have long ago observed to you) it is the fundamental Mistake of Grammarians and Writers on the philosophy of Grammar and Language [to assume] that words and their syntaxis are the immediate representatives of *Things*, or that they correspond to *Things*. Words correspond to Thoughts; and the legitimate Order & Connection of words to the *Laws* of Thinking and to the acts and affections of the Thinker's mind (*Letters*, VI, 630).

The world of objects only lives for Coleridge in so far as it is 'moving, acting, or being acted on'; only then are 'things'

> first brought into notice, so as to become the distinct objects of human Consciousness—that is, *Thoughts*—and the words *immediately* refer to our *Thoughts* of the Things, as Images or generalized Conceptions, and only by a second reflection—to the Things in themselves (*ibid.*, p. 817).[3]

This causes problems, as we shall see, when it is intimated that there might yet be a world of 'things' which language and perhaps perception itself is in some sense misrepresenting; but Romantic theory is predominantly nominalist, as part of the movement away from the materialist or realist idea of the world. A symptom of this, I believe, is the relative scarcity of onomatopoeia in Romantic poetry. Blair (*Lectures*, I, 128), commending de Brosses, saw the origin of all naming in the imitation of sounds, with words representing, 'as much as they could, the nature of the object which they named, by the sound of the name which they gave to it'. And Stewart (*Works*, IV, 74) is prepared to admit this in the case of some words, though by no means all. A. W. Schlegel points to the lapse when he argues for the justification of punning and word play as an attempt to reinstate the *lost* 'resemblance between the word and the thing',[4] and this lapse is the crucial element in the Romantic formulation, whether it be between outer object and word, or inner vision and word, the two alternatives which Shelley itemised in his reference to the mysterious lacunae between 'sensation' and 'reflection', and between 'inspiration' and 'composition' (*Complete Works*, VII, 64, 135).

Coleridge, in what looks like a reference to the old idea of the physical world as the language of God, declared that 'The Omnipotent has unfolded to us the Volume of the World, that there we may read the Transcript of himself',[5] but implicit in his very metaphor is the obligation of reading into or out of; the necessity of deciphering meaning by an active response of the sort which

Coleridge hoped for from his own readers. Much of Coleridge's best poetry, in fact, seems to me to be about the difficulty of deciphering this transcript, and putting it into some 'publishable' form. There often appears to be a tension between 'nature', whatever it might be, and the meaning, theological or otherwise, which the narrator seeks to place upon it, or read out of it. In 'Frost At Midnight', for example, the inarticulate child is spoken *into* a relationship of oneness with nature precisely because it resides, for the narrator, in the same realm of the unknowable, having not yet grown into the linguistic community. While the frost performs entirely without wind, without the breath of utterance, and without offering any 'correspondent breeze', the child provides a mediation, a point of contact, as its breathings (which are prophetic of language, potentially)

> Fill up the intersperséd vacancies
> And momentary pauses of the thought! (*Poetical Works*, p. 242)

thus supplying a continuity which the speaker in his own meditations does not have. The assertive 'Therefore' (l. 65) seems to me to suggest that both the child and the film on the grate are being turned into 'companionable forms'

> Whose puny flaps and freaks the idling Spirit
> By its own moods interprets, every where
> Echo or mirror seeking of itself (ll. 20–2).

Not that I wish to turn the poem into a stringent critique of intentionalism; but the theme is there, and it is one which I shall return to. The paradox must stand; that it is the very absence of apparent communication among natural forms which creates the gap which can be occupied by the poet's speculations, but that within these speculations he feels compelled to try to close that gap. The movement is very close, I think, to that represented by the end of 'Tintern Abbey', where Wordsworth hands the reins over to his sister; and both sister and child can appear as analogues of the reader.

The speaker of 'Frost At Midnight', then, in his predication of the child's future happiness, seems to be trying to get away with taking his words for 'things', for states in the world, rather than for the thoughts which they properly are; and this is, I shall be arguing, one of the cardinal sins for the Romantic mind.[6]

As I have hinted, the sign in poetic language of a lively faith in language as involving some roughly direct embodiment of 'things' in words, would be onomatopoeia, and this is noticeably absent from large stretches of Romantic verse. There is the odd line in Blake—for example, the description of 'loud Horns wound round sounding' (Erd. 304, K. 274)—and there is Wordsworth's assonant homage to Spenser (*The Prelude*, III, 281–2); but this is a piece of the 'literary', a self-conscious repetition of the master's style within the highly self-conscious tour around Cambridge. As such, it might even be that the passage represents a rite of exorcism, the expunging of a predecessor by means of the mastery of his style. For it is a clue to the concept of the 'natural' in *Lyrical Ballads*, for example, that one almost never finds onomatopoeia. Indeed, I would wish to argue that it is precisely the attention lavished on words as things in themselves, embodying directly the 'things' they describe, instead of on their imperfect functions as signifying tools, which constitutes the viciousness of what Wordsworth calls 'poetic diction'. As he writes to Wilberforce:

> When the material forms or intellectual ideas which should be employed to [rep]resent the internal state of feeling, are made to claim attention for their own sake, then commences Lip-worship, or superstition, or disputatiousness, in religion; a passion for gaudy ornament and violent stimulants in morals; and in our literature bombast and vicious refinements.[7]

It is never implied, or at least it is never positively suggested, that the poet's attention to 'the real language of men in a state of vivid sensation' (*Prose*, I, 119) duplicates the relationship of such men to 'things in themselves'. Rather, we are again in the realm of rhetoric rather than epistemology. What the poet pays attention to is the exact delineation of the *responses* of such men as they are revealed in language; far from implying any community with natural objects, the *Lyrical Ballads* often seem to dramatise man's predicament of disconnection from them, as we have seen already and shall see again. Indeed, the active and reactive coexistence of mind and nature, working so as to produce 'an infinite complexity of pain and pleasure' (*ibid.*, p. 140), makes the prospect of our ever perceiving (let alone communicating) things in themselves a somewhat remote one. Given 'the manner in which we associate ideas in a state of excitement' (pp. 123–4), and the disruptive and disordering function of the imagination which is 'sufficient to produce such changes even in our physical nature as might almost appear miraculous' (p. 150), we only ever have things as they are seen, or as they are intentionally projected. The poet must be, inevitably, one who looks for and delights in companionable forms in the world around him, and one who is 'habitually impelled to create them where he does not find them' (p. 138). The point about the 'simple and unelaborated expressions' (p. 124), then, is not that they embody a world of objects, but that they reveal more honestly and clearly the extent of what language *cannot* effect. Paring down the scope of poetic diction, whose complications involve the reader in a secondary 'creative' activity which he tends to regard as a parallel to, or an enactment of, some similar process going on in the 'real' world around him, Wordsworth plans to reveal, not the totality of what language can say, but rather the enormity of what it cannot. Whereas Shelley, for one, chooses to upset any imported stability of meaning by what Wordsworth might have called a 'motley masquerade of tricks, quaintnesses, hieroglyphics, and enigmas' (*Prose*, I, 162), baffling us with the sheer density and proliferation of the linguistic medium, Wordsworth himself creates mystery and stimulates self-consciousness through simplicity, through the use of language in its minimal state. As so often extremes meet, and strategies which seem to be at opposite ends of the spectrum turn out to be aiming at the same thing. Wordsworth's is quite definitely a heuristic method, but it is an alinguistic one; as far as it can be without sinking into silence. The drama of 'Anecdote for Fathers' happens between the lines, and what is 'said' is said by the adult and is part of his self-deception and his ignorance of the implications of his own behaviour. He thinks that his monologue is making him intelligible to himself, whereas it is only carrying him further from seeing the real state of affairs, the emotional logic of his mood. It is only the disruption caused by the child's inability to handle convincingly the distancing, symbolising functions of language which makes him aware of this.[8]

Wordsworth was always ambivalent, perhaps purposely so, about the precise watershed between the mind making nature, and nature making the mind (see, e.g., *The Prelude*, XII, 286–93), and this pertains to the implicit presentation of language in *Lyrical Ballads*. As Wordsworth says,

> . . . it is proper that I should mention one other circumstance which distinguishes these Poems from the popular Poetry of the day; it is this, that the feeling therein developed gives importance to the action and situation and not the action and situation to the feeling (*Prose*, I, 128).[9]

This is to my mind one of the most radical aspects of the poems, and of the theory built around or out of them; that 'meaning' is rhetorical rather than epistemological, existing only in the mind of a character or persona and not at all 'in itself'. I shall make this point again in discussing 'The Thorn' at a later stage of the argument, and in discussing the darker implications of the intentionalist position. For the moment, it is enough to signal the paradox in Wordsworth's idea of language, that it communicates a 'meaning' based on the intuition that all linguistic meaning is at best partial and at worst corrupted and distorted. Nor should we expect him, as the transcriber of the epistemological dramas of *The Prelude*, to rest easily in a posture of exclusive subjectivism, separating meaning from a context which might well, he considers, determine it. At the very moments when words are successfully communicating something, then they are founded back into the same mysterious context as nature itself, equally far beyond exact cognition:

> Visionary Power
> Attends upon the motions of the winds
> Embodied in the mystery of words.
> There darkness makes abode, and all the host
> Of shadowy things do work their changes there,
> As in a mansion like their proper home:
> Even forms and substances are circumfus'd
> By that transparent veil with light divine;
> And through the turnings intricate of Verse,
> Present themselves as objects recognis'd,
> In flashes, and with a glory scarce their own
> (*The Prelude*, V, 619–29).

The apparent evocation of sinister forces in this passage, combined as it is with a more conventional reference to the ennobling functions of language, is perhaps not accidental. The traditional poetic diction is tyrannous, in that it provides its users and readers with an illusion of substantial meaning which dissuades them from looking within and beyond, and the Wordsworthian alternative, simplicity, does not 'say' its meaning, but leaves it to be inferred from what is left out.

The process of translation or distortion which threatens the reader's reception of the word is also often described as having occurred within the poet's mind in the passage from inspiration to composition; 'when composition begins, inspiration is already on the decline' (Shelley, *Complete Works*, VII, 135).[10] The ambiguous, compromised nature of composition is one of the themes of the 'Introduction' to Blake's *Songs of Innocence*, where the passage from

piping, to singing, to writing involves the disappearance of the child
(*Songs*, 3). The connection of this little lyric with the larger structure
of *The Prelude*, or that reading of it for which I have argued already,
will be apparent. Wordsworth's metaphor for lifelessness, the
'written book' (VIII, 727), is no accident. Throughout the account of
life in London, we find the linguistic metaphor used to suggest
exhaustion and overdetermination, the absence of meaning through
the very oversupply of possible meanings. The city is a sort of
semiotic inferno, with so many signs demanding attention, that all
chance of signification disappears. We see 'files of ballads dangle from
dead walls', and advertisements which 'Press forward in all colours on
the sight'; there are so many 'written characters' that all communication is doomed from the start (VII, 209, 211, 222). This is the
corollary in urban civilisation (perhaps even the cause) of that
corruption in poetic diction which offers stimulation precisely as a
means of preventing real thought, and it makes demands on the
imagination which are far harder to meet than even the most
fearsome among nature's disciplines. The corruption of manners in
urban society is not simply a piece of poetical ranting, but has a
profound connection with and implication in the impossible demands
made upon the mind in its basic urge to understand.

With Blake, one of the most common metaphors of repression is
the binding process which goes into the production of a book (see
Songs, 44), suggesting as it does determinate beginnings and endings.
Cyclic form functions to try to induce us into a process of continual
re-reading, fighting off the moment of closure. But, prior to this, the
written word itself is one of the most familiar forms of tyranny in the
fallen world. The tablets of the law received on Sinai are 'forms of
dark delusion' (Erd. 66, K. 245), and the 'articulate' utterances of the
Shadowy Female in 'Milton' promise that the authority of the letter
will be inscribed upon the mill of slavery:

I will have Writings written all over it in Human Words
That every Infant that is born upon the Earth shall read
And get by rote as a hard task of a life of sixty years (Erd. 110, K. 499).

The institution of language as it is handed down is thus a repository of
vested interests, and must be unsettled from its place in the minds of
Blake's own readership.

The mythical images behind this general dissatisfaction with
language include not just the model of a prelapsarian unity, a 'lingua
adamica', but also the projection of a state which had no need for the

written text at all. Monboddo describes a time at the height of the Pythagorean teaching when nothing was committed to writing; it was only dispersal and persecution, a fall from innocence on the part of civilisation as a whole, which produced texts (*Origin and Progress of Language*, II, 260). It is in fact exactly the intrusion of tonality, with the implied primacy of speech over writing, which renders the literary form an 'ironic' one, supplying hints and half meanings which the written word alone cannot satisfy or bring to completion. This problem is implicit in all forms of 'dramatic' presentation and is, for example, part of the disturbance caused by the last lines of 'Ode on a Grecian Urn', where we are unsure both of the speaker and of the status and tonal quality of what is spoken; it is also a familiar tactic in *Lyrical Ballads*, where the exact 'meaning' of direct speech, as we have seen in 'The Two April Mornings', seems almost impossible to pin down. This becomes, therefore, a precaution against closure, in that as long as we have no such pinning down we have no secure 'interpretation'.[11]

As I have said, the metaphor of the fall is applied not simply to the act of writing, but bears also upon the very act of utterance, or outering, that prior stage of objectification and division which is intimated in Blake's 'Infant Joy' and in the 'Introduction' to *Songs of Innocence*. Hegel's theory of expression, threaded through various parts of *The Phenomenology of Mind*, is of great interest in this context. He says that

> Language and labour are outer expressions in which the individual no longer retains possession of himself *per se*, but lets the inner get right outside him, and surrenders it to something else (p. 340).

In this process

> the inner turns itself into something else, into an other, and thereby puts itself at the mercy of the element of change, which tranforms the spoken word and the accomplished act, and makes something else out of them than they are in and for themselves as actions of a particular determinate individual (p. 340).

However, it is only in this projection beyond itself that the psyche comes to know itself *as* a self:

> This disappearance is, therefore, itself *ipso facto* its continuance; it is its own cognition of itself, and its knowing itself as something that has passed into another self that has been apprehended and is universal (p. 531).

In other words, the act of utterance and its reception in a

communicative relationship is the means whereby we establish our identities, both for others and for ourselves, so that the moment of self-discovery is also the foundation of the social contract. But there is a paradox involved, in that the outering of the self brings with it the experience of ontologocial insecurity, it is a 'mediating process of alienation (die entfremdende *Vermittlung*)' (p. 531).[12] The extraordinary metaphor of 'absolute self-identity in absolute disintegration' (p. 540—1) points to a radical insecurity at the heart of the communicative process:

> It is the oneness expressed in the identical judgment, where one and the same personality is subject as well as predicate. But this identical judgment is at the same time the infinite judgment; for this personality is absolutely split in two, and subject and predicate are entities utterly indifferent one to the other, which have nothing to do with each other, with no necessary unity, so much so that each has the power of an independent personality of its own (p. 541).

These last passages I have quoted are discussed by Hegel in terms of an ongoing process, the hypothetical reunification of 'the spirit in self-estrangement (der sich entfremdete Geist)' (p. 509, *Werke*, II, 347), and thus might seem to belong to a particular historical moment; but, as we have said before, for Hegel, the metaphor of history is but a metaphor, which is to be re-enacted in the experience of every individual consciousness. Perhaps we are entitled therein to step outside the ongoing progress of the argument, and to wonder whether Hegel's preoccupation with self-division might be related to his sense of its presence in his own culture. He goes on to resolve this moment of double identity when he projects language as the embodiment of the ongoing spiritual development of society and nation (see, for example, pp. 660—1, 716—7). But I am suggesting that the Romantic mind was still committed to a working through of this experience of division which Hegel seems so eager to get beyond, and that such redemptive possibilities as are intimated along the way are continually threatened so long as one remains *within* the activity of reading. 'La Belle Dame Sans Merci', for example, allows us only half the process which Hegel describes. We can read out of ourselves—indeed, I think that we have to if 'meaning' is to appear—but we are not permitted the return movement, or at least not in any ultimate, closural sense. Wordsworth, resident in London, looks upon

> a blind Beggar, who, with upright face,
> Stood propp'd against a Wall, upon his Chest

Wearing a written paper, to explain
The story of the Man, and who he was.
My mind did at this spectacle turn round
As with the might of waters, and it seem'd
To me that in this Label was a type,
Or emblem, of the utmost that we know,
Both of ourselves and of the universe;
And, on the shape of the unmoving man,
His fixèd face and sightless eyes, I look'd
As if admonish'd from another world

(*The Prelude*, VII, 611–22).

Blindness confronting blindness, identity in difference; we stumble when we see. The beggar has only words, which he cannot see, to describe himself; he is 'for others'. But, in so being, he reminds them of what they cannot 'see'. The poet too stands with his words, distanced from himself and awaiting some attribution of meaning in the eye of a passer by. Like the beggar, he has only language, and it is in language that he must deposit the seeds of any redemption he might hope to encourage:

English, the rough basement.
Los built the stubborn structure of the Language, acting against
Albions melancholy, whom must else have been a Dumb despair

(Erd. 181, K. 668).

This is the thesis of Schelling's essay 'Concerning the Relation of the Plastic Arts to Nature', where he argues that the artist cannot shun the

separateness nor the pain, indeed the torment, of form . . . Only by the consummation of form can form be destroyed . . . without bounds the boundless could not be manifested . . . if unity is to be made palpable this can only be done through singularity, isolation, and conflict.[13]

It is the key to the apparent paradox in Blake's admiration for the 'bounding line', which at first seems odd in the light of his sensitivity to the restricting functions of form:

expression cannot exist without character as its stamina; and neither character nor expression can exist without firm and determinate outline (Erd. 540, K. 585).

Seeing clearly is analogous to clear intellectual perception; we have to see ourselves reflected with some exactness before reform is possible or productive of something beyond fresh errors. The poet must, then, be prepared, as Shelley puts it in one of his homophone puns, 'To dye in hues of language' (*Poetical Works*, p. 75). He must dye his inspiration in the colours of composition, but he must also himself die, in the hope that his reader will find the sparks among the ashes, in a gesture akin to self-sacrifice. I have used the phrase before: he becomes as we are, that we may become as he is; the heuristic contract.[14] Language may be 'a thing subject to endless fluctuations and arbitrary associations' (Wordsworth, *Prose*, III, 82), but it is all we have, and it must be employed. In becoming as we are, the poet is always looking for a way to communicate which does not involve giving up what *he* is, and the tension is always between the integrity of that vision and the habitual slumber within which our spirits are sealed. He is looking for a mechanism—I should say 'organism'— which can demand that our thoughts, in Coleridge's words,

> be taken up again into the circulation, and be again and again re-secreted in order to ensure a healthful vigor, both to the mind and to its intellectual offspring (*Biographia*, I, 160n.).

The search is for a language which resists to the highest possible degree being cast into any system of institutional presuppositions which would become the tyrant over that language and interpose between it and its readers. There must be, as Shelley put it, 'A subtler language within language wrought' (*Poetical Works*, p. 113), and it is towards a delineation of the features of this 'subtler language' that I shall now move.

II

I shall employ a crude distinction in what follows between the word and the sentence as units of meaning, attempting to argue that both these categories are put to work in the general task of deconstruction. Word and syntax, name and context, can seem to represent two different processes in the attribution of meaning, the one speaking to us 'off the page' through selecting and substituting mechanisms, the other suspending its selective options until the contextual qualifiers have been supplied. I am not, needless to say, trying to make any sort of professional distinction here, but mean merely to divide up language, which works in both these ways (and probably many others) at once, for the limited purpose of an exposition.

We have already seen, in the reading of 'La Belle Dame Sans Merci', that the provision of the proper name achieves the exact opposite of its habitual social function, implicated, for example, in the darker reading of 'Infant Joy'. Announced as it is in a foreign language, offering as context only the title of the poem itself, and compounded as it is of various potential 'meanings' which might be found in the literary tradition and in the words taken by themselves (what about, for example, 'belle dame' as 'belladonna', deadly nightshade, a narcotic producing loss of breath and dilated eyes?),[15] it makes the bearer more mysterious and ambiguous than she might otherwise be, and completely fails to fulfil the habitual nominative function of specification. The act of naming is conventionally a conferring of stable meaning, and at the same time an assertion of power and control: 'Sweet joy I call thee'. It is no accident that the knight of mediaeval romance is reluctant to reveal his name; or, if he does so, offers only a pseudonym, a vacant sign which must be tenanted by the hearer and leaves him as puzzled as before. Thus Keats's lady, who is unidentifiable in being named; like Shelley's 'Mont Blanc', white mountain, blank mountain, untenanted by colour, culture, and signification, and so overtly so that it reflects the beholder's fantasies back upon himself, asking him the questions he would ask of it. At the same time as naming, from the point of the nominee, threatens a loss of self-control, the other side of Hegel's paradox must also apply. Naming the world outside, carrying through the gestures of definition and discrimination, is a relief from the whiteness, playing out the level of control which must exist if the subject is to 'identify' himself reflexively within that world. Martha Ray, in 'The Thorn', transfers her affection for Stephen Hill to her fixation on the mountain, hill to mountain, in a movement which speaks for the hoped for repetition of some control, through language, of the very despair to which she is abandoning herself.[16] This repetition is not to be attibuted to any intrusive authorial concern for poetical symmetry, but rather to a dramatic propriety in Martha's (or the sea captain's, or the villagers') behaviour, an attempted ordering of the landscape of experience through language. It sets the tone of the whole poem, which is, as I shall later argue, an examination of intentionality.

This reminds us again of the basic nominalist argument, that phenomena are taxonomically graspable by virtue of the class name they have in common; if things 'in essentia' are different, then it is language which holds them together. Hence Coleridge's parable of the patient who derives comfort from 'some new symptom or product, that had at once determined the name and nature of his complaint . . . even though the discovery did at the same moment preclude all hope of restoration' (*Biographia*, II, 208), and his sense of 'the calming power which all distinct images exert on the human soul' (p. 254). The act of naming stands in a paradoxical position in the Romantic spectrum; it can be either a gesture of tyranny and limitation, or a saving necessity in the process of self-constitution.[17] That it can be both at once is certainly, I shall argue, implicit in Wordsworth's poetic intelligence, and quite overt in Blake's model of the ego educating itself through successive lapses into limitation and closure. The stabilising function of naming must be upset, even if it be subsequently reintroduced, in order that we shall be committed to becoming rather than 'being'. The oscillation between stability and deconstruction must be always a process, never a product. Martha Ray, or whoever 'speaks' her, can be seen to be the type of the reader in her need to achieve coherence through the name; but at the level which might be thought to apply to most readers, the gesture of intentionalising meaning is simply a confirmation of habitual values and perceptions, and an avoidance of all thought. The paradox must not be reduced in Wordsworth, I think, but Hegel saw the impulse towards stability as part of the mind's desire for the false god objectivity, a desire which must be refused if philosophy is to begin:

> In the question: what *is* this? or: what kind of a plant *is* this? *what* is often understood by the *being* enquired after, is merely the *name*, and when this is learned one is satisfied and now knows what the thing *is* . . . it must be conceded that we have not the least conception of the 'I', or of anything whatever, not even of the Notion itself, so long as we do not really *think*, but stop short at the simple, fixed *general idea* (*Vorstellung*) and the *name* (*Science of Logic*, pp. 624, 777).

Properly speaking, we can learn nothing in this way; the reification of the world reflects back and produces a reified ego, which means either passive self-abandon or the tyranny of the 'Ichphilosophie', since the ego

> is, because subjectivity, at the same time the power over the different names—the link which, having nothing in itself, fixes in itself series of them and keeps them in stable order (*Philosophy of Mind*, p. 222).

Disruption of the stability of objects and names thus unsettles the subject whose tools they are; poetry is indeed, as A. W. Schlegel said (*Lectures*, trans. Black, II, 135), a 'playing with words', but not so much with the aim of restoring the relationships of word and thing, as of unsettling our fantasies in that direction, and bringing them to consciousness through the articulation of disjunctions. The habitual

notion against which any such ambition has to fight is the familiar one
that the pre-established exactitude of its terminology is the measure of
the success of language in communication. This view held significant
sway at the time, and may be among the reasons why Hegel, with his
careful taking to pieces and reassemblage of the German philosophical vocabulary, was so slow to gain attention from foreign readers.[18]
The accompanying presupposition is that the substantive is the
beginning of all discourse. Dugald Stewart, in an attempt (which to
his credit he saw as impractical) to exclude from a necessarily semiotic
communicative process all its ambiguities and heuristic elements,
regarded the task of enquiry as the establishing of a pure sign system:

> . . . the necessity of this task can never be superseded, till every word
> which we employ shall be as fixed and invariable in its signification as an
> algebraical character, or as the name of a geometrical figure (*Works*, III,
> 107).[19]

It is against this sort of background, where the name is a short cut to
ontological and epistemological certitude, thus operating simply as a
confirmation of habitual values and perceptions, that we must
understand the Romantic polemic. Naming comes to seem a part of
what we now tend to call 'mystification', a habit familiar to the
eighteenth century as the taking of metaphor for reality. As Diderot
put it:

> Gradually we became used to believing that these names represented real
> beings; we regarded sensible qualities as simple accidents, and thought of
> the adjective as really subordinate to the substantive, even though the
> latter is in fact nothing, and *the adjective everything*.[20]

Residence within the name comes to be seen as part of the materialist
conspiracy of fixed identities, the repository of a conservatism which
inhibited both the health of the mind and the life of the state. 'You
take a name', says Hamann, 'and need no proof of *your* existence.'[21]
The first reaction of the Romantic poet to the name is negative. The
cultural conspiracy which Shelley describes in 'Queen Mab' is one
where naming is a prelude to maiming, a dismembering of
brotherhood into difference and distinction:

> specious names,
> Learned in soft childhood's unsuspecting hour,
> Serve as the sophisms with which manhood dims
> Bright Reason's ray, and sanctifies the sword
> Upraised to shed a brother's innocent blood (*Poetical Works*, p. 776).

When Keats's Lycius begins the insidious process of trying to institutionalise his love for Lamia, to fix it within a stable social framework and to clip its wings, the first thing he asks of her is her name (*Complete Poems*, p. 638). The words he hears in reply are 'blind and blank' (p. 102) to him, but Lamia's denial of friendship and parentage is a clue to the necessary nature of imaginative experience, could he but see it, as Wordsworth did before his highland girl.

Wordsworth's poems 'On the Naming of Places', included in the second edition of *Lyrical Ballads*, give us important versions of the process of naming. I should like to discuss the fourth of these, 'A narrow girdle of rough stones and crags' (*Poetical Works*, II, 115–7), in the context of the argument so far.

> A narrow girdle of rough stones and crags,
> A rude and natural causeway, interposed
> Between the water and a winding slope
> Of copse and thicket, leaves the eastern shore
> Of Grasmere safe in its own privacy: 5
> And there myself and two beloved Friends,
> One calm September morning, ere the mist
> Had altogether yielded to the sun,
> Sauntered on this retired and difficult way.
> —Ill suits the road with one in haste; but we   10
> Played with our time; and, as we strolled along,
> It was our occupation to observe
> Such objects as the waves had tossed ashore—
> Feather, or leaf, or weed, or withered bough,
> Each on the other heaped, along the line   15
> Of the dry wreck. And, in our vacant mood,
> Not seldom did we stop to watch some tuft
> Of dandelion seed or thistle's beard,
> That skimmed the surface of the dead calm lake,
> Suddenly halting now—a lifeless stand!   20
> And starting off again with freak as sudden;
> In all its sportive wanderings, all the while,
> Making report of an invisible breeze
> That was its wings, its chariot, and its horse,
> Its playmate, rather say, its moving soul.   25
> —And often, trifling with a privilege
> Alike indulged to all, we paused, one now,
> And now the other, to point out, perchance

To pluck, some flower or water-weed, too fair
Either to be divided from the place 30
On which it grew, or to be left alone
To its own beauty. Many such there are,
Fair ferns and flowers, and chiefly that tall fern,
So stately, of the Queen Osmunda named;
Plant lovelier, in its own retired abode 35
On Grasmere's beach, than Naiad by the side
Of Grecian brook, or Lady of the Mere,
Sole-sitting by the shores of old romance.
—So fared we that bright morning: from the fields,
Meanwhile, a noise was heard, the busy mirth 40
Of reapers, men and women, boys and girls.
Delighted much to listen to those sounds,
And feeding thus our fancies, we advanced
Along the indented shore; when suddenly,
Through a thin veil of glittering haze was seen 45
Before us, on a point of jutting land,
The tall and upright figure of a Man
Attired in peasant's garb, who stood alone,
Angling beside the margin of the lake.
'Improvident and reckless,' we exclaimed, 50
'The Man must be, who thus can lose a day
Of the mid harvest, when the labourer's hire
Is ample, and some little might be stored
Wherewith to cheer him in the winter time.'
Thus talking of that Peasant, we approached 55
Close to the spot where with his rod and line
He stood alone; whereat he turned his head
To greet us—and we saw a Man worn down
By sickness, gaunt and lean, with sunken cheeks
And wasted limbs, his legs so long and lean 60
That for my single self I looked at them,
Forgetful of the body they sustained.—
Too weak to labour in the harvest field,
The Man was using his best skill to gain
A pittance from the dead unfeeling lake 65
That knew not of his wants. I will not say
What thoughts immediately were ours, nor how
The happy idleness of that sweet morn,
With all its lovely images, was changed

To serious musing and to self-reproach.   70
Nor did we fail to see within ourselves
What need there is to be reserved in speech,
And temper all our thoughts with charity.
—Therefore, unwilling to forget that day,
My Friend, Myself, and She who then received   75
The same admonishment, have called the place
By a memorial name, uncouth indeed
As e'er by mariner was given to bay
Or foreland, on a new-discovered coast;
And POINT RASH-JUDGMENT is the Name it bears.

The poem is among Wordsworth's finest, and repays all the scrutiny we might be able to bring to bear upon it. The superficial course of events seems apparent enough. The narrator and his sophisticated friends are rambling through the countryside in that 'vacant mood' (l. 16) whose dangers have already been intimated in the 'Anecdote For Fathers', when they see through the mist the figure of a man fishing. This becomes the occasion for a self-satisfied meditation upon the vicious habit of idleness among working folk, but as they approach they realise that the man is too old and crippled to be doing anything else, and is, moreover, fishing for his food rather than for any vicarious pleasure. The mood becomes one of self-reproach, as the idleness which they have projected into the old man is seen properly to belong in their own minds and habits; in memory of this realisation, the place is christened 'POINT RASH-JUDGMENT', and the poem comes to an end. The presentation is much more subtle than this, of course, but what I have said will serve as a beginning. Beyond this, I would argue that the poem does not simply *describe*, in the course of its narrative, an act of selfish appropriation and wilful intentionalising which is overcome in the conclusion, all living happily ever after,[22] but actually embodies *as a whole*, and in the entire activity of its expression, variously overt and subtle versions of the same crime that occupies the centre of attention on a fast reading. The second act of appropriation is the naming of the place itself, which simply repeats in a finer tone the prior nomination of the old man as an emblem of idleness. The gesture of self-correction is thus surreptitiously implicated in the same problems as determined the initial crime, and once again the closural ambitions of the reader are thwarted. The metacomment which appears to consist in the naming of the place, capitalised as it is and set off typographically from the rest of the poem, comes to seem something of an act of transgression. There is no privileged language, and the moment of correction must itself involve an occluded repetition of egotism and self-satisfaction.

It will probably seem that I am pushing the case a little hard, and it certainly could be argued that the irony, if it exists, is a benevolent and tolerant one. But further clues can be found, if we read back in the light of this argument. A landscape which has begun life as 'a rude and natural causeway' (l. 2) which is 'safe in its own privacy' (l. 5) has ended up by being identified as an emblem of perhaps rather grandiose self-discovery in the minds of three itinerants. Its 'meaning' has been established, but that act is also a ravishing, akin to the speaker's designs upon the urn. The fisherman is not guilty of this, because his relationship to the landscape is not one of implicit ambition but of subsistence. Note that both the landscape (l. 7) and fisherman (l. 45) are on the other side of the veil of perception from the speaker and his friends, separated by the mist. The dispersal of this mist is not simply a metaphor for the growth in self-consciousness of the speaker, but is also a reductive act which brings a self-subsisting and independent world under the rule of the adverting mind of the ramblers. The poem describes a series of ravishings; there is the reading of the harvesting as a mirthful activity ('feeding thus our fancies'), which can be seen as an explicit piece of sentimental voyeurism; there is the plucking (which is, let us note, grouped with the act of 'pointing', which will be repeated at the end and changed from a verbal to a nominal sense) of the flowers, which bears, I think, explicit comparison with 'Nutting'; there is the reading of the old man; and, finally, the definition of the place. It is worth pointing out also the yet more subtle gesture of symbolising which the speaker enacts in the first flush of his shame:

> his legs so long and lean
> That for my single self I looked at them
> Forgetful of the body they sustained (ll.60-2).

Here again, the making of emblems and the selection of parts to stand for the whole involves the forgetting of that whole. The speaker's mental processes move immediately beyond the object which inspires them into levels of selection and distancing, here implicitly revealed as an act of division as the old man's body comes apart from his legs. The making of symbols, as Wordsworth well knew, may well have been the only way we have of rendering things intelligible and communicable, but it was also liable to lapse into, or even to be indistinguishable from, an act of epistemological aggression. The progress of the ramblers through this landscape, in fact, could almost be made compatible with the urban encroachment upon rural sanctities which Wordsworth in his public voice spent so much energy discouraging. Once again, I think that the poet who writes this poem has a very critical view of the poet who speaks it. The 'single self' (l. 61), which appears simply to identify the speaker as distinct from his companions, may also beg reference to a condition of egocentricity and disconnection. [23]

It is in the context of Blake that the concept of 'naming' as part of the metaphor of the Fall, which becomes thereby a fall into language, is already best-established as part of the critical vocabulary. In the words of one scholar, writing of 'The Book of Urizen':

> Namings in Genesis express God's benevolence and his intimate involve-
> ment with man. The namings that take place in Urizen carry exactly the
> opposite meaning. [24]

The problem becomes a communicative one, how to alert the reader that this is what is happening, how to turn fixity into fluidity, limitation into expansion. There must be contraction if expansion is to be possible; there must be a name if language is to come into being. Blake's undertaking begins, notoriously, with the proper name itself. Let me take the best example of all, the etymology of the name 'Urizen'. Many critics have commented on this, but almost all of them have been content to note only one or two possible derivations or interpretations. Kathleen Raine, *Blake and Tradition*, II, 53–6, suggests a derivation from 'Uranus', and also from the Greek οὐρίζω = to bound, limit (hence English 'horizon'), which is much the most frequently repeated explanation. In fact, the list of homophonal substitutions which can be made into this name seems almost infinite. Let me just list those I am able to come up with myself: you reason (imperative), you reason (descriptive, 'you are reasoning'), you, reason (vocative), your reason (attributive), your eyes in ('the text as you see it'), your eyes end ('the limits of your perception') you rise in (imperative, or descriptive), you rising, your rising (descriptive, actually or potentially), you risen ('your resurrection') . . . [25] Fanciful perhaps, but, turning to the first chapter of Urizen's book, we find the following opening lines:

> Lo, a shadow of horror is risen
> In Eternity! Unknown, unprolific!
> Self-closed, all-repelling . . . (Erd. 69, K. 222).

Is it an accident that we can read 'Urizen' in 'is risen', that we find also 'horror' (out of 'horizon'?), that we can compound the form 'hor (ror is r)isen'? Is Los, who becomes Urizen in the course of the book, seen to be prefigured in 'Lo'? Not matters for scholarly proof, perhaps, and what I have suggested will no doubt be accorded various degrees of probability by different readers. But this could be exactly the point. In the fallen world which Urizen, and our reason, represent, dominated as it is by intentional projections and inflictions of the self into the world (a process which Blake the artist does not consider himself immune from), is not this fronting of the altering eye the most important meaning of all? Blake, of course, offers us no determinate methodological clue to the deciphering of his proper names. This would be to ease the burden of responsibility, to sell short the heuristic obligation, which must work, it will be remembered, in contexts where there is an insufficient supply of determinate information. And the names are, after all, not really signs for the determinate identities we tend to see in habitual experience. Blake's figures become what they behold, in a continuous process of lapsing and rebuilding which is an obvious analogue both of the behaviour of people in the world, and of the rise and fall in imaginative self-confidence which the reading mind goes through in its search for meaning. The name 'Urizen' is an obvious and a particularly important speculation or in-vestment which this reading mind must go through, embedded as it is within the overdetermined design of the frontispiece.[26] Urizen's commitment to the medium of stone, if that is what it is—he is often described as 'petrific'—seems to suggest a regression to a higher degree of linguistic fixity which may threaten to carry with it the writer's own book. In the words of Hugh Blair, *Lectures*, I, 170:

> Writing was long a kind of engraving. Pillars, and tables of stone, were first employed for this purpose, and afterwards, plates of the softer metals, such as lead. In proportion as writing became more common, lighter and more portable substances were employed.

Urizen is moving in this direction in a movement which we are to see as inversely related to the direction of our own salvation, which accords exactly with the reading of his book as an 'antithetical' version of the creation myth. But, as I have said, we should not expect the same process to work for all Blakean names, and in the light of this it can seem surprising how often they do work, or begin to work. S. Foster Damon, *A Blake Dictionary*, p. 124, notes that Enitharmon brings together the names of her earthly parents, Enion and Tharmas, and sets this against other possible etymologies, classical and homophonal. Raine (II, 139) suggests a different Greek root from Damon, in ἐν ἁρμονίᾳ . Los is an anagram of Sol (in fact, a backwards reading), among other possibilities.²⁷ Blake was very fond of perverse palindromes whose similarity embraces antithetical perspectives, on the lines of dog/god, was/saw. The latter is especially intriguing given Blake's polemic, shared as we shall later see by other Romantics, against the tyranny of the eye, imposing as it tries to do a single vision on the mind and acting improperly as the chief among the senses. Optics was at the front of attention as a metaphor of limitation and geometrical abstraction, and the convertibility of ontology and epistemology, was/saw, might well have been of special interest for a craftsman who was committed to a medium which involved the painstaking process of producing on copper an inverse image, writing and all, of what would eventually be printed.²⁸ To return to proper names, 'Thel' might be connected to the Greek θέλω = will—her drama is very much one of an act of will posited but then retracted—but the name is also an approximate anagram of Leth(e), and forgetfulness might well be the form of repression she will choose in fleeing back to the protection of her valley. Let us call it coincidence that Blake, as he often does, signs his name in the contracted form 'Willm'.

The name 'Los' provides Blake with a host of opportunities for breaching the conventional semantic distinctions in the cause of deconstruction and confusion. Not only is he the inverted Sol, a fiery prophet antithetically related to the world in which he finds himself, whose salvation must literally involve a turning inside out, and outside in—as his Spectre perceives,

He saw now from the ou[t]side what he before saw & felt from within
He saw that Los was the sole, uncontrolld Lord of the Furnaces

(Erd. 150, K. 627)

but his dismembering in and through language goes beyond anagram and beyond the proper name itself. We read, in 'Jerusalem', of Albion

Rending the fibres of Brotherhood & in Feminine Allegories
Inclosing Los: but the Divine Vision appeard with Los
Following Albion into his Central Void among his Oaks (Erd. 191, K. 656).

The passage can be seen as a dense example on the level of language in action of what it describes; it inscribes what it describes. Los as noun form is inc-los-ed in the verb form, but that disintegration of brotherhood is also a setting into action, into movement, so that we can come to an antithetical reading of the passage through attention to the material texture of language; as we are told, the 'Divine Vision' is with Los in his imprisonment within the word, which itself becomes prophetic of his salvation and redemption. It is hard not to speculate, moreover, upon the fact that Los is also 'ink-los-ed', imprisoned in the wider sense within the artist's medium and the text as an object; to witness his final salvation, we must follow not simply his progress through the text, from page to page, but must allow for his passage out of that text into our reading imaginations, following his own habit of becoming what he beholds. This device is a popular one with Blake, and occurs quite often (see, for example, Erd. 200, 211, K. 684, 696), though as we should expect the word 'inclosd' is also found when no obvious nominal implications come to mind. But the name, in most of the examples I have described, is made into something momentary rather than material, open to reformation and recreation, time after time. Blake is using the fantasy of turning words into things as a way of stimulating self-consciousness, trying to encourage a state wherein 'Urizen' will indeed be seen to involve 'our eyes in' the text (to invoke yet another near-homophone, this time from the perspective of community instead of singularity). The naked figure on the title page of the poem 'Milton' seems to part the name with his hand, Mil-ton, just as the figure in plate 18 sunders 'Selfhood' into 'Self-hood' with his foot, a movement repeated in the tablets held by the Urizen figure (see Erdman, *The Illuminated Blake*, pp. 217, 234, and comments). The annihilation of the selfhood is presented as a visual analogue or consequence of the stony 'texts' which the old man grasps.

On the level of words other than the proper noun, examples of disintegration and remembering abound; little hope, indeed, for those of us who might share Urizen's fantasy of achieving 'a solid without fluctuation' (Erd. 70, K. 224). Take this example from 'The First Book Of Urizen', in some ways the most densely overinscribed text of all, being the artist's explicit confrontation with his own medium:

> Ages on ages rolled over them
> Cut off from life & light frozen
> Into horrible forms of deformity (Erd. 76, K. 230).

Not only is 'form' contained within 'deformity', but what is left

when it is removed is 'de-ity', and it is the fallen deification of Urizen
which forms the main subject of the book; deity is deformity. Not for
nothing did Blake call this 'The Book of my Remembrance' (Erd.
662, K. 262), not simply in the memory, but putting together in a
new way, re-membering.[29] I can only touch upon the scope of
Blake's verbal ingenuities, which operate well beyond the standard
devices of punning and ambiguity. There is a moment in 'Milton'
when

> Los puts all into the Press, the Opressor & the Opressed
> Together, ripe for the Harvest & Vintage & ready for the Loom
> (Erd. 120, K. 510).

Blake's own printing activities aside, the latent metaphorical roots of
the oppressors and the oppressed are reactivated, but in such a way
that we have to recognise that the same fate bears upon master and
slave. Antithetical usages of verbs whose active or energetic construction had long since lapsed from common awareness are also
common:

> And loud the Souls howl round the Porches of Golgonooza
> Crying O God deliver us to the Heavens or to the Earths,
> That we may preach righteousness & punish the sinner with death.
> But Los refused, till all the Vintage of Earth was gatherd in (*ibid.*)

What Los is refusing is nothing less than division and distinction,
which it is the purpose of the harvest to abolish; thus he is, in the
antithetical sense, 're-fusing', putting together again. One can look at
Los's beholding of the 'first female form now separate' in the same
light:

> He embrac'd her, she wept, she refus'd (Erd. 78, K. 231).

It is his pitying her which makes re-fusing possible, at the same time as
there is a refusal (denial) of that pity from the state of separation,
dualism; pity divides the soul. In a similar way, Blake will use
'involv'd' to mean something like 'surrounded by' (Erd. 312, K. 283),
as an activity habitually described as introspective is made to seem
external, an infliction upon the world, just as Albion turns his eyes
'outward to Self' (Erd. 309, K. 280). The 'confusion' which to the
fallen vision signifies only chaos and disorder is used in the antithetical
sense to suggest 'fused together with', for the merging of singularity
into brotherhood is indeed chaos to the tyrant eye:

Then fell the Legions of Mystery in maddning confusion
Down Down thro the immense with outcry fury & despair
Into the wine presses of Luvah . . . (Erd. 388, K. 376).[30]

Blake's use of 'disorganiz'd', similarly, is to be read not just in its metaphorical sense of 'disordered', but at the same time in its reactivated literal meaning, 'dismembered', 'taken to pieces', the lapse from organic coherence which is the prelude to re-organisation, putting together in a new way:

> Like fetters of ice shrinking together
> Disorganiz'd, rent from Eternity,
> Los beat on his fetters of iron (Erd. 74, K. 228).[31]

One of Shelley's reviewers, writing for the *Quarterly Review*, 26 (October, 1821), complained that the meaning of *Prometheus Unbound* had to be 'obscurely conjectured by the reader', and that words 'hover on the verge between meaning and no meaning' (quoted in Zillman, p. 710; and in Hayden, *Romantic Bards*, p. 401). Homage to Shelley's implicit purpose, I think. It is not the poet's business to provide these meanings; he aims rather at deconstruction, at the creation of vacancy.[32] In a similar manner Thomas Taylor, in an essay of 1804, argues for the grotesque and surprising in fiction as that which excites its readers

> to the investigation of the truth, attracts us to recondite knowledge, and does not suffer us through apparent probability to rest satisfied with superficial conceptions, but compels us to penetrate into the interior parts of fables, to explore the obscure intention of their authors, and survey what natures and powers they intended to signify to posterity, by such mystical symbols.[33]

Apparent probability is the last thing which these poets deal in, and the last canon of satisfaction which can be derived from their work.

III

I shall not take a great deal of space to indicate the presence of a strategy of deconstruction and reconstruction as it operates at the level of syntax. Any number of aesthetic writers could be consulted as representatives of the 'plain sense' school of thought, though they mostly, as with the word, allow for a measure of controlled poetic licence as a means of exciting the reader to take notice.[34] Language, as I have said, was not felt to 'reflect' the world but rather to offer an organised and useful modification of it; it mirrors the mind, more than it mirrors things. Thus it was a significant moment when the status of conventional syntax was challenged on the grounds that it no longer represented the natural order of strictly *mental* events, as it was in the arguments about the status of inversions. The classical languages were appealed to as mediums wherein passion could rearrange word order without loss of specifiable meaning; expression could follow what Coleridge (*Philosophical Lectures*, p. 290) called 'the order of thought', which in modern languages is often in tension with the demands of grammar.[35] If poetry be considered as the vehicle of this tension, then we can see the makings of a prototypic Imagist theory in these remarks, one where words are placed and stressed according to their importance in the mind of the poet; or, within the heuristic contract, in the mind of the reader who has to recompose them into meaning. I do not mean to imply that all Romantic poets wrote poems radically subversive of normative syntax, nor that those who did were the first poets to do so.[36] I would, however, argue that one of the strategies of reader activation and of the elision of authority is the recognition and provision of syntactic indeterminacy, often resolvable only by a choice of self; and this is of special importance in a climate of thought which can conceive of poetry as the organon of *all* knowledge, and not simply as an entertaining variation on a basically stable system of meanings. Lord Bacon was a poet, for Shelley (*Complete Works*, VII, 114).

I shall give just two examples from Shelley, the first of which is taken from the conclusion of Asia's speech in 'Prometheus Unbound', II, iii:

> Hark! the rushing snow!
> The sun-awakened avalanche! whose mass,
> Thrice sifted by the storm, had gathered there
> Flake after flake, in heaven-defying minds
> As thought by thought is piled, till some great truth
> Is loosened, and the nations echo round,
> Shaken to their roots, as do the mountains now
>
> (*Poetical Works*, p. 234).

The simile in the middle of this passage, which in normative syntactical patterning would read 'as thought by thought is piled in heaven-defying minds', and function therefore simply as an illustration within a larger narrative movement, is here split into two and the parts inverted; this has the effect of making the 'heaven-defying minds' the virtual centre of attention and the nub of rhetorical 'meaning', creating an expectation which is fulfilled when we recognise that the larger presentation of landscape is indeed as a metaphor of the mind. Thus it seems entirely appropriate that the 'heaven-defying minds' should be pushed into a relationship with its antecedent which is that of a predicate rather than a simile. To militate as far as he can against the deadening of metaphor, or in this case simile, Shelley sets it firmly against the normal scheme of narrative expectation which must arise every time we read through the argument, however well we may know the techniques in advance. The complexity is a warrant against decay.

Any number of examples of the same strategies can be found in Shelley; consider, for example, the opening lines of 'Mont Blanc', and the problems which have been indicated by Wasserman in his reading of them (*Shelley: A Critical Reading*, p. 222f.). Shelley is offering a syntax which indeed, as he announces in his advertisement to 'Rosalind and Helen',

> only pretends to be regular inasmuch as it corresponds with, and expresses the irregularity of the imaginations which inspired it (*Poetical Works*, p. 167).[37]

I shall choose one more among the less familiar examples of purposeful disjunction, this time from 'The Revolt of Islam':

> We know not where we go, or what sweet dream
> May pilot us through caverns strange and fair
> Of far and pathless passion, while the stream
> Of life, our bark doth on its whirlpools bear,
> Spreading swift wings as sails to the dim air;
> Nor should we seek to know, so the devotion
> Of love and gentle thoughts be heard still there
> Louder and louder from the utmost Ocean
> Of universal life, attuning its commotion (*Poetical Works*, p. 101).

Once again, in a passage buried in the middle of the stanza, positioned by its context as but a subordinate clause in a sequence of loose paratactic organisation, Shelley has inverted the expected order and established a frictional contact between an apparent subject and an apparent predicate. Instead of describing 'the stream of life' as simply bearing 'our bark' upon its whirlpools, he has pushed the verb to the end of the line, thus bringing 'the stream of life' into play as a possible object of that verb, within the context of a standard poetic inversion. We are forced to evaluate, if we are reading attentively, the relation of subject and object, a local syntactical decision which can be seen to bear upon the larger argument of where we are going and how we are getting there. The paradox is pushed forward though not resolved, but the 'either/or' turns into a 'both/and' in the second half of the stanza; we should not seek to know the answer so long as the synthesis is maintained in the experience of love. There is another Shelleyan reading of 'commotion', which in the fallen vocabulary indicates violent disturbance or mental unrest (*OED*. 1592, 1768), but can here be read as co-motion, 'moving together with'.

It is with Blake that the function of syntax and syntactical expectation seems to me to be used with the fullest versatility within the performative artifact; there is a demand for punctuation, for an interference which must be carried out in the light of a conscious realisation of its nature and consequences. In 'The Everlasting Gospel', for example, Blake has been talking about Socrates and Caiaphas, in a retrospective tense. He goes on:

> Both read the Bible day & night
> But thou readst black where I read white (Erd. 516, K. 748).

The preceding four lines have been explicitly in the past tense, so that when we come to 'read' we are caught between two tenses, an uncertainty which is only resolved with the last line. An everlasting gospel indeed, one which resists our attempts to push it into the past, into history; an attempt which the poem up to a point encourages in order to stimulate some purposeful investigation of the contrast. This is not strictly a 'syntactical' point, perhaps, but if we regard syntax as that which embodies and demands decisions about connection and coherence, then it comes to the same thing. Many of Blake's famous aphorisms depend on their being seen to be read in, at least, two ways. Thus with

> Damn. braces: Bless relaxes (Erd. 37, K. 152).

Does he mean 'damn things which restrain, bless things which relax' (imperative), or that 'the act of damning is invigorating, the act of blessing relaxing'? These two possibilities polarise active and passive readings. An even more famous example is the following:

> Sooner murder an infant in its cradle than nurse unacted desires
> (Erd. 37, K. 152).

I can remember wondering until quite recently how the author of 'Auguries of Innocence' could put his name to such an unabashed justification of that much-quoted persona, the 'romantic superego', and advocate, from whatever perspective, the murdering of babies. Perhaps it is the shock of this which forces us to look for another reading; the nursing does not refer to our internal feelings, but to the child itself, figuratively embodied as 'unacted desires'. 'Sooner murder the child you are nursing than allow *its* desires to remain unacted'. Still slightly troubling, until we realise that the only reason for these desires to remain unacted is our own supervision, and the enforcing of our own inhibitions on the infant. The teasing out of this reading is in fact a fine little exercise in decentering the selfhood. Our first tendency—perhaps I should say 'my' first tendency, so as not to involve those further along the road to salvation—is to appropriate the 'free' or indeterminate word, 'nurse', to an egocentric reading, and it is the ego which is unseated when that reading is complicated. Our self-satisfaction, which is implicated in the gesture of denial we make after the first reading ('Oh no! how can he say that? I would not do such a thing'), gives way to a darker sense of responsibility in the recognition of the deeper level of egotism involved in the second reading. Not that we can escape even now in the sure knowledge that we have exhausted Blake's 'purpose', for it is possible to read the personification from the other direction, stressing the priority of unacted desires rather than children. Thus, to paraphrase, unacted desires are 'like' infants in cradles; if they are never allowed to grow up, they may as well be murdered, and not to act them is akin to murder. The point is, of course, that there is no simple reading, and recognising the reflexiveness of this line may well be the closest we can get to its author's purpose. As a performative aphorism, it demands a context to decide its credibility, what Austin might have called its 'happiness', and we must bring that context with us. In other words, we become its author.

There are, then, always decisions to be made. Sometimes the syntax, in the most overt sense, gives us a hint that the persona who is speaking is not to be invested with the authority to which he aspires. In 'The Voice of the Ancient Bard', for example, the syntax falters, stumbles, collapses, and comes close to sinking into a formless murmur (deliberately unstopped, left suspended), to warn us that this bard is of dubious integrity, and is not to be taken at face value (*Songs*, 54). 'Face value', indeed, is a metaphor Blake may well have in mind, as the design seems to indicate that the bard has two faces, looking in different directions. Often we are caught between 'objective' statement and dramatic predication,[38] or between closed and open

forms, finality or incompletion. Note the way in which the last line of
'A Little BOY Lost' (*Songs*, 50),

> Are such things done on Albions shore

refuses us the question mark (alas, inserted in K. 177) which would
allow us to align ourselves, as we do so easily, with the righteous,
interrogative faction, and turns a line which we try to read as a
question into an uneasy statement or insinuation of complicity
(which is the feeling we have, I think, when the interrogative is
denied). This atmosphere of ambivalence and potential discomfort,
involving as it does the intrusion of indeterminate 'tones of voice'
which upset the apparent precision of the written word, is evident
right from the beginning of *Songs of Innocence*. I have already touched
on some of the implications in the 'Introduction' (*Songs*, 4). It is well
known now that the status of the artist and his function as transcriber
and communicator are not untroubled. His reed is hollow, and is the
articulation of his message staining waters which would otherwise be
clear, or staining them into a state of clearness?[39] Both, I think,
depending on whether the events are viewed from a hypostatised
innocence or an actual experience which must be played through if
some higher innocence is to be achieved. All of which is to give an
uneasy tonality to the last line of the poem, again unpunctuated and
unstopped:

> Every child may joy to hear

Every child may, if he so wishes, or are there other options? Certainly,
to read this line imperatively as 'every child will joy to hear' is to
identify oneself with the tyrannous adult, imposing predications on
the infant world, whose appearance provides, I think, one of the
prominent ironies of the volume, as in 'Infant Joy'. Responding to the
demand made by the lack of end stopping, and turning the page, we
come to 'The Shepherd', which follows the 'Introduction' in ten out
of the twenty known separately published editions of *Songs of
Innocence*, and in fifteen out of twenty-two of the complete *Songs of
Innocence and of Experience* (Erdman, *The Illuminated Blake*, pp. 69,
96–7). Here is the poem:

> How sweet is the Shepherds sweet lot,
> From the morn to the evening he strays:
> He shall follow his sheep all the day
> And his tongue shall be filled with praise.

For he hears the lambs innocent call.
And he hears the ewes tender reply.
He is watchful while they are in peace,
For they know when ther Shepherd is nigh. (*Songs* 5)

What looks at first like a happy little poem about protection begins to fragment under careful scrutiny. Carrying over the tone of un-certainty from the page before, one is justified in stressing the first line, with its strange tautology, 'How sweet *is* the shepherd's sweet lot?' He strays, instead of the sheep, and he follows, instead of leading. But he is watchful, and the implication is that this has something to do with their being at peace. What is the connection? Are they at peace precisely because he is watchful, waiting to restrain them at the first sign of unrest, as an adult overseeing children? Or is the shepherd watchful of things other than the sheep, ready to fend off any threat from outside the flock? The latter reading makes him the perfect authoritarian, prepared to follow where he is led until such time as protective functions might be called upon; he is not nursing unacted desires. This reading, moreover, seems to fit in best with the details of the first stanza. If he is simply an inept shepherd, following rather than leading, then it is hard to incorporate the fact of his watchfulness into a coherent relationship with this imbecility.[40] But to answer the question of what sort of a shepherd we are being faced with, we must first ask it, and we can come to see that the lot of this shepherd is 'sweet' only because he has submitted his role to a higher examination than that implicit in the metaphor of leadership at its crudest. The turn of meaning, one might almost say the 'joke', is at the expense of the experienced reader and his expectations of what the business of shepherding involves, and it is the contradiction of these expectations in the presentation of a passive authoritarian which begins the quest for a different sort of meaning. The first line, then, can be punctuated 'How sweet is the shepherd's "sweet lot"?', where 'sweet lot' represents the traditional pastoral trope and its place in the standard poetic diction, which is precisely what Blake is qualifying. Thus we end up punctuating the text for ourselves, in a gesture of 'filling in' wherein the 'unfinished' state of the poem operates as a metaphor of inclusion inducting the reader into a creative relationship with the page before him—and this must work whether or not my 'in-terpretation' be admitted as the correct or exclusive one. For the shepherd is also one of the familiar metaphors for the author, or poet; in turning around the expected order of priorities, Blake is also pointing out that he himself, imprisoned on the page or bound to the tree in a sense which is as positive as it is negative, is obliged to follow where his reader leads him, providing the raw materials of a 'meaning' in whichever interpretative pastures the flock might happen upon. What the larger protective function might be for the author as shepherd is a teasing question, touching as it does on the issue of where the author can determinately intervene to block interpretation, and where he is totally under the control of his reader's intentionality. On this point, more later.[41]

A great many of the decisions we have to make in reading Blake can be seen to depend upon active or passive options. Deployed tensions between subject and object, touching upon their possible identification, has often been noticed as an important feature of the Romantic lyric.[42] With Blake in particular, this often takes the form of an insight into the artist/reader's responsibility or culpability—for the two go together within the metaphor of language as fall, but necessary fall—as touched upon in the 'Introduction' to *Songs of Innocence*. Take the first stanza of 'London', for example:

> I wander thro' each charter'd street,
> Near where the charter'd Thames does flow
> And mark in every face I meet
> Marks of weakness, marks of woe (*Songs*, 46).

The passage involves not just the suggestion of 'charted' in 'charter'd'—for the city and the river are mapped by reason as they are licensed and hired out by commercial interest—but also a possible double reading of 'mark', which can be read either as 'notice' or, following the more active and intentional content of the main clause to which it is subordinated, as 'inscribe' or 'determine'. The question of the implication of the 'I' in the fallen or corrupt world which it at first appears only to describe, as outside itself, is thus brought into focus. For the speaker/reader of experience, such a decision is obviously crucial: Blake may indeed, as Bloom suggests (*Poetry and Repression*, p. 38), be other than a 'prophet'.

The incidence of this sort of strategy at the beginning of 'The First Book of Urizen' is well known, and has often been remarked upon by critics.[43] Let me give just some brief examples:

> what Demon
> Hath form'd this abominable void
> This soul-shudd'ring vacuum?—Some said

'It is Urizen', But unknown, abstracted
Brooding secret, the dark power hid (Erd. 69, K. 222).

Here, we are torn between reading Urizen as the creator of the void, and as the void itself. The 'is' belongs grammatically to the vacuum, but stands syntactically as the response to the question. Looking for an answer, we tend to superimpose the present descriptive 'is' upon the past tense 'hath'; and both readings are correct, for Urizen is the creator of himself, and his self is his world. Again, in the lines

strong I repell'd
The vast waves, & arose on the waters
A wide world of solid obstruction (Erd. 71, K. 224)

if we are hunting for an 'externalised' reading, then we will take the wide world of obstruction as the subject of 'arose'. But the uninverted sense also holds good, in that Urizen is this world, this obstruction, being self-created. The participatory obligation of puzzling out the syntax stimulates recognition of this gesture of division and synthesis. Consider the encounter of Los and Urizen:

The bellows & hammer are silent now
A nerveless silence, his prophetic voice
Siez'd; a cold solitude & dark void
The Eternal Prophet & Urizen clos'd (Erd. 76, K. 230).

The 'nerveless silence' appears both as the object of 'siez'd', and as an amplification of the preceding line, in which case the verb describes the seizing-up of the voice, in a reflexive sense. The next verb, 'clos'd', also demands attention, for we must ask whether Los and Urizen are actively closing off the dark void; or whether they are being enclosed by it. Taking the last of the quoted lines separately, Los and Urizen are also closing in the sense of coming into conflict, a conflict sharpened by their desire to preserve the separate identities which are gradually being fused.

This irony in Urizen's position, that he sees as existing objectively and outside him a world which he is himself continually producing, is brought to the front again and again by Blake wherever the tyrant appears. In 'The Four Zoas' he laments:

O what a world is here unlike those climes of bliss
Where my sons gathered round my knees O thou poor ruind world
Thou horrible ruin once like me thou wast all glorious
And now like me partaking desolate thy masters lot
(Erd. 342–43, K. 317).

thus expressing as casual or coincidental a relationship which is in fact causal. What is described is also performed, what is done to others is simultaneously inflicted upon ourselves. Blake's prophetic books show the same things happening again and again, even to the same 'characters', the same names. There is no alternative to a continuous rising and falling, self-creation and self-destruction. In the same spirit Demogorgon's words at the end of 'Prometheus Unbound' 'waken Oblivion' (*Poetical Works*, p. 267); they wake us from oblivion, and consign us to it at the same time, as the result of the poem, an awakening in one sense, a heightening of consciousness, is inevitably compromised by the return to habitual consciousness which must succeed the end of the poetic experience. The challenge, the success, and the defeat are held together in the one expression.

Indeterminate syntactic relationships are then part of the range of options open to a poet who is committed to a heuristic method. Conventionally the embodiment of normative hierarchies and stable progressions based on explicit subject/predicate relationships, syntax becomes, for Blake and Shelley particularly, a mode of displacement and confusion. We are denied 'progression', in so far as we might assume it to be the vehicle of reading through time, a process based, for these poets, on the false securities of accumulated information and the hegemony of unexamined and pre-established codes within which all new items of potential 'meaning' take their place. Instead, we are made aware that all meaning is partial, even after it has been filled out by the reader's performative activity; this is demonstrated in the tension between what we create and what we receive, which is only ever a hypostatised point of contact *between* reader and text, always open to readjustment and realignment in the light of subsequent readings, and even during the same reading, as patterns of coherence appear and disappear.

As beginnings are never 'stated' but must always be inferred, and as we always begin our meditations upon meaning from a point *within* those meanings,[44] thus rendering our apprehension of their limits and scope a necessarily incomplete and partial one (this is what I have described as the absence of the metacomment), so one of the formal artifacts open to the poet becomes that of the fragment. Many among the *Lyrical Ballads* are in this sense 'fragments'; they imply antecedents and consequents outside the denotative scope of the language in which they are written. Southey felt it to be of 'the very essence of passion to speak in hints and fragments',[45] and the fragment, in one form or another, is an important feature of Romantic discourse, as it is at the centre of the Romantic practice of the discipline we now know as 'criticism', which is characterised above all by attention to the 'image'. Gordon McKenzie, in his *Critical Responsiveness: A Study of the Psychological Current in Later Eighteenth-Century Criticism*, p. 97, chooses to attribute this to what he calls the 'psychological method' deriving from Locke:

> Its weakness lies in an inadequate account of large structures of thought and emotion . . . The account of memory and imagination implies that only small sections of experience can be attended to at the same time, and the principle of association which plays so large a part in all these critics loses its significance when applied to very large contexts.

But whatever the determining factors may or may not be, and however passive the poet may be under their influence, necessity can yet appear as virtue, and it is for the integrity of that most famous of all Romantic 'fragments', 'Kubla Khan', that I shall now argue.

Arguments about the degrees of spontaneity and premeditation which might have gone into the poem seem ultimately somewhat unsatisfying; there is no way of deciding absolutely between the two, nor does the distinction matter to a theory of mind which regards the spontaneous expression as itself embedded in an infinitely proliferating context of possible determinants. Lowes has been criticised for having left the hierarchies and orderings unspoken or unsought in his vast compendium of source materials, *The Road to Xanadu*;[46] but it may be that critical opinion will come to declare an intuitive wisdom in this procedure, when it recognises that the determination of 'meaning' can never be presented without the implicit exclusion of possibilities which are felt to inhibit that particular meaning. Thus, excluding a great deal more than I include, I shall offer an argument for viewing the poem as a careful structure of recession and diminishing perspective which is overlain and dialectically complicated by successive heightenings of imaginative perception and co-ordination.

To begin with, the verse itself is specified as a 'fragment' by the prose preface. This relationship of verse to prose, the one within the other, is enacted again and again in the internal relationships between the parts of the poem alone. The first five lines culminate in the disappearance of the sacred river, and it is this disappearance which is fought off and tentatively pre-empted in the next twenty-five lines.[47] The 'ceaseless turmoil' of the fountain is throwing up the fragments of a prior material or substance which has been digested and decomposed, presumably, before the poem's narrative begins. The reappearance of these fragments is interspersed with the reappearance of the sacred river whose descent into invisibility has already been described; the second 'stanza' of the poem, up to line 30,[48] is thus a wager against time, a momentary (and eternal) staying of the final disappearance of the river (and we cannot be sure from textual evidence alone whether the poet is redescribing the river *before* it disappeared in line 5, or its spasmodic reappearance *after* that descent). Again, in the 'third' stanza lines 31–6, we are reintroduced, not to the pleasure-dome itself, but to its 'shadow', with the object being recomposed, as it were, into a new nominal phrase, 'dome of pleasure'. This crucial passage, which in any simple reading of the poem as a progressive celebration of the powers of poetry or imagination, would have to be glossed as the point of the mediation of all contraries and oxymoronic juxtapositions, is once again a re-enacting of images previously introduced. The fourth stanza, introducing the damsel and the poet's conditional declarations, are very overtly 'after the event', and again speak for a further degree of distancing from any immediate descriptive intensity. The availability of the vision of Xanadu seems to depend on the vision of the damsel which is only loosely connected to it, any causal link being left, apparently, vague. Once again, the 'once I saw' (l. 38) seems to invoke a time outside of and prior to the vision of Xanadu.

On this reading, then, the poem is composed of a series of regressing visions or groups of images, each moving further and further away from the primary descriptive 'reality' of the first stanza, and each bringing the poet closer to the wishful, conditional mood of the last lines. But there is another argument to be attended to. This poem is, as J. B. Beer has capably argued in *Coleridge the Visionary*, pp. 199–276, fundamentally a dialectical construct. Each stage of the regression I have described above also introduces a new image; the first introduces the fountain (recollected in stanza three), and the second the caves of ice (recollected in stanza four). These images provide a rising counterpoint to the declining intensity of the opening ones, those of dome, river, and caverns. Loss and gain are happening simultaneously, overlapping.[49] As the speaking voice moves further from its beginnings, there is an accretion of detail and a re-organisation of priorities. The first stanza does render images which are not at all recaptured—walls, gardens, incense-bearing trees—or recaptured only briefly, as the 'forests ancient' reappear as the 'cedarn cover' (l. 13) and the 'wood and dale' (l. 26). But the general patterning seems to be one of the superimposition of loss and gain, slippage and re-creation.

The conclusion is, then that the 'fragment' which Coleridge was able to transcribe is itself fragmented, and divided up with a complexity which is sufficient to indicate that it is already a model of the only 'whole' which it could possibly ever be, an infinite working and re-working of details already lost to immediate perception but regained and intensified through imaginative recollection. In terms of structure, and in this barest sense, Wordsworth did no more in the thirteen books of *The Prelude* than Coleridge is doing in fifty-four lines. The disappearance of the river, whatever it might 'represent', and of the attendant images, are redescribed as a means of prolonging their life in the imaginative mind. Alph stands to Coleridge much as the Duddon, and the experience of childhood in general, stands to Wordsworth. It seems an appropriate coincidence to find Wordsworth writing, towards the end of his long poem:

> we have traced the stream
> From darkness, and the very place of birth
> In its blind cavern, whence is faintly heard
> The sound of waters; follow'd it to light
> And open day, accompanied its course
> Among the ways of Nature, afterwards
> Lost sight of it, bewilder'd and engulph'd,
> Then given it greeting, as it rose once more
> With strength, reflecting in its solemn breast
> The works of man and face of human life,
> And lastly, from its progress have we drawn
> The feeling of life endless, the great thought
> By which we live, infinity and God (*The Prelude*, XIII, 172–84).

'Kubla Khan' does not pursue this meditation to its crescendo, and nor, I think, does Wordsworth himself in one implicit voice of the poem, which is that in which he wrote to Sir George Beaumont in June, 1805, after having finished it:

> . . . it was not a happy day for me I was dejected on many accounts; when I looked back upon the performance it seemed to have a dead weight about it, the reality so far short of the expectation; it was the first long labour that I had finished, and the doubt whether I should ever live to write the Recluse and the sense which I had of this Poem being so far below what I seem'd capable of executing, depressed me much (*Letters: The Early Years*, rev. ed., p. 594).

Wordsworth too, it will be remembered, saw his poem as but 'a sort of portico to the Recluse' (ibid.), but a fragment of the whole. *The Prelude* is in one light a sort of double negative; it is but a promise of the future, and it cannot regains its own past, the poet's earlier years. For both poets, verbal facility comes only after the experience which it has to describe; the ensuing 'meaning' is necessarily out of step with the events which made it possible, but at the same time is of equivalent value. I take that state which Coleridge describes, wherein 'all the images rose up before him as *things*' (*Poetical Works*, p. 296), to have ceased by the end of the first stanza, and perhaps even before the beginning of the poem; the succeeding passages are variations upon these themes, those images, rehearsed in the mind alone, or in the mind's eye.

What I have been suggesting, perhaps rather laboriously, is that the fragmentation within the poem makes the poem a 'whole'. Any further development would have to have been a repetition of the dialectical interplay of loss and gain which is already fully exemplified in what we have.[50] The fragment has the logic of wholeness; it says all that there is to be said. One wonders, in fact, if it might not be the vehicle of that fantasy which Coleridge recorded in one of his notebooks:

> To have a continued Dream, representing visually & audibly all Milton's Paradise Lost. (N. 658).

If it is, then it must be said that that paradise, like the innocence of the child, is lost as soon as posited, and the process of description is the chronicle of the attempt at regaining.

In this context, the choice of names and images may be seen to have an almost mantric significance. Whatever the streamy associations which might have fed into the naming of 'Alph', it seems beyond doubt that it has something to do with the alphabet, the gift of language, or ordered speech.[51] As such, it has connections within the poem as well as sources outside it. 'Abora' and 'Abyssinian' both begin with the first two letters of the alphabet, connecting back across the stanzas to the sacred river of words, and providing some sort of coherence overlaying the general pattern of syntactical ebbing and flowing.[52] Further, there is an 'abyss' in 'Abyssinia' (which, like 'Abora', also ends with the first letter of the alphabet, where it began), an image which occurs in striking conjunction with that of the river in a later passage by Wordsworth:

Never did a Child stand by the side of a running Stream, pondering within himself what power was the feeder of the perpetual current, from what never-wearied sources the body of water was supplied, but he must have been inevitably propelled to follow this question by another: 'towards what abyss is it in progress? what receptacle can contain the mighty influx?' and the spirit of the answer must have been, though the word might be Sea or Ocean, accompanied perhaps with an image gathered from a Map, or from the real object in Nature—these might have been the *letter*, but the *spirit* of the answer must have been *as* inevitably, a receptacle without bounds or dimensions, nothing less than infinity (*The Friend*, II, 337).[53]

Language, however compromised it may be, is all that the poet has between himself and oblivion, struggling as he is to close, for the apprehending reader, the gap between inspiration and composition. In terms of the primary experience he describes, indeed, he is himself in the position of that reader, or that child by the side of the stream, providing symbols towards infinity, and he has only the letter to do it with. Thus I regard 'Kubla Khan' not as 'a symbolic expression of his inability to realise his power as a poet',[54] but rather as a recognition of all that the power of the poet can ever be as it conveys an experience inevitably contained within the various limitations imposed by narrative time, memory, and language.

If 'Kubla Khan' speaks for the inevitably partial nature of poetic communication when set against the vision which inspires it, then it demonstrates also, as I have argued, the value of the reconstituted images and meanings which accrue out of that vanishing and that incompletion. The poem can stand in one of its guises as an emblem of the heuristic method, which Coleridge is able to employ on so many occasions. What the artist in the primary, authoritarian sense cannot do is presented to the reader as an invitation or temptation, an empty space which he must fill for himself in the cause of kindling his own torch. The central chapters of *Biographia Literaria* seem to me to make some sense in this context. Chapter XIII promises to be the answer to all our questions, the central argument to which the long and complex preceding chapter is but a preface. In fact, we are presented with three epigraphs (in three different languages), a discourse on negative quantities and polarity, a letter from a 'friend' (who was in fact Coleridge himself) on the feasibility of continuing what he has begun, a promise of some future account of the build-up to the conclusions about to be presented, and the conclusions themselves, the famous comments on imagination and fancy. The chapter seems to me to be a parody of a deductive method, in that what is dealt with is not discursively explicable but only 'presentable'; that is to say, it cannot be provided as a body of objective information, but only communicated as a living process, wherein only participation will produce meaning, and only imagination define imagination. All the hints are there. The philosopher does not deal with what is 'existing and complete', but rather contemplates intelligence 'in its growth, and as it were represents its history to the mind from its birth to its maturity' (*Biographia*, I, 196). The move from the 'notional to actual' in 'the process of our own self-consciousness' will only be apparent in the process itself:

> By what instrument this is possible the solution itself will discover, at the same time that it will reveal to and for whom it is possible (p. 198).

And so on. The prose 're-presents' what we might think it ought to 'explain', and imagination, far from being the logical deduction to be derived from it, is in fact the prerequisite for achieving any understanding at all.[55] This is no mere excuse for a loose methodology, but is in fact the strictest method of all, making the highest demands both on the author and the reader. And Coleridge knew well what he was doing. In August, 1817, the year of publication, he wrote to Tulk:

> In my literary Life you will find a sketch of the *subjective* Pole of the Dynamic Philosophy; the rudiments of *Self*-construction, barely enough to let a thinking mind see *what it is like* (*Letters*, IV, 767).

We can indeed see the results of this philosophy as applied to certain areas of inquiry, as he goes on to tell us; but in itself, seeing 'what it is like' is all we can ever achieve from the outside. The intrinsic recognition is available only to the participating mind, as the enduring vision of Xanadu demands the flashing eyes and the floating hair.

4 Intimate Voices

> But our thoughts have generally such an obscure implicit language, that
> 'tis the hardest thing in the world to make them speak out distinctly.
> For this reason, the right method is to give them voice and accent.
> Shaftesbury, *Soliloquy or*
> *Advice to an Author*

I

I have so far tried to describe the metaphorical vehicle of the
imperative towards deconstruction, the image of childhood, and also
its embodiment in linguistic techniques. I shall now attempt to
demonstrate and explain the incidence of the division which has
already been frequently posited between author and narrator,
'speaker' and 'poet'.

This division has a great deal to do with tonality, with the intrusion
of implied inflections and intonations into a written discourse which,
by definition, can never completely satisfy or complete the probable
or possible 'meanings' which that tonality might demand. It is always
very difficult for the critic to pinpoint, even in a partially unambiguous sense, the 'meaning' of a dialogue, the degree to which the
'author' behind the whole artifact might himself be endorsing the
views of either party. Shaftesbury saw this as the appeal of the
dialogue form for an open debate uncompromised by the strident
prejudices of author and reader: '*the Author* is annihilated; and *the
Reader* being no way apply'd to, stands for No-body. The self-
interesting partys both vanish at once'.[1] Something 'truthful' might
then be thought to emerge from it. The Romantic version of this
argument, however, would have to take account of the complicated
and perhaps indistinguishable mixture of argument and persuasion,
logic and rhetoric (which in the lowest terms means needs and
desires), which can be seen to lie behind any attempt to convince. Any
employment of the strategy of 'voices' asks questions about the
authority of the subjectivities which they enunciate, and there is no
sure concept of an ultimate truth whose articulation they might be

working towards. When meanings are presented within overtly or implicitly signified spoken voices, we have to estimate, not just *what* is said, but also by and for whom, and on what particular occasion it is said. This makes for a necessarily unstable structure whose complete meaning is probably unattainable, and whose partial meanings themselves demand large contributions from the reading mind, disposed according to its own needs and convictions.[2]

This is an important part of what I want to call 'irony'. Allemann (*Ironie und Dichtung*, p. 16) regards 'literary irony' as involving a tension between what the speaker appears to *say* and what the reader/hearer deduces that he really *means*; but, in the Romantic context, the qualification must be made that the deduction about what is really 'meant' cannot be accomplished on the evidence of the text alone; the reader must intrude, even manipulate, in his own person, and often constitute something of a different order from what is before him.[3] Along with this, there goes the suggestion that the personae of author and speaker, like those of 'Ode on a Grecian Urn', cannot ultimately be kept apart with the exactness necessary if the one is to provide a critical overview of the other; though, of course, it is only through the working out of the distinction that its redundancy can be made apparent. Only after the positing of the metacomment does the questioning of its integrity begin; this often becomes clear in the attempted identification of this 'author' figure, whom we try to locate somewhere behind and outside of the ironised speaker. It is in this context that I shall pass on to a discussion of 'The Rime of the Ancient Mariner', with special reference to the nature and status of the marginal prose commentary which appears in the later versions.

The only critic I know of who has gone at all deeply into the question of the commentary is George Watson, in his *Coleridge the Poet*, pp. 85–104, and his account must stand as a signpost to any further discussion of the theme. Watson notes (p. 91) the 'Jacobean-Caroline' nature of its language, and that it is, 'in the broadest sense, pastiche'. He describes also how the historical positioning of this diction locates it half way between the pretended action (c. 1500) and the date of composition (c. 1800), so that the action 'is seen through a double historical lens'. (p. 95) If I may summarise his argument by a quotation:

> I suggest that the purpose and effect of the gloss can only be to intensify the historical, dramatic, 'as if' element in the poem, both in the action of the poem and in its stated morality. Its effect is deliberately to enlarge doubt concerning what the Mariner says, to remind the reader that, in

spite of the textual modernization of 1800, the poem is an historical exercise which asks not to be taken literally (p. 93).

There is nothing in this fine account, I think, which is essentially at odds with what I am about to say. Watson makes the crucial observation that the status of the 'I', of the old sailor's utterance, is dramatically qualified by the commentary.[4] If the poem and its gloss display themselves as a historical exercise, however, then they can be seen at the same time as a 'hermeneutic' exercise, a demonstration of the speaker-reader relationship and its bearing on the location of a possible 'author'. The first reaction to the commentary, I think, and one which would certainly explain why so many critics have ignored it, is that it is a summary and a guide to what the poem enacts in verse. But, where the verse offers an 'immediate' rendering, full of unspecified details brought out of the consciousness of the recollecting 'I', the prose stands at a greater distance from the events related, and purports to put them into place, not infrequently by invoking something very close to the language of the Authorised Version of the Bible. Where the verse seeks to place us 'on the spot', forcing us to orient ourselves within the landscape of the poem:

> The Sun came up upon the left,
> Out of the sea came he!
> And he shone bright, and on the right
> Went down into the sea (*Poetical Works*, p. 187).

the prose flattens all this out into a pseudo-objective description of how the ship 'sailed southward', adding the extra locating details which fix the sailor's message within the most conventional codings of seafaring language, 'with a good wind and fair weather'. Such reductions, or explanations, of slightly mysterious details into very matter-of-fact descriptions is one of the most common tactics of the commentary. For example, the Mariner's assertion that

> We were the first that ever burst
> Into that silent sea.

is converted by the prose into the direct account of how 'the ship enters the Pacific Ocean' (p. 190). The prose adds details and specifications, be they geographical or moral, which remain indeterminate in the Mariner's narration. Thus it conspires to reduce to the 'ordinary' those aspects of the narration which strike the deepest mysteries. What we have is the tension between a primary experience and an 'objectively' presented account of it in another voice. In the transition from one to the other, there is an evident process of loss and gain; some details are added—and not always as overtly as the references to the learned Michael Psellus (p. 191)—while others are left out. There is nothing in the verse which tells us that the albatross is to be regarded as a 'pious bird of good omen' (p. 189), and one may even wonder whether this sort of attribution is to be seen as an example of the fickle superstitions and confident causal connections which the other sailors indulge in. The verse consistently plays upon ambiguities and tensions which completely escape the voice responsible for the prose gloss. Thus, where the prose describes how the Mariner is made the scapegoat (p. 191), the verse reads

> Instead of the cross, the Albatross
> About my neck was hung.

Cross is an elided version of 'cross-bow', but it also surreptitiously suggests the protagonist's identification with Christ, and the redemptive potential which is, mysteriously, implicit in his very crime. One could go on within the terms of the prose-verse relationship which I have outlined here. The prose description of the Mariner's loneliness, for example, with its rhapsodical passage into the vault of heaven (p. 197), seems completely out of place in juxtaposition with the terse under-statement of the Mariner's own summary. This seems to be one occasion where the prose voice drastically goes beyond the authority of the verse, into an extended variation of its own, derived from its own prior and extraneous disposition. Again, at the beginning of Part V, the prose connects into a causal sequence two events left separate or merely conjunctive by the verse; Mary sending sleep, and the rain which falls upon the ship. Perhaps I have said enough to make the point. It can be argued that the prose commentary stands as a conscious, albeit gentle, parody of the habit of overinscription and reductive explanation which the poem undoubtedly attracted from its first readers. As such, the effect is not simply, as Watson suggests, to place the Mariner's own conclusions in doubt, but also to ironise the status of the prose voice. In terms of the reading experience, it reminds us that the process of paraphrase and explanation which goes on, implicitly, every time we read, must of necessity involve a level of misprision. The primary experience, which is within Coleridge's aesthetic the proper material for torch-kindling, is threatened and reduced by secondary discourse, and the level of closure, of 'metacomment', which that discourse might be thought to provide, is in fact only a faded version of the events which made it possible. If, therefore, we see that prose language as spoken by an 'author', then it is one who has lapsed from the pitch of intensity which produced the verse within it, and this is not any simple confession of failure but, in terms of Shelley's distinction between inspiration and composition, a carefully wrought analogue of the relation of both reader and author to the text before them. Coleridge is ironising his own voice to wake up his readers, by being both 'speaker' (the mariner himself') and commentator. Each voice casts doubt on the other, and we are asked to choose between them, not necessarily in the same way as I have chosen in reading the poem as an anatomy of primary and secondary experience. But there is evidence for this reading, and in this context it is hard to resist the urge to quote the passage so often quoted in discussions of this poem:

> Mrs. Barbauld once told me that she admired the Ancient Mariner very much, but that there were two faults in it,—it was improbable, and had no moral. As for the probability, I owned that might admit some question; but as to the want of a moral, I told her that in my own judgement the poem had too much; and that the only, or chief fault, if I might say so, was the obtrusion of the moral sentiment so openly on the reader as a principle or cause of action in a work of such pure imagination. [5]

This being the opinion of the mature Coleridge, it seems hardly likely that he would have employed without some irony a technique which appears to add to the specificity of that moral. Consider also the following comment, or self-interrogation:

> Quaere, whether or no too great definiteness of terms in any language may not consume too much of the vital and idea-creating force in distinct, clear, full-made images, and so prevent originality. For original might be distinguished from positive thought. [6]

The prose commentary does nothing if it does not add 'clear, full-made images' to a verse language of indefinite attributions.

I shall now say something about 'The Eolian Harp' (*Poetical Works*, p. 100) in the context of the argument about the division of the narrative voice. It is a commonplace of criticism that the last paragraph, beginning 'But thy more serious eye . . . ', represents a drastic change of tone from the rest of the poem; so much so that Watson, *Coleridge the Poet*, p. 66, finds that 'Sara is merely a nuisance in the poem, which ought to have closed on the penultimate paragraph'. It seems to me that the passage referred to does offer a real contribution to the poem, especially when it is seen to speak for a faltering of confidence which is intimated also in the opening lines.

There are, I think, at least two sorts of discourse at work here, corresponding roughly to the prose and verse conventions of 'The Rime of the Ancient Mariner'. The first, and dominant one is that of the easily flowing, 'conversational' descriptions; the second occurs in the two parenthesised passages of the first twelve lines. Each of these stands as a secondary commentary (an apparent metacommentary) on the first discourse, pushing it into place, moralising it, and specifying it, yet in such a way as to at least suggest its insecurity within, or conscious incompatibility with, that first discourse. After the first paragraph, these parenthetic intrusions disappear from the poem—it is as if the poet gains confidence in the viability of the first discourse—but they reappear, I think, unparenthesised (yet implicitly additive, as Watson's response shows), in the prolonged version of the 'second' discourse which forms the final paragraph. It provides an affirmative (and negative) full stop where before was only tentative punctuation. I agree with McFarland, *Coleridge and the Pantheist Tradition*, p. 107, that his 'inability either really to accept or wholeheartedly to reject Pantheism' is an abiding theme throughout Coleridge's career, and particularly in his mainstream poetic career. In this context, it is hard to take the last paragraph in literal good faith as a strenuous self-rebuke moving toward a finally achieved fixity of purpose.[7] It demands a judgement of some sort about its tonality, because it clearly represents a change of mood from what comes before, but at the same time we do not have enough information to determine that judgement in any absolute and unambiguous way. It could well be read, for example, as a passage of mock sententiousness and ironised self-deprecation, paying only literal lip-service to Sara as the spokesman of orthodoxy. If Coleridge did intend any final closure, it is hard to imagine why he would have added, in 1828, one of the most overtly pantheist passages of all (lines 26–33), contributing as it must to undermine the authority of that closure.[8] As with 'The Ancient Mariner', then, what is offered seems to be a structure founded in a deliberate discontinuity embodied in the presentation of two sorts of discourse which do not meet except frictionally and ironically at certain points. One discourse offers or appears to act as a closural force upon the other—offering itself as a 'metacommentary'—but this gesture is not vindicated when we begin a closer survey and an attempted reconciliation of divergent meanings. The voice which is superficially authoritative is thus seen not to belong to the 'author' at all, because it does not meet the demands of interpretive coherence. The author, who at this point is a true 'ironist', has abdicated his habitual role and left an empty space which the reader must occupy (but only in order to leave free once more?) with his own triangulations.

Perhaps it will not be over-enthusiastic to point to one more Coleridgean example of the fronting of incompatible perspectives within an apparently homogeneous poetic discourse, the 'Hymn Before Sun-Rise, in the Vale of Chamouni' (*Poetical Works*, p. 376). Even if the poem be described as a translation, we must still account for Coleridge's interest in the theme, and for what he produced out of it. The task is, I think, to explain the process whereby a tentatively questioning speaking voice located amidst silence and darkness is able to aspire to a condition where all passive bewilderment is left behind, and within which he feels able to orchestrate the cosmic symphonies of nature. Do the natural forms of the valley really respond to the call to 'join my Hymn' (l. 28), and do they, or can they, really answer the questions which the speaker puts before them? Do they speak forth the praise of their creator, or is the speaker simply throwing his voice? Take lines 47–8, for example:

> And who commanded (and the silence came),
> Here let the billows stiffen, and have rest?

Is this the silence which accompanied the creator's fiat, or the silence which, in the same time scale as the questioning voice, accompanies or even precedes the speaker's appeal for knowledge? Are we listening to the unison chorus of a thousand voices, or to one voice which has run wild and mistakes, or tries to mistake, the echoes of itself for an external reality?[9] With both these poems, the decision about how we re-perform their actions is not to be made by authoritative references to their 'texts'. This is true of all poetry to a certain extent, of course; but here the point is crucial because of the way in which the voices within the poems seem to be antithetical.

As has been said before, Wordsworth was explicit about the dramatic design of 'The Thorn'; the 'loquacious narrator' (*Prose*, I, 117) is to be distinguished from the voice of the poet himself. The poem has received a great deal of attention, and there are several basic accounts from which beginnings can be made. One of the more recent, that of Michael Kirkham (already cited), stresses the importance of the perspective represented by the visiting stranger to whom the retired sea-captain is telling his story. His function, Kirkham argues, is to force us 'to seek a solution at another level of significance' (p. 77) beyond that which the captain himself is able to identify. This is certainly the invitation which an explicitly dramatic presentation extends to its reader, and it is useful to ask whether such a possibility can be fulfilled.[10] It is worth bringing to mind the case already argued for the fourth of the 'Poems on the Naming of Places', where the moment of self-redemption and correction actually repeats the moment of the crime itself, albeit at a less culpable level. In that poem, the protagonists use the landscape as the vehicle for their (idle) need to symbolise all that they see; here, while the old sea captain pretends to deny all responsibility for the account he is conveying, the most noticeable feature of his discourse is that beneath this disavowal he is, by the very terms and details of his description, in fact exercising a surreptitious control over what we can *do* with the information he is giving us. We are invited to perform a 'heuristic' function, to build up for ourselves a balanced case, but there is a prior process of selection and intentionalising going on right from the start of the captain's narration which we would be gravely in error to read as the truth. He tries to prescribe the terms in which our reformulation of his information can operate. His language is threaded with subjunctives, hesitant similes, and reports and opinions to which he claims to attach no weight; but at the same time he has tried to foreclose the conclusions in the very first stanzas. The hints of burial and ominous intention in stanza II (*Poetical Works*, II, 241) are fed into what is supposed to be a 'description' well before we have been told any of the human details. Again, the description of the moss upon the little hill,

> As if by hand of lady fair
> The work had woven been;
> And cups, the darlings of the eye,
> So deep is their vermilion dye (p. 242)

introduces under the cover of 'observation' the primary images and metaphors of the human drama to which all this is supposed to be but a preface. The anthropomorphic description of the moss is a persuasive gesture rather than a description; it tries to insinuate the suspicion that human hands have been at work here. Similarly, the 'darlings of the eye' demand that we make a comparison with children (who might well be thus described), and the 'vermilion dye' begs reference to blood. The trick is, from the speaker's point of view, that having allowed in these details under the guise of preliminary description, we as readers will later tend to use them as 'fact' in confirmation of the details of the story of Martha and her child. To do so, then, would clearly be to participate in the superstition which the narrator is seeking to proliferate at the same time as denying his desire to do so. He is deceiving himself about the nature of his own discourse, failing to realise that what looks like the acceptable language of vivid personification is in fact corrupted by its being founded in already established ideas. The intentional simile which tells us that the hill of moss is 'like an infant's grave in size', for example, occurs twice in two successive stanzas (p. 242). Surely this is the deepest level at which Wordsworth is concerned to attack the credibility of the old captain? He denies the interpretive gesture when it is overtly called for, but provides it at the more insidious level under the cover of observation. Take these lines from the last stanza

> I cannot tell how this may be,
> But plain it is the Thorn is bound
> With heavy tufts of moss that strive
> To drag it to the ground (p. 248).

Here, the fresh disavowal of accurate insight (about whether or not the child is buried there) is immediately followed up by another intentional observation which tries to turn the objects of the landscape into symbols. The insidious thing about this use of figurative language is that it is just ambiguous enough to make the casual reader think that he is making genuine connections and finding things for himself; whereas all the time he is simply falling into the trap laid by an unconsciously cunning narrator. Once again, we can see displayed here the terms of Wordsworth's objection to what he called 'poetic diction'; to engage with the self-substantiating meanings of the captain's language and to take them for some sort of reality—as we very easily do because we contribute some of our own active intelligence to its unravelling—is to commit the crime into which 'poetic diction' tempts its reader.

What, then, is the 'level of significance' beyond all this? What options are there for getting beyond, in our own voices, the sorts of misprision which the old sea-captain inflicts on the landscape, and on the human beings who are dragged into it? There is, of course, seeing for ourselves, as the narrator directs us in lines which were left out of the poem after 1815:

> But to the Thorn, and to the Pond
> Which is a little step beyond,
> I wish that you would go:

> Perhaps when you are at the place
> You something of her tale may trace (pp. 243–4).

There are two points here; firstly, this represents a directive to leave the poem, to move out into a real world from within which we can no longer question the speaker of a printed text. This is a heuristic imperative, of course, a demand for self-verification, and it may be that we can treat it as a hint that any descriptive act which we might perform in our real worlds had better be an improvement on those of the captain. Secondly, however, one must carry on to wonder whether there are any alternatives in kind to the sorts of intentional descriptions dramatised in the poem. It is noticeable that Wordsworth does not include any rejoinder by the visiting stranger about his own perceptions of the thorn bush. What would they have been, if he had? Some passages in Wordsworth's own voice come to mind. Among the notes which he dictated to Isabella Fenwick in 1843, de Selincourt (p. 511) quotes the following on 'The Thorn':

> Arose out of my observing, on the ridge of Quantock Hill, on a stormy day, a thorn which I had often passed in calm and bright weather without noticing it. I said to myself, 'Cannot I by some invention do as much to make this Thorn permanently an impressive object as the storm has made it to my eyes at this moment?'

Wordsworth has undergone in himself, in other words, through the agency of a change in the weather, a slighter version of the change in the narrator's perceptions which has been wrought by the influence of superstition and local gossip. Something has happened to both of them to make them 'see differently', and it begins to look as if Wordsworth has for some reason dramatised his own change in perceptions as an act of violent intentionality, almost a crime (given that Martha is still alive, and must suffer from rumours). Is the sea-captain a persona of the poet? We can fill out this argument even without recourse to the obvious details of Wordsworth's affair with Annette Vallon. We know from his familiar statements that

> the array
> Of outward circumstance and visible form
> Is to the pleasure of the human mind
> What passion makes it (*The Prelude*, XII, 286–9),

even where, as in this case, he goes on to talk of a reciprocal influence. The *Lyrical Ballads* are about 'the manner in which we associate ideas in a state of excitement', and about situations wherein 'the feeling therein developed gives importance to the action and situation and not the action and situation to the feeling' (*Prose*, I, 122–4, 128). This is a positive manifesto as much as it is a crime. We can cite also the poet's confession of the need for symbols through which experience can be mediated (though, as I have argued before, one can see behind this a deep fear of experience):

> first I look'd
> At Man through objects that were great and fair,
> First commun'd with him by their help (*The Prelude*, VIII, 450–2).

A certain intentional constituent is thus, we might conclude, implicit in all perception and description. Is it then the poet's task to minimise this, to restrain it from reaching the extreme which I have argued to be dramatised in 'The Thorn'? Coleridge, in pointing out that 'language is framed to convey not the object alone, but likewise the character, mood and intentions of the person who is representing it', argues also that it is possible in poetry to eschew all the vicious associations which an age of 'corrupt eloquence' would thrust upon the writer (*Biographia*, II, 115–6). But is it possible to overcome also the limitations of the inner man, which only rise to conscious recognition, if at all, at the very *moment* of perception or expression? Wordsworth has this to say:

> The powers requisite for the production of poetry are: first, those of Observation and Description,—i.e., the ability to observe with accuracy things as they are in themselves, and with fidelity to describe them, unmodified by any passion or feeling existing in the mind of the describer; whether the things depicted be actually present to the senses, or have a place only in the memory. This power, though indispensable to a Poet, is one which he employs only in submission to necessity, and never for a continuance of time: as its exercise supposes all the higher qualities of the mind to be passive, and in a state of subjection to external objects, much in the same way as a translator or engraver ought to be to his original (*Prose*, III, 26).[11]

The indeterminacy which characterises even this, a finished piece of prose, is worth noting. Wordsworth starts out by a strong declaration of faith in 'things in themselves' (clearly, even by 1815 he cannot be thought of as a scrupulous Kantian), but then commits himself to a near-total retraction based on an announced faith in the higher powers of the mind. It may well be that what is here presented as some sort of moral decision really masks a much more painful and uncontrollable epistemological predicament. Far from the description of 'things in themselves' being the easiest and most available of all poetic strategies, is it not truer to say that this sort of description is absolutely impossible, so that we see Wordsworth making a virtue of necessity? How can the mind learn to keep

In wholesome separation the two natures,
The one that feels, the other that observes (*The Prelude*, XIII, 330–1)?

I would suggest that Wordsworth at some level of expressive consciousness knew well enough that this sort of elegent schism within the mind was impossible to enact in any complete way, and that 'The Thorn' can be seen as an enacting of that consciousness. The sea-captain is an emblem of the poet in that he claims not to judge or interpret, and indeed tries not to do so, but yet he ends up by closing off the possibilities for the production of meaning in a much more deceptive and secretive way. He is offering us the chance to make up our own minds, but is at the same time trying to predetermine the decision we must come to. At this level of involvement, it may well be that the poem is suggesting that there is *only* complicity, at the same time as showing the cruelties and misappropriations inherent in that complicity where human lives are involved. The old sailor is not so far from those who give 'Point Rash-Judgment' its name, except that he never corrects himself because he never realises the nature of his transgression. We are left wishing to do otherwise, but unsure of how to go about it. And, like the ramblers in that poem, he is also from this perspective a proxy of the poet himself; 'poet' and 'speaker' come together again. What Wordsworth bravely describes as a volitional contract prompted by the desire to experience 'real and substantial action and suffering',

So that it will be the wish of the Poet to bring his feelings near to those of the persons whose feelings he describes, nay, for short spaces of time, perhaps, to let himself slip into an entire delusion, and even confound and identify his own feelings with theirs (*Prose*, I, 138),

may well be an inevitable coalescence of personae. Just as he was at times content—though I have already tried to argue that it always caused him concern—to admit that objects in nature could not be thought of as separate from the eye of the beholder, so he is here faced with the awkward implication that dramatically presented narrators may be no more than versions of the poet behind them. Hence his confession and his warning; that if his own language should be seen to have suffered from 'those arbitrary connections of feelings and ideas with particular words, from which no man can altogether protect himself', then his reader too 'ought never to forget that he is himself exposed to the same errors as the Poet, and perhaps in a much greater degree' (p. 152).

As far as poet and speaker go, it may be that there is only ever what Coleridge describes as 'a species of ventriloquism, where two are represented as talking, while in truth one man only speaks.' (*Biographia*, II, 109)[12]

The same technique operates in an even more baffling way in 'Endymion'. Keats seems to have been conscious of the bewildering transitions between the different voices (see his remarks on punctuation, *Letters*, I, 271); and he was also conscious, as he shows with a strange mixture of jest and earnest, of the dubious status of personal identity:

> it is a very fact that not one word I ever utter can be taken for granted as an opinion growing out of my identical nature—how can it, when I have no nature? . . . But even now I am perhaps not speaking from myself; but from some character in whose soul I now live (*Letters*, I, 387–8).[13]

I have mentioned already that the 'poet' of 'Endymion', unlike the poet of 'The Eve of St. Agnes', seems to want to keep his distance (and thus his reader's distance) from the narrative by intruding into it in his own voice, as a commentator. It is worth looking closely at one or two instances of this technique, which can be seen to cast an interesting light on the suppressed continuity within the apparent difference. There is a point in Book II where the poet, using the mention of 'Helicon' as a touchstone, intrudes in his own voice on a moment of high rapture between the characters:

> O fountained hill! Old Homer's Helicon,
> That thou wouldst spout a little streamlet o'er
> These sorry pages! Then the verse would soar
> And sing above this gentle pair, like lark
> Over his nested young. But all is dark
> Around thine agèd top, and thy clear fount
> Exhales in mists to heaven. Aye, the count
> Of mighty poets is made up; the scroll
> Is folded by the Muses; the bright roll
> Is in Apollo's hand; our dazèd eyes
> Have seen a new tinge in the western skies.
> The world has done its duty. Yet, oh yet,
> Although the sun of poesy is set,

These lovers did embrace, and we must weep
That there is no old power left to steep
A quill immortal in their joyous tears
                    (II, 717— 32; *Poems*, pp. 193— 4).

This passage, as is well enough known, speaks for the poet's insecurity before a tradition which he has no hopes of emulating, and for the weakness of his own powers. But, remembering that in a later poem the capacity to enter into a mythologised world is exactly the fantasy which has such ambiguous consequences for Madeline and for the reader who follows her (and who, if I read it rightly, cannot help following her), it may be worth wondering whether there is more at stake here. What the poet is asking for is a level of privileged insight, a mythologised perspective from which the events might be seen to have a stable or architectonic signification. He wants to deliver his message from 'above' the lovers, to look down upon them (both literal and metaphoric senses of this phrase will work here). What makes him uneasy is the sense that there is only identification, that he can only comment from ground level, within the experience he describes. What is at stake is not just Keats's place in the gallery of immortal poets, but also the whole status of 'poetry' as an institution mediating experience to a passive and subservient readership. This early poem speaks, I think, for a Keats who has not yet come to embrace the undesirability of such authoritarianism, which is what the invoked mythological dimension can be taken to represent. At the beginning of Book III, after the poet's critique of political tyranny, he delivers in his own voice an address to the moon (III, 52f.), which is repeated by Endymion himself as soon as we rejoin the course of the dramatic narrative (l. 142f.). Book IV begins with the poet addressing the 'Muse of my native land!' and Endymion's own first words invoke exactly the same theme:

'Ah, woe is me that I should fondly part
From my dear native land! . . . (IV, 30— 1).

In each case, the voice of the dramatic persona repeats, in a more or less elided way, the voice of the 'poet' which has preceded it. The distance between them is thus only partial and tentative, as it is between the various characters who are properly seen to be 'inside' the poem, where the problem of naming makes this identity theme even more apparent than does the occluded poet/speaker relationship. Cynthia herself bears a mythologically overdetermined

name, which does not help Endymion in his problem of definition
among Cynthia, Phoebe, and the Indian Maid (or, rather, it repeats
for the alerted reader his immediate crisis of determination). Phoebe is
also Diana (IV, 430– 1); are Diana and Cynthia then synonymous at
IV, 563–6? Diana is traditionally called Artemis, and 'Cynthia' is a
possible pseudonym of Artemis, goddess of chastity . . . and so on.
The reader is put through, at the level of mythological attribution,
the same dramas as Endymion experiences at the level of primary
perception.

II

Thus the distinctions which do appear to be offered, in the poems
discussed, between dramatic and distanced personae, those involved
and those standing above and outside pulling the strings, are undercut
in variously explicit or surreptitious ways, in a movement which
undermines also the reader's separate self, and leaves everybody
loitering at roughly the same distance from the silent borders of the
lake. This is one more among the techniques of deconstruction. If I
may borrow the words of a modern commentator on a modern
predicament:

> Identifying narrators is one of the primary ways of naturalizing fiction.
> The convention that in a text the narrator speaks to his readers acts as
> support to interpretive operations which deal with the odd or apparently
> insignificant. . . . the reader may treat anything anomalous as the effect of
> the narrator's vision or cast of mind . . . the most radical works set out to
> make this kind of recuperation an arbitrary imposition of sense and to
> show the reader how dependent his reading is on models of
> intelligibility . . . In Barthes's words, writing becomes truly writing only
> when it prevents one from answering the question 'who is speaking?'[14]

Romantic poetry, or much of it, is about such resistance to
'naturalising', and we have already seen the purpose of its obtrusion of
'the odd or apparently insignificant'. We are indeed meant to sense
the oddness of the narrators' visions, but we are denied any easy access
to a predetermined and confirmed competence with which to unseat
that oddness. We are not permitted the 'metacomment' and its
attendant self-satisfactions.

This reidentification of separate and single voices can be related to a
crisis in epistemological speculation which becomes increasingly
evident throughout the second half of the eighteenth century, and it

can be seen also to imply that the passing on of the responsibility for
meaning from author to reader is as much a necessity as it is a virtue. If
there is no certainty about what is known and how we know, then
there is no determinate content to communicate at all. Eighteenth-
century philosophy had tended towards the unseating of epistemology as the source of any degree of truth. German philosophy
after Kant was particularly anxious to insist that the mind is
intrinsically *with* objects, and thus to avoid the problem of articulating some area of correspondence between mind and object, or some
degree of translation between the one and the other.[15] This has the
effect of locating the possibility of philosophical coherence in a
mediated area of 'consciousness in the world' which is impossible to
relate definitively to 'things to themselves'. As Coleridge put it:

> During the act of knowledge itself, the objective and subjective are so
> instantly united, that we cannot determine to which of the two the
> priority belongs. There is here no first, and no second; both are
> coinstantaneous and one. While I am attempting to explain this intimate
> coalition, I must suppose it dissolved (*Biographia*, I, 174).[16]

And there is the problem; that description can only ever approach this
moment, and furnish the materials, but it can never *make* it happen.
This must be left to the reader/perceiver, who is thus in a similar
position as regards perception itself as he is in the context of poetic
meaning. There is no language for describing—indeed, no means of
apprehending—the exact relation of self and other as anything other
than a simultaneous synthesis, which must be so in order for it to be
possible for us to think of perception as existing at all.[17] Experience
proves nothing, except what we must presuppose in order for
experience to be possible at all. The 'source' is always outside and
beyond, and we can 'know' nothing of it except as we experience it at
the *moment* of perception. Hence, for Blake

> Knowledge is not by deduction but Immediate by Perception or Sense at
> once Christ addresses himself to the Man not to his Reason Plato did not
> bring Life & Immortality to Light Jesus only did this (Erd. 653, K. 774).

This is what Coleridge means by 'the act of knowledge itself', at
which time there is no problem of explanation in that one simply
gives way to the self-evidence of experience. In such conditions, we
cannot apprehend both the experience itself and the means whereby
we have come to it, or are able to undergo it. There is no
'metacomment', no perspective outside which is not in fact within.

This is in part why Romanticism chooses to disorganise the metaphor of optics as an expression of the mind's relation to its world. I shall discuss this again in the context of metaphor, below; suffice it to say, here, that in a model based on the transmission or translation of data, it becomes very difficult to preserve the balance from tilting in the direction either of passive reception or of active tyranny and interference.

As authors, speakers, and readers come together within the sojourn around poetic meaning, so mind and nature are posited as identities in difference, simultaneously contributing to the moment of perception. Within this formulation, the function of causality as a mode of explanation is necessarily displaced; it becomes, not an account of how real things relate, but a convenient mental construct which we are obliged to make use of at the same time as remaining aware that its coherence is unverifiable in terms of things as they might be in themselves.[18] Instead of cause and effect we have constant conjunction; not truth, but probability,[19] and epistemology in general is placed under strain as a viable way of producing meaning. This identification or con-fusion of cause and effect can be related to the strategy of deconstruction which has already been described at some length. To upset the easy attribution of cause and effect is to disturb the reader's orthodox orientation in the world about him, what Coleridge called the 'consolatory feeling that accompanies the sense of a proportion between antecedents and consequents' (*Biographia*, II, 207):

> Even in large assemblies of men highly educated it is too often sufficient to place impressive images in juxta-position: and the constitutive forms of the mind itself aided by the power of habit will supply the rest. For we all *think* by causal connections. (*Lay Sermons*, p. 153).

Thus it is precisely to avoid these normative habits of organisation that Coleridge expresses all his most important philosophical propositions in terms of the identity of cause *in* effect. As the symbol replaces the metaphor at the centre of his theory of representation, being an integral part of the whole which it represents and therefore avoiding the implications of a semiotic system, so the idea

> is its own evidence, and is insusceptible of all other. It is necessarily groundless and indemonstrable; because it is itself the ground of all other possible demonstration (*ibid.*, p. 32).

This removes the 'idea' from any position which would be vulnerable to disproof or questioning through sensationalist criteria. Blake's syntactic and semantic techniques are similarly designed to impress upon the reader that

> every Natural Effect has a Spiritual Cause, and Not
> A Natural: for a Natural Cause only seems, it is a Delusion
> Of Ulro: & a ratio of the perishing Vegetable Memory
>
> (Erd. 123, K. 513).

For Shelley, the whole habit of casting experience into patterns of inner and outer, cause and effect, is simply a linguistically instituted delusion:

> It imports little to inquire whether thought be distinct from the objects of thought. The use of the words *external* and *internal*, as applied to the establishment of this distinction, has been the symbol and the source of much dispute. This is merely an affair of words, and as the dispute deserves, to say, that when speaking of the objects of thought, we indeed only describe one of the forms of thought—or that, speaking of thought, we only apprehend one of the operations of the universal system [of beings] (*Complete Works*, VII, 65).

Mind *in* nature becomes mind *with* nature (see Kant, *Pure Reason*, p. 140). And applied to the theory of poetry, the causal model turns into that process of reciprocity which Coleridge praised in Wordsworth under the phrase 'meditative observation' (*Biographia*, II, 118). We have already suggested, in the account of 'The Thorn' as elsewhere, that this theoretical interpenetration of self and other involves, for Wordsworth at least, problems of intentionality and consequent intimations of culpability which are technically manifested as 'traps' wherein reader and (attributed) author are left in sojourn. Is it not also tempting and instructive to locate Coleridge's affirmative statements of synthesis within the context of such poems as the 'Hymn Before Sun-Rise', already discussed? What appears in a notebook entry as a moment of symbiosis:

> Thought and Reality two distinct corresponding Sounds, of which no man can say positively which is the Voice and which the Echo (N 2557)

becomes in the system of poetic tensions a strenuously maintained conjunction whose credibility is undermined by the hesitancy of the speaking voice and the gap between its performing and its summarising attitudes.

What I am suggesting, then, is that the indeterminate or synthesised presentation of the traditional and common-sense dualisms of inner and outer, cause and effect, can be located not only as a rhetorically directed attack upon the reader's presuppositions, of the sort which has been described at great length, but also as a rather more urgent response to a problem of knowledge which some of the poets, albeit against their better judgements, were still trying to solve. Virtue and necessity, then, come down to the same thing; nor would I wish to suggest which is prior to the other.[20] Of course, we could put forward the argument that the uncertainty of the speaking voice of the 'Hymn Before Sun-Rise' is a deliberate presentation of incompletion which the reader is expected to fill out with the deduction that, in pantheistic terms, there is only *one* voice, so that the attempt on the speaker's part to divide himself from God must be seen as a conscious irony in the mind of the poet. But there are two distinct processes at work in this sort of argument. The first is the consciousness of the tonal uncertainty of what is spoken, and in the context of my argument so far, any *tonal* indeterminacy in the *written* word is *per se* unspecifiable, unresolvable into a closed system of reference. The second *is* such specification, which, although it is a perfectly natural and perhaps even desirable thing to do, yet involves a sortal crossing which must make the reader himself responsible for the meanings elicited, and the recovery of the 'poet' or the authoritative voice at best only conjectural.[21] We are left, then, I think, with the immanence of the tonal confusion, which seems to reassert itself before *and* after the cycle of attempted metacomment has played itself out in our minds. The same model will work for *The Prelude*, where the variety of epistemological standpoints adopted by the narrator is so multiform as to defy inclusion within any simple model of synthesis, because we are presented with no moment at which the process can be seen to stop once and for all. As the balance swings back and forth between mind and nature, intention and reception, we begin to suspect that the point of rest is nothing more than an ideal construct which the mind makes for itself, if it achieves it at all. Wordsworth dramatises this very honestly, to my mind, in the passage describing the 'spots of time', so often felt to be the uncomplicated saving moments which pull together the chaos of events. In fact, as the narrator admits, these moments are bought only at a price:

> This efficacious spirit chiefly lurks
> Among those passages of life in which

> We have had deepest feeling that the mind
> Is lord and master, and that outward sense
> Is but the obedient servant of her will (XI, 269–73).

What the narrator accepts here as a 'beneficent influence' (279) is precisely what I have argued to be implicitly qualified by so many of the *Lyrical Ballads*, the dubious (albeit inevitable) insurrection of the centre from its proper relationship to the circumference. Earlier in the poem, we are told of the narrator's preservation of his own 'first creative sensibility' within the reception of natural forms:

> A plastic power
> Abode with me, a forming hand, at times
> Rebellious, acting in a devious mood,
> A local spirit of its own, at war
> With general tendency, but for the most
> Subservient strictly to the external things
> With which it commun'd (II, 381–7).

This seems to be the other extreme, that of strict subservience, and it creates an oscillation or a tension usually solved by Wordsworth with an indeterminate vocabulary of 'affinities', (II, 403) 'sympathy', (II, 409) and 'dim similitude' (mss. V and U, qu. p. 582). Can poetry reconcile these extremes of tyranny and passivity, self and other? Shelley describes how those in the states of reverie and childhood

> feel as if their nature were dissolved into the surrounding universe, or as if the surrounding universe were absorbed into their being. They are conscious of no distinction. And these are states which precede, or accompany, or follow an unusually intense and vivid apprehension of life (*Complete Works*, VI, 195–6).

But, as the argument for 'La Belle Dame Sans Merci' has shown, the dissolving of distinction brings with it a host of problems connected with the implication of the aesthetic experience in time, and its intelligibility in terms of the habitual consciousness which must succeed it. To remain within the visionary state is to be deprived of self-intelligibility, but to pass out of it is to lose the very thing which has given rise to the urge to describe. Moreover, as soon as the mind finds itself describing nature as an object in the reflexive recognition of itself, then it risks internment within a discourse whose terms allow only for perpetually moving between opposite poles. Synthesis is either a hypothetical point between persistently disjunctive extremes, or, when actual, it is incommunicable except *through* disjunction; and this distinction amounts to the same thing from the reader's perspective. Wordsworth finds that he prefers the 'living thought' of Mont Blanc to the 'soulless image' which the 'real' mountain offers him (*The Prelude*, VI, 454–5); things are 'other' than expected. He tramps up Snowdon, the object of so much mystery and veneration from below, only to discover that what he has left behind has become equally remote and inaccessible, swallowed in a sea of mist, except for

> a fracture in the vapour,
> A deep and gloomy breathing-place through which
> Mounted the roar of waters, torrents, streams
> Innumerable, roaring with one voice (XIII, 56–9).

The sense of fixity we might wish to derive from this is challenged by having the 'homeless voice of waters' (63) presented as the centrepiece, along with the breach itself, of the 'Imagination of the whole' (65). That wholeness should emanate from the hole is itself notable; that point of disappearance which must perhaps itself be nothing that other things shall be, but which also stands as the vortex drawing out (and down) the adverting mind of the climber into the dissolution whose preclusion has been the very object of his ascent. In the context of what has been said already, we need only touch upon the aptness of this incident as an emblem of Wordsworth's larger journey through the poem, which sends him further and further from his beginnings in the very act of trying to find them. Equally apt is its availability as an image of the urge towards metacommentary which has been described throughout this account. In all of these 'mountain' poems, as in the famous passage from *The Prelude* where the crossing of the Alps is described (VI, 487f.), the narrator puts himself into a position from which 'meaning' is expected to appear, in the shape of a perspectivally determined grouping of landscape forms laid out before him (it is no accident that Blake's designs generally refuse to allow themselves to be ordered in this way), but finds instead that the promised 'overview' offers nothing more than a new set of mysteries. [22]

The expression in aesthetical theory of the gulf between mind and nature is to be found in the accounts of 'the sublime'. I shall not go into the subject in great detail, [23] except to mention that it can be seen as an attempt to assimilate those aspects of nature which at first glance seem to make mockery of any synthetic ambition in the mind. Kant puts this very well:

In fact, without the development of moral ideas, that which, thanks to preparatory culture, we call sublime, merely strikes the untutored man as terrifying. He will see in the evidences which the ravages of nature give of her dominion, and in the vast scale of her might, compared with which his own is diminished to insignificance, only the misery, peril, and distress that would compass the man that was thrown to its mercy.[24]

The experience of the excesses of nature serves to encourage a recognition of human insignificance, as a prelude, within the usual hypothesis of the 'sublime', to the aesthetic satisfaction which comes with being subject to such enormous forces. It is not enough, I think, to see the Lisbon earthquake as a causal factor in this cast of mind; after all, there have been equally catastrophic natural disasters since that time. What seems more to the point is to suggest that there was established, in the second half of the eighteenth century, a framework of expectation and an a priori formulation within which such an event could take on enormous significance. If the earthquake can be said to have exposed the dubious status of the doctrines of rational self-sufficiency which the public voice of Enlightenment thought put forward, then it could also be said that it re-emphasised the priority of the gaps upon which that voice was founded; it was the all too apt emblem of the disruption of cause and effect which, from Hobbes onwards, so many of the philosophers had felt compelled to point out. This remained a prominent feature of the Romantic experience of nature. Wordsworth, in particular, who described himself as one 'Foster'd alike by beauty and by fear' (*The Prelude*, I, 306), gives expression to a whole range of confrontations with malign or overwhelming nature; low breathings, open boats, dead men, strangers in the night, and so forth. Coleridge, though he wrote to Sara Hutchinson in terms of the standard definition of the sublime—'I have always found this *stretched & anxious* state of mind favorable to depth of pleasurable Impression' (*Letters*, II, 853)—was at the same time well aware that this pleasurableness depended upon the hegemony of 'the powers of Reason & the Will, which remaining no Danger can overpower us' (p. 842). These are the faculties most threatened by the experience of unmediated nature and, as will be argued later, by the poetic activity itself. Shelley described 'Mont Blanc' as

composed under the immediate impression of the deep and powerful feelings excited by the objects which it attempts to describe; and as an undisciplined overflowing of the soul, rests its claim to approbation on an attempt to imitate the untameable wildness and inaccessible solemnity from which those feelings sprang (*Complete Works*, VI, 88).

It is, if we accept this in good faith, indeed an imitation of its object, but only insofar as it repeats the incoherence and chaos which that object (those objects) conveyed to the would-be creative consciousness. The letters written from the Alps are full of the frankest confessions of a sentiment 'of ecstatic wonder, not unallied to madness'.[25] Shelley saw in the Bossons glacier 'the most vivid image of desolation that it is possible to conceive' (I, 499), and nature in this landscape is described very much as an emblem of his own aesthetic principles:

> In these regions everything changes & is in motion. This vast mass of ice has one general progress which ceases neither day nor night. It breaks and rises for ever; its undulations sink whilst others rise (I, 500).[26]

Once again, virtue and necessity are hand in hand as the ethic of perpetual renewal is exactly compatible with the impossibility of fixing the experience of the landscape within a determinate epistemological framework; and the reader is led to regard the strategy of his 'author' as one of transference.

This is the sort of movement of thought which runs parallel to Blake's contention, already quoted, that knowledge is 'Immediate by Perception or Sense at once'. It is thereby placed beyond the reach of this deductive and explanatory language which seems to succeed only in introducing a gap between the suppositions we *act* upon and those we can prove to be 'truthful' in speculative terms. Philosophy itself is only of use to 'point out a good which by philosophy is unattainable' (Coleridge, *Philosophical Lectures*, p. 226).[27] 'REASON AND RELIGION ARE THEIR OWN EVIDENCE' (*Biographia*, II, 215). How do these propositions come to appear viable to a non-believer, to someone who does not start out from a basic faith in these self-evident things? The answer, for Coleridge as for Kant, consists in the demonstration of the exhaustion and self-defeat which any purely speculative inquiry will incur when it is pushed to its limit. Thus the grain of affirmative response which exists in all men, it is hoped, will find itself out of the deconstruction of every other approach. Coleridge was at all times very anxious to keep this special version of the 'self-evidence' method well away from contagion by the exponents of mere 'common sense' as advocated by 'the amiable Beattie, and other less eloquent and not more profound inaugurators'

(*Biographia*, I, 182); rather, as we have seen before, the posture of simplicity must be constructed, through the deconstruction of our habitual ways of thinking. The conclusions which accrue from it do not, therefore, stand in that fixing relationship to the problems of speculative inquiry which we have nominated the 'metacomment'. On the contrary, they depend upon a radically different *sort* of procedure whose necessity can only be perceived *as* it is enacted. Because it is related to speculation precisely as a negative, as 'not speculation', then we are not able to reconstruct using the same materials as have carried through the deconstruction. There is difference in kind, not just in degree. As Coleridge puts it, we have a choice. Either we remain within the realm of speculation, in which case

> We must be whirl'd down the gulf of an infinite series. But this would make our reason baffle the end and purpose of all reason, namely unity and system. Or we must break off the series arbitrarily, and affirm an absolute something that is in and of itself at once cause and effect (causa sui), subject and object, or rather the absolute identity of both (*Biographia*, I, 187).

This break is a sortal one, and the practising writer can never be sure that the act of reconstitution will occur in his reader's mind, or occur in the way he would wish it to. It relies upon a power of self-generation, and this is why the will is at the centre of Coleridge's philosophy. But if verification is to be looked for in primary experience rather than in theoretical exposition, it is therefore committed to the process of change through time which characterises all contingent experience. If at one pole we are beset with

> an over-anxious eye
> That with a false activity beats off
> Simplicity and self-presented truth (*The Prelude*, I, 249–51),

then at the other we are threatened by the state of identity itself, which, it is implied, can only be maintained momentarily without plunging the mind into entropic confusion, a different sort of fixity, of the sort experienced by Keats's wretched wight. Wordsworth describes the 'blank confusion' of the inhabitants of London,

> Living amid the same perpetual flow
> Of trivial objects, melted and reduced
> To one identity, by differences
> That have no law, no meaning, and no end (VII, 701–4).

Once more, the terms of the argument have cast themselves into dialectical contraries wherein each must be present in the other. Without difference there is no identity, and vice versa. It is man's need, or compulsion, to interrupt the pure identity or self-involvement of natural processes with his own dialectic of outering and innering which constitutes for Coleridge man's highest faculty:

> The wisdom in nature is distinguished from that in man by the co-instantaneity of the plan and the execution; the thought and the product are one, or given at once; but there is no reflex act, and hence there is no moral responsibility. In man there is reflexion, freedom, and choice; he is, therefore, the head of the visible creation (*Biographia*, II, 257).

Freedom means risk, and choice can manifest itself as aggression, as Wordsworth has (implicitly) demonstrated. Moreover, communicative isolation always threatens at the end of the line, but only he who draws the knife gets Isaac. Does the 'Ha, Ha, He' of Blake's 'Laughing Song' (*Songs*, 15) ask to be read as the spontaneous participation by the children in nature's prelinguistic, unformulated, and unfallen expression of well-being? Or does it dramatise the sterile tautology of human language which, even at its least corrupted level, can only repeat itself, self-regardingly, as at odds with the variety and plenitude of nature's natural voices? Innocent joy, or are Har and Heva lurking behind 'Ha' and 'He'? To make this 'decision' is to decide about one's self; meaning is a function of being, and being is discovered in meaning. In Shelley's formulation, 'neither the eye nor the mind can see itself, unless reflected upon that which it resembles' (*Complete Works*, VII, 121).[28] At the same time as the epistemological problem is being satisfied by the model of the necessary synthesis of self and other, the idea of personal identity itself is subsumed under epistemology.[29] The theory of being thus becomes tied into the moment of *realising* meaning in just the same way as the theory of perception has been. We know ourselves *as* we see; and Kant added the qualification that *what* we thus know is phenomenal rather than noumenal (*Pure Reason*, p. 369f.; see also pp. 153–5, 331–3, 557–8). What answers can be found to refute Hume's famous contention (*Treatise*, Bk. I, pt. IV, sect. 2, p. 207).

> that what we call a *mind*, is nothing but a heap or collection of different perceptions, united together by certain relations, and suppos'd, tho' falsely, to be endow'd with a perfect simplicity and identity?

We have really only the choice between self-evidence (and hence an *assumption* of common or shared experience which can never be proven *ab extra*) or recourse to some relational explanation such as causality (with all its regressive and infinitely proliferating levels) in order to explain ourselves to ourselves, and these options can be seen to represent the two sides, roughly speaking, of the Romantic aesthetic as it is applied to techniques of communication. Often they seem to occur together; the regression is proffered as a way of encouraging the 'leap', the sortal crossing which would locate the argument on a new level, in fact one outside argument, a higher species of self-evidence. In the lowest terms, self-evidence was, as might be expected, the formulation of personal identity adopted by the mainstream 'common sense' tradition.[30] Hume himself set out to describe coherence *in* the mind as the alternative to knowledge of objects in themselves, and in at least one of his voices he could argue that 'the perceptions of the mind are perfectly known' (*Treatise*, Bk. II, pt. II, sect. 6, p. 366), a supposition which could not so easily be maintained by a generation which, even though it often came to place its faith in a communicable psychology, was yet increasingly aware of the unconscious and of the existence of the mind in an essential but indefinable relation to its world. To posit the absolute inherence of the one in the other is to risk the intentionalist predicament dramatised, it has been argued, by Wordsworth in such poems as 'The Thorn'. But to posit a gap between mind and nature, as is done in all the deductions of the higher faculties, is to risk incommunicability and rely, ultimately, upon self-evidence. Coleridge describes man contemplating his image in nature

> till finding nowhere a representative of that free agency which yet is a *fact* of immediate consciousness sanctioned and made fearfully significant by his prophetic *conscience*, he learns at last that what he *seeks* he has *left behind*, and but lengthens the distance as he prolongs the search (*The Friend*, I, 509).

There were those to whom this free agency was not a fact—as it was not to Coleridge himself at his darkest moments—as well as those, like the wretched wight, for whom the reflexive movement between self and world was cut short or complicated beyond control.

The point which emerges, I hope, out of this rather technical summary of certain developments in eighteenth-century philosophy is that the personae of 'speaker' and 'poet' are connected by more than mere coincidence. The very vocabulary and concept of distinction are rendered unstable, and speculation can no longer satisfy itself with an account of the transfer of data between a mind and a world pre-established as separate entities. Each is present, or absent, simultaneously with the other, and this model of complex interdetermination applies also to the relation of mind to itself, to its possible 'parts'. We do not have, as Hume once famously tried to maintain that we have, a privileged perspective from which we see ourselves in the third person. Speaker and poet come together as distinguished in degree rather than in kind.

There is an important way in which at least some among the Romantics would have answered Hume's description of the mind as 'a heap or collection of different perceptions'. They would have invoked the faculty of the will; though here again it is crucial to note that the will is the ultimate performative faculty. Wordsworth, responding to Mathetes' letter written by John Wilson to *The Friend*, delivered as his advice to the youthful mind a 'steady dependence upon voluntary and self-originating effort, and upon the practice of self-examination, sincerely aimed at and rigorously enforced' (*The Friend*, I, 394). The context for the second part of this rubric has already been plotted: the pressures and presuppositions which have been collectively associated with the 'heuristic method' are within its constellation. The first part bears directly upon the status of the will, as well as being a *sine qua non* for the application of these heuristic methods. Wordsworth's 'spots of time', it will be remembered, are those in which the mind is most assured of its control, its status as 'lord and master'. Coleridge regarded the will, properly distinguished from mere 'volition' and uncomplicated by the confrontation with the intentionalist heresy so deeply felt by his brother poet, as 'the true and only strict synonime of the word, I, or the intelligent self' (*The Friend*, II, 279).[31] At the same time, he is prepared to argue for mankind as being within the fallen state precisely because of a disease of this faculty, this 'obscure Radical of the Vital Power' (*Letters*, V, 406), this 'mysterious Ground of all things visible and invisible.' (*Letters*, VI, 641). The will is, with reason, one of 'the two great component parts of our nature' (*Philosophical Lectures*, p. 112), yet only available for identification in the activity itself; it 'knows its own State in and by its Acts alone' (*Aids to Reflection*, p. 89).[32] We can draw two basic points out of this; that the will is of absolute importance, and that it can only be apprehended *as* it operates, through self evidence. As Rousseau says (*Émile*, p. 236), 'The will is known to me in its actions, not in its nature.[33] Coleridge certainly knew of the 'mysterious diversity between the injunctions of the mind and the elections of the will' (*Aids to Reflection*, p. 344), a condition wherein the most vital of the faculties constituting personal identity is most unattainable; and the warnings of various of the *Lyrical Ballads* about the dangers of appropriation are there to point out the threat of the decline of pure will into volition or desire. The belle dame's entourage—knights, wights, questioners and readers—also comes to mind once more. Expecting to find and establish themselves, they lose the habitual modes of self-reference which they already had. Overtly enough, the will is a part of this loss. It is the will as the principle of authoritarian control within the self, in the sense in which Coleridge connects it metaphorically to the Father, the Godhead (*Letters*, VI, 641), which is incapacitated. Coleridge himself is eloquent on the subject of the necessity of the will, and of the reason and judgement which go with it, in his account of the consequences of Hartley's theory:

> our whole life would be divided between the despotism of outward impressions, and that of senseless and passive memory . . . one or other of two consequences must result. Either the ideas, (or relics of such impression,) will exactly imitate the order of the impression itself, which would be absolute *delirium*: or any one part of that impression might recall any other part, and . . . *any* part of *any* impression might recall *any* part of any *other*, without a cause present to determine *what* it should be (*Biographia*, I, 77).

It is the will which must 'controul, determine, and modify the phantasmal chaos of association' (p. 81), and where the consciousness of freedom which it supplies is lacking, then for the man so afflicted, all

> spiritual intercourse is interrupted, not only with others, but even with himself. No wonder then, that he remains incomprehensible to himself as well as to others. No wonder, that, in the fearful desert of his consciousness, he wearies himself out with empty words, to which no friendly echo answers . . . or bewilders himself in the pursuit of *notional* phantoms, the mere refractions from unseen and distant truths through the distorting medium of his own unenlivened and stagnant understanding (p. 168).

These descriptions have a force of conviction which suggests that Coleridge himself had at times entered the landscape of 'La Belle Dame Sans Merci', and that he was himself unable to answer the question why the will, like poetic inspiration for Shelley, should be indubitable when it is in action, and unimaginable while it is in abeyance. [34]

If there is an aspect of Romanticism which inhibits either ethically or practically the exertion of the will, then there is also a significant polemic directed at that yet more familiar constituent of the personality, the memory.[35] The disorganisation of poetic language for which I have already argued is a symptom of this, as it serves to demand continual re-reading and reformulation of meaning. Not that the memory alone is enough; the threat of total recall is as disrupting as its complete absence, and we have seen Coleridge describing the state where the order of ideas would 'exactly imitate the order of the impression itself' as one of 'absolute *delirium*'. The protagonist of 'La Belle Dame Sans Merci' is unable to organise his experience into a hierarchical sequence, because he is unable to make the exclusions necessary for the constitution of 'meaning'; no item or detail signifies any less than any other. What is really called for, then, is an active mind working over the material in the memory, producing a balance of intention and reception.[36] This is the sort of balance which Wordsworth's theory of 'emotion recollected in tranquillity' could be seen to be aiming at, but which is itself embedded in the paradox that the more perfectly the memory functions, the more it obtrudes experiences whose immediate intensity was at the time unassimilable. It thus disturbs the very tranquillity which the passing of time had purported to provide. Wordsworth himself explains this in a passage already quoted:

> the emotion is contemplated till by a species of reaction the tranquillity gradually disappears, and an emotion, similar to that which was before the subject of contemplation, is gradually produced, and does itself actually exist in the mind (*Prose*, I, 148).

This is one extreme; but there is a paradox implicit in this reading back. The 'spontaneous overflow' is best applied by the poet who has 'also thought long and deeply', a habit whereby 'our continued influxes of feeling are modified and directed by our thoughts' (*Prose*, I, 126). It is this which makes the past meaningful, which brings out things

> doom'd to sleep
> Until maturer seasons call'd them forth (*The Prelude*, I, 622– 3).

Standing against the most confident of these assertions of control— and even they are dearly bought—we may refer again to the final irony whereby the summary of meaning is pushed forward out of the poem, for 'future restoration' (XI, 343) at a time 'surely yet to come'

(XIII, 441), in a grand repetition of a recourse already sketched out in the closing movement of 'Tintern Abbey'.[37]

Blake seems never to have dallied with the temptation to incorporate the memory into his account of the creative mind, trying as he was to bring about a condition in which 'the Daughters of Memory shall become the Daughters of Inspiration' (Erd. 94, K. 480). It was the confusion of the two, a basic mistake which he ascribed to the Greeks, which was held responsible for such opinions as that of Reynolds 'that Genius May be Taught & that all Pretence to Inspiration is a Lie & a Deceit to say the least of it' (Erd. 632, K. 452):

> The Imagination is not a State: it is the Human Existence itself
> Affection or Love becomes a State, when divided from Imagination
> The Memory is a State always, & the Reason is a State
> Created to be Annihilated & a new Ratio Created (Erd. 131, K. 522).

The notion that man is a 'fortuitous concourse of memorys accumulated & lost' has its place within the limited vision of humanity as 'but a Worm seventy inches long' (Erd. 173, K. 659).[38] Everything in Blake's poetry contributes 'To cast off the rotten rags of Memory by Inspiration' (Erd. 141, K. 533), the necessity of which has been well put by Donald Ault in his *Visionary Physics*, pp. 97, 122:

> Memory is the enemy of novelty, for it brings the energy of the present moment into adjustment with the abstract past. In this way, for Blake, memory is the source of causal feelings, causality being 'a Ratio of the perishing Vegetable Memory'. Memory is in a war with the emergent novelty of process . . . a tool of the delusive Satanic power which attempts to fix things in a constantly fluctuating context.[39]

These arguments about will and memory have a place in the general crisis of authority and control for which I have been arguing, but Blake's view, as so often, is an extreme one, denying the authenticity of both.[40] This is certainly one way of solving the problem of the potential lapse of will into desire (about which I shall have more to say in the next chapter) and of necessary retention of information into the tyranny of past experience. This displacement of will and memory is widely typified in Romantic poetry by emphasis on the metaphors of dream and madness, the two categories of experience which had always shared the status of exclusion in the rationalist tradition;[41] they erode quite explicitly the control over experience established by will and memory.[42] It is worth noting the conjuction voiced by Hume:

and this is common both to poetry and madness, that the vivacity they bestow on the ideas is not deriv'd from the particular situations or connections of the objects of these ideas, but from the present temper and disposition of the person (*Treatise*, Appendix, p. 630).

Take out the word 'madness', and this could be Wordsworth describing *Lyrical Ballads*. Once the illusory fixity of a language of objectivity is given up, then there is, as has been seen before, no ultimate way in which the process of closing off meaning can be enacted, short of the transposition of sorts or classes represented by such devices as the categorical imperative, related negatively and uncontingently to the problems which have given rise to their own necessity. And, of course, it is exactly this element of chaos and confusion, taken for granted in madness and dream, which renders them the appropriate vehicles of a discourse based on anti-authoritarian and continuously self-creating modes:

> The joy, the triumph, the delight, the madness!
> The boundless, overflowing, bursting gladness,
> The vaporous exultation not to be confined!
> > (Shelley, *Poetical Works*, p. 261).

Madness becomes the analogue of poetry in its search for a metaphor of deconstruction, at the same time as it is excluded along with it by a status quo concerned to deny that deconstructing function. Blake recognised this in looking forward to a time when we might

> cast aside from Poetry, all that is not Inspiration
> That it no longer shall dare to mock with the aspersion of Madness
> Cast on the Inspired, by the tame high finisher of paltry Blots,
> Indefinite, or paltry Rhymes; or paltry Harmonies (Erd. 141, K. 533).

In the context of an aesthetic and an ethic with a declared policy of 'make it new', dream and madness become positive states in that they both function by erasure, creating vacancies and empty spaces, uncommitted images, an intermediate area of pure determinability, anarchy:

> The imagination of the waking man is a well-policed republic, where the voice of the magistrate keeps everything in order; that of the *dream* is the same republic in a state of anarchy.[43]

They are the two states whose very definition depends upon a radical dislocation of space and time, the stability of which was the organising myth of the materialist model of mind, for those who, as

Shelley put it, 'follow the footsteps of poets, and copy the sketches of their creations into the book of common life', and thereby 'make space, and give time' (*Complete Works*, VII, 132). Blake describes his poem 'Milton' as conceived and executed in a period 'less than a pulsation of the artery' (Erd. 126, K. 516). It is a moment between time, opening into infinity, the moment that neither Satan, nor his 'Watch Fiends' (Erd. 135, K. 526)—and Blake means this in two ways, adverting to the despotism of the Urizenic eye as well as to the dominant organising metaphor of the materialist world view—can find. Thus the imagination can be redeemed from the trammels of the Urizenic creation, from the 'strong delusive light of Time & Space' (Erd. 228, K. 715), whereby

The Visions of Eternity, by reason of narrowed perceptions,
Are become weak Visions of Time & Space, fix'd into furrows of death;
Till deep dissimulation is the only defence an honest man has left [.]
(Erd. 196, K. 679).

The dream creates emptiness and infinity, the medium of eternity, preserving the mind from fixity and objectification, albeit that, in terms of the paradox we have seen before, limits must be drawn in order to encourage their removal:

The Daughters of Beulah follow sleepers in all their Dreams
Creating Spaces lest they fall into Eternal Death
The Circle of Destiny complete they gave to it a Space
And named the Space Ulro & brooded over it in care & love
(Erd. 299,K. 267).

Eternal death is the threat of a vision limited to the distinctions and satisfactions of a vegetable, sexual world, the spaces they create are the reminders of what is beyond and outside this world, at the same time as the *one* space, the Ulro, is the reduction of those plural spaces into illusory singleness; care and love are ambivalent for the inhabitants of that space, simultaneously contracting and expanding their visions, a limit to contraction imposed so that expansion may occur again.

The narrator of Shelley's 'The Triumph of Life' exists also at a sort of zero point outside of and between the habitual categories of spatial and temporal organisation:

before me fled
The night; behind me rose the day; the deep

Was at my feet, and Heaven above my head,—
When a strange trance over my fancy grew
(*Poetical Works*, p. 508).[44]

Dream and madness, then, offer themselves as metaphorical embodiments of the distance which poetry seeks to establish between itself and habitual experience. But at the same time the criteria are eroded by which we might seek to distinguish them sortally *from* such habitual experience. Dreaming and waking, madness and sanity, come to be theorised as differences of degree rather than kind.[45] As Hartley put it, 'it is impossible to fix precise Limits, and to determine where Soundness of Mind ends, and Madness begins' (*Observations*, I, 390). Once again, it is the metacomment which is undercut, the position outside and above what is being described, from which one can comment without the possibility or threat of implication. Once these extreme states are seen to interpenetrate, the one can no longer be used to define the other; as in 'La Belle Dame', there is no sure sense of separateness out of which 'identity' can be reflexively constituted. Keats could write begging

> that our dreamings all of sleep or wake
> Would all their colours from the sunset take,
> From something of material sublime,
> Rather than shadow our own soul's daytime
> In the dark void of night (*Poems*, p. 323).

In the 'dark void of night' there are none of the established protective functions available, none of the defences which soften the waking experience. Such dreaming can only be a repetition, in no finer tone, of the discomforts of the day. When he was not being tortured by his dreams, Coleridge could complain that his sleep was 'made up of Ideas so connected, & so little different from the operations of Reason, that it does not afford me the due Refreshment' (*Letters*, II, 707) and, after a lifetime of scholarship, experiment, and speculation, he still felt that he knew nothing of the real nature of dreams (*Letters*, VI, 715). The lady of Shelley's poem 'Marianne's Dream' makes a pact with the dream in which it promises to let her see the secrets hidden by the day; see them she does, but seeing is not 'meaning'. At precisely the moment when one of the figures she meets 'seemed to speak' (*Poetical Works*, p. 538), she is woken up, lifted out of the 'stream' in which the vision occurred. We may agree

> That sleep has sights as clear and true
> As any waking eyes can view (p. 539),

but sight alone is not enough, it merely compounds the mystery. What Keats's wretched wight is 'told' tells him nothing.

None of the standard causal or substantial models held out much security for the establishment of personal identity, and the habitual constituents of the personality, will and memory, have been seen to be eroded by a poetic experience forming itself by means of the images of dream and madness. The caverns whose depth can only be imagined or guessed at from the spasmodic reappearances of Alph the sacred river, which is also the river of language, are in this respect the caverns of the mind, those which, for Wordsworth, sun 'Could never penetrate' (*The Prelude*, III, 247). It is the implicit assumption of, for example, Kant's treatment of personal identity that the mind can always in some sense bridge the gaps which its own speculations open up for itself, that

> beyond the characteristic of his own subject which is compounded of these mere appearances, he [man] necessarily assumes something else as its basis, namely, his ego as it is in itself (*Foundations*, p. 70).

Though he can have no 'knowledge' of this noumenal identity, man must nevertheless postulate its existence and act upon the assumption of its reality. But the Romantic 'imagination' works to question the security of even this limited option. The power which came upon Wordsworth in the Alps as a 'usurpation' (*The Prelude*, VI, 534) was also experienced by Coleridge in the English Lake District. He wrote to Wedgwood of how

> my spirit courses, drives, and eddies, like a Leaf in Autumn: a wild activity, of thoughts, imaginations, feelings, and impulses of motion, rises up from within me—a sort of *bottom-wind*, that blows to no point of the compass, & comes from I know not whence, but agitates the whole of me; my whole Being is filled with waves, as it were, that roll & stumble, one this way, & one that way, like things that have no common master (*Letters*, II, 916).

It seems worth pointing out here that the 'imagination' was not simply seen to be that 'synthetic and magical power' which functioned by 'the balance or reconciliation of opposite or discordant qualities' (Coleridge, *Biographia*,II, 12); it could produce discord and disruption, challenging not just the standard conservative ethic of the avoidance of excess,[46] but also the basic movement of innering and outering which constitutes the selfhood in the Romantic experience. It can operate antithetically as well as synthetically, negating whatever state prevails at the moment when it is brought into play. Thus Wordsworth describes imagination not simply as 'consolidating numbers into unity', but also as 'dissolving and separating unity into number' (*Prose*, III, 33), the activity of a mind which delights not just in the 'perception of similitude in dissimilitude' but also in the opposite perception of 'dissimilitude in similitude' (*Prose*, I, 148). In this context we may set Coleridge's definition (or demonstration) of the 'secondary imagination' as that which

> dissolves, diffuses, dissipates, in order to re-create; or where this process is rendered impossible, yet still at all events it struggles to idealize and to unify (*Biographia*, I, 202).

As has already been argued at great length, the movement of diffusion, or deconstruction, proceeds to the point where any re-creation must involve a new approach, a change of key, so that the methods which characterise the one will not do for the other. Thus the reunification is not to be taken for granted, it is indeed a 'struggle', and even where it succeeds it risks establishing nothing more than a different system of fixed qualities which must themselves be disturbed by subsequent imaginative activity. This is where the theory of the imagination comes very close to the general tenor of Friedrich Schlegel's descriptions of irony, for example as 'permanent parekbasis';[47] it becomes a principle of pure transference, and nothing in itself. Coleridge himself at one point formulates exactly this model of imagination in speaking of

> A middle state of mind more strictly appropriate to the imagination than any other, when it is, as it were, hovering between images. As soon as it is fixed on one image, it becomes understanding; but while it is unfixed and wavering between them, attaching itself permanently to none, it is imagination . . . a strong working of the mind, still offering what is still repelled, and again creating what is again rejected . . . (*Shakespearean Criticism*, II, 103–4).

Moreover, even if it is granted that the primary function of the faculty known as 'imagination' was a synthetic one, then this purported synthesis must itself be set against that breach in the mind's defences which had been exposed by Hartley and the tradition for which he spoke; Drummond felt that, if Hartley's theory were held to be true, then the human 'bundle of vibrations would be liable to perpetual derangement' (*Academical Questions*, p. 293). Kant based his entire system on a normative concept of psychology, taking for granted the absurdity of experiencing 'a blind play of representations' (*Pure Reason*, p. 139), or of having 'as many-coloured and diverse a self as I have representations of which I am conscious to myself' (p. 154); as Reid put it, 'all mankind place their personality in something that cannot be divided' (*Works*, p. 345).[48] But such division was a familiar experience, and poetry both expressed it and inspired it. What Hegel called the 'unhappy consciousness (unglückliches Bewußtsein)', that which is 'divided and at variance within itself (*in sich entzweite*)', was not simply a historical phenomenon peculiar to the Middle Ages (*Phenomenology of Mind*, p. 251; *Werke*, II, 158) but also a stage along the way for the contemporary consciousness, and one where it ran the risk of being trapped for ever. Young Werther, whose sorrows provided some of the most popular reading matter available to European Romanticism, described himself as 'a whole litany of antitheses' (*Werke*, VI, 87), and his career offers some evidence that the 'walking paradox' was not always held at the safe, contemplative, and satirical distance which marks the tone of Shelley's 'Peter Bell the Third' (*Poetical Works*, p. 358). And Shelley too knew the mind at times as 'a picture of irreconcileable inconsistencies, even when perhaps a moment before, it imagined that it had grasped the fleeting Phantom of virtue' (*Letters*, I, 109).

The division of the selfhood, of course, must be embedded in a strictly paradoxical context for the Romantic mind. As in the one sense it presents a threat, a divided consciousness which risks being perpetuated in its division and robbed of the new synthesis which it had been the apparent purpose of the techniques of deconstruction to make possible, so in the other sense it is the only way in which such a synthesis can ever be achieved. In this scheme of identity in difference, aesthetical theory and practice finds itself constantly oscillating between self and symbiosis, ego and eros. There is no way to the one without the other, no redemption without dismembering. Blake related this to reflexive vision, the elevation of space into infinite space:

> O search & see: turn your eyes inward: open O thou World
> Of Love & Harmony in Man: expand thy ever lovely Gates
>
> (Erd. 185, K. 675).

To remain undivided is to accept as authoritative the state of single vision which constitutes the natural man; so that division is both the obligation imposed on man by eighteenth-century culture and at the same time his only hope of transcending it, the positive within the negative. Vala is a tyrannous principle, 'Dividing & Uniting at will in the Cruelties of Holiness', but she also contains and demands the terms of her own redundancy:

When viewd remote She is One when viewd near she divides
To multitude as it is in Eden so permitted because
It was the best possible in the State called Satan to save
From Death Eternal & to put off Satan Eternally (Erd. 364, K. 348).

Blake is also, it seems, implicitly commenting on the theory of 'imagination' as he saw it expressed by his contemporaries; we have seen it to involve a similar balance of dividing and uniting. As Hegel put it:

Before the ego, this concrete Being, can be made the beginning and ground of philosophy, it must be disrupted—this is the absolute act through which the ego purges itself of its content and becomes aware of itself as an abstract ego (*Science of Logic*, p. 76).[49]

What this means is that the self-other, subject-object relation is always constituted from two directions at once; Coleridge's 'heaven descended' maxim, the Socratic 'know thyself', is thus always a self-finding through self-division, as Shaftesbury had earlier described it:

THIS was, among the Antients, that celebrated *Delphick* Inscription, RECOGNIZE YOUR-SELF: which was as much as to say, *Divide yourself*, or *Be* TWO (*Characteristicks*, I, 170).

Knowing one's self is knowing an 'other', with the moment of recognition poised, ideally, between the two extreme options dramatised in Keats's poems; the loss of self implicit in 'La Belle Dame Sans Merci', and the obtrusion of self which is the attempted gesture of the speaker of the 'Ode on a Grecian Urn', as it is the theme of so many of the incidents in *Lyrical Ballads*. That both these extremes themselves can come to incorporate their opposites is simply to begin the cycle again. Ideally, centre and circumference must be held in tension, neither usurping the other. Schelling describes how

the ego, or individuality, is indeed in general the basis, foundation or natural center of every creature's life; but as soon as it ceases to be the ministering center and enters as sovereign into the periphery, it burns in it like Tantalus' malice in its selfishness and egoism. ⊙ now turns into ◯ —.[50]

To displace the proper relation of centre to circumference is, paradoxically, to rob the self of its centrality at the very moment it would seem to be asserting itself most forcefully. Thus poetry for Shelley is 'at once the centre and circumference of knowledge' (*Complete Works*, VII, 135), the ideal synthesis of innering and outering, proving on the pulses the notion that

> The words *I* and *you*, and *they* are grammatical devices invented simply for arrangement, and totally devoid of the intense and exclusive sense usually attached to them (VI, 196).[51]

But this moment of ideal synthesis is located in time, and within a framework of experience which is always building up to it, and falling away from it. The passivity before outer events and objects which represents the materialist model of the mind itself incurs the threat of a reaction towards the other extreme. Thus the fascination with figures of uninhibited free will which marks so much of the 'public' voice of Romanticism was for the most part critical, warning against the excesses of unchecked appetite. This is a dominant theme in the drama, centre usurping circumference, found, for example, in 'The Borderers', 'The Cenci', and in Coleridge's translations from Schiller, 'The Piccolomini' and 'The Death of Wallenstein', all of which in some sense display the workings of unrestrained egotism, that which Wordsworth calls

> The freedom of the individual mind,
> Which, to the blind restraint of general laws
> Superior, magisterially adopts
> One guide, the light of circumstances, flash'd
> Upon an independent intellect (*The Prelude*, X, 826–30).

But there is a paradox residing in this position, well indicated by the terms in which Coleridge describes the early Wallenstein:

>   yet I have known him
> Transported on a sudden into utterance
> Of strange conceptions, kindling into splendour
> His soul revealed itself, and he spake so
> That we looked round perplexed upon each other,
> Not knowing whether it were craziness,
> Or whether it were a god that spoke in him
>   (*Poetical Works*, p. 767).

This recalls nothing so much as the figure of the poet as described at the end of 'Kubla Khan', and it must serve as a reminder that the very qualities of self-determination and self-investigation which impel these Napoleonic figures into ruining themselves and those around them are also those necessary to respond to and participate in the poetic experience as it is characterised by what have been called 'heuristic methods'. This may go some way towards explaining why it is that such methods tend to involve also the abolition of the 'metacomment', the undermining of the stable self which seeks to replace the authority it has itself deconstructed. If Bonaparte had displayed the darker options available to the political vacuum, then the closing mind represents the same process at work within the reading experience. Hence the suspicion directed at men of power, and everything involved with what Shelley called 'the dark idolatry of self' (*Poetical Works*, p. 120). Wordsworth and Coleridge themselves came in for some criticism based on their appearances as men of power. De Quincey complained of the latter that he was too prone

> to project his own mind, and his own very peculiar ideas, nay, even his own expressions and illustrative metaphors, upon other men, and to contemplate these reflex images from himself, as so many characters having an absolute ground in some separate object (*Works*, II, 94).[52]

But it was above all Wordsworth who came in for this sort of attack from the poets who followed him, and in a much more precise way than is often recognised. Besides the explicit Wordsworthian echoes in 'Alastor' and the yet more overt message of the 'Verses Written on Receiving a Celandine in a Letter from England' (Rogers, *Complete Poetical Works*, II, 80), it is tempting to regard the movement of 'Prometheus Unbound', involving as it does the education of the hero away from his 'self-torturing solitude' (*Poetical Works*, p. 214), as an appeal for a reborn Wordsworth. Keats distinguished his own lack of identity 'from the wordsworthian or egotistical sublime; which is a thing per se and stands alone' (*Letters*, I, 387). This might seem strange in the context of the argument I have put forward for the *Lyrical Ballads* as investigations of the problems of power and intentionality, anatomies of the tyrant eye. But these poems themselves are the complicated version of that posture of mastery and control which Wordsworth's critical voice so often commends, as we have seen. Besides what has been discussed already—the 'spots of time' passage, for example—there is the fascinating account of one of his own sonnets, included in a letter of 1807 (*Letters: The Middle Years*, I, 145f.).[53] He describes how he casts his eye over a multitude of ships on the sea, but is at the same time obliged to focus his 'I' upon one in particular. This it is which provides the point of fixity from which selection and unification is possible. Wordsworth asks who is there that has not felt that the mind can have no rest among a multitude of objects, of which it either cannot make one whole, or from which it cannot single out one individual, whereupon may be concentrated the attention divided among or distracted by a multitude? (p. 148).

As the one ship pushes all the others into a secondary role, so the mind itself then dispenses with that ship, which is 'merely a lordly Ship, nothing more'. Once the mind is 'fixed and rouzed, all the rest comes from itself', and it 'wantons with grateful joy in the exercise of its own powers' (p. 149). What Wordsworth is here describing, with absolute honesty (conscious or otherwise), is precisely the 'egotistical sublime', the intrusive and reductive, intentional aspect of perception which is presented as a necessary concomitant to description and communication. The eye uses one object to reduce the whole scheme to order, and then builds its own identity upon the dismissal of that object, in a process marked by a double distancing and displacement. What the poet is really doing is establishing his empire over the field of vision, constituting himself at the expense of the world which makes him possible; and the reader who follows this is repeating this gesture. At the same time, the issue is presented within the implication that there is no alternative. There is a very close parallel in Coleridge:

If in the midst of the variety there be not some fixed object for the attention, the unceasing succession of the variety will prevent the mind from observing the difference of the individual objects; and the only thing remaining will be the succession, which will then produce precisely the same effect as sameness . . . In order to derive pleasure from the occupation of the mind, the principle of unity must always be present, so that in the midst of the multeity the centripetal force be never suspended, nor the sense be fatigued by the predominance of the centrifugal force (*Biographia*, II, 262).

We have reached a crucial point in the argument I am trying to put forward. From various sources, it can now be seen that there is a mainstream problem for Romantic aesthetics developing around the conjunction of intentionality and personal identity, presented as dangerous in excess but necessary to a degree. The question which must be asked is, can there be a 'rouzing' without the corresponding 'fixing' which Wordsworth has described? The issue has been before us ever since the case of the speaker of Keats's ode; Bonaparte and the reader of poetry alike dramatise the ubiquity of desire. 'La Belle Dame Sans Merci' does offer a rouzing without a fixing, but the price paid for the absence of the fixing is nothing less than fixation. This is the context in which I wish to introduce a discussion of the status and function of metaphor in Romantic poetics.

5 Metaphor

I

It is with an account of metaphor, and its place in the Romantic aesthetic, that I shall start to try to bring together the themes and ideas which have been expounded, or hinted at, in what has been said already. Within the exploration of a project of metaphor may be grouped will, intention, personal identity, deconstruction, freedom and constraint; all the antithetical implications of the processes of 'rouzing' and 'fixing' which we have dealt with so far. If the activity of the making of metaphor has been traditionally canonised as the *sine qua non* of poetry, then it must be suggested that the endorsement or recreation of this view by Shelley seems to be in tension with the conclusions we can drawn from an examination of Wordsworth, Coleridge, and Blake, where metaphor does not seem to be accorded this status.[1] One of the purposes of this chapter is to explain this apparent contradiction, which has its roots in two different sorts or applications of metaphor, and to examine why it should be that this habitually endorsed poetical trope, one which might appear at first sight to play a constitutive part in any 'heuristic method',[2] is held in apparent suspicion by the major poets of the first generation of Romantics.

It has been argued that the search for a determinate or describable relation to the outside world, which is the problem that the poets inherit insofar as they are committed to the language of standard epistemological speculation, is at the same time the search for an identifiable concept, or even experience, of selfhood. Augustan discourse was usually content to insinuate the unquestioned verification of the perceiving subject by never describing it, never suggesting that it might be responsible for what it sees. It exists as an unspoken but implicitly central presence from which, and not through which, the landscape is organised, and the precision-crafted gallery of general specificities, visual and psychological, which it conveys, are deployed through the rhymed couplet.[3] Romanticism, on the other hand, seems fundamentally committed to a model of 'reciprocal causality', wherein self and object are articulated coinstantaneously, and poetic description, with its implication in and dramatisation of temporality, must then tend to provide an unsettled rhetoric out of which this synthetic moment emerges 'negatively', if at all, from a context of surrounding qualifications and blunted approaches. Thus I have put forward a version of Coleridge which cannot resolve its poetic oppositions and multiple voices into an ongoing process (see, for example, the account of the 'Eolian Harp' poem), and have suggested a version of Wordsworth as a poet compelled to oscillate between mastery of the landscape (and the consequent retraction into guilt) and absolute passivity (which in turn risks passing into terror). Not that these poets do not offer their fair share of epiphanies; but such things usually arise out of the reader's choice, rather than from the demands of any didactic discourse. The voice of assertion, insistence, and achievement is almost always undermined, and this commits the poet-reader whom I at least am compelled to construct as part of the reading act (see p. 228, n. 21) to a confrontation with the question of whether an ethically foolproof act of perception is possible.

Before concerning ourselves with the positioning of metaphor as it was understood 'literally' by the poets and their tradition, it is worth hazarding some remarks about its general place within the configuration of ideas dealing with mimesis and with the making of symbols, images, icons, and such other devices as the mind uses in its relationship to language and the world. I want to suggest a working distinction between metaphor and analogy. In one sense, analogy relates to metaphor as the conscious to the unconscious; it stresses the making of ratios and similitudes as a *way* of conducting the rational activity; it is explicitly heuristic, and therefore less likely to be taken as 'reality'. But there was a lingering theological version of analogy which posited the adequacy of all relational perception within the perfectly created cosmos, and it is this sense that the post-Enlightenment philosophers sought to displace. The discussion of analogy in this period must then be understood in the context of the attempt to modify the concept from the theological to the rational usage. The concept of 'metaphor' can be distinguished from this by regarding it as the mode of perception appropriate to the phenomenalist aspect of the Romantic aesthetic, whereby the mind is in a constitutive (and problematic) relation to its world, which it creates as it creates its own identity. Metaphor is thus much more liable than analogy (in its new 'rational' sense) to 'naturalise' itself by virtue of its importance and its immediacy for the perceiving subject, and this is why the making of metaphor comes to be an ambivalent activity for the Romantic poet, and is often cast as the trope of guilt and desire, necessary to creation but risking false creation, liberating the mind but threatening at the same time to establish its own extrinsic tyranny.

What I have called the 'analogical' perspective was not one which was felt to be very convincing during these times. It was still felt to be able to solve certain issues in Berkeley, but even here there is an insistence that analogy be rendered scrupulous and specific; it will not do to indulge in merely random connections. Generally, analogy comes to be admitted as productive only of probability; the closer together the analogised items, the more secure such probability becomes.[4] For Hartley, it is preferable to 'mere Imagination' (*Observations*, I, 435), but must be disciplined and controlled lest it run away with itself:

> For the Mind once being initiated into the Method of discovering Analogies, and expressing them, does by Association persevere in this Method, and even force things into its System by concealing Disparities, magnifying Resemblances, and accommodating Language thereto (I, 296).

Reid (*Works*, p. 201f.) identifies the progress of philosophy with the progress from 'analogy' to 'reflection', whilst recognising the uses of the former. In fact, the limitations placed on the use of analogy in philosophical method are very closely akin to those placed on metaphor by the rhetoricians. As the editors of the *Encyclopédie* put the case, 'Reasonings by *analogy* can serve to expound and illustrate certain things, but not to demonstrate them.'[5] This, as we shall see, is exactly the standard restriction upon metaphor, that it can illustrate but not prove, embellish but not embody. Nor is this similarity a casual one, for 'analogy' is at this time being 'psychologised', recognised as a mode of explanation rather than an authoritarian demonstration. Instead of being a way of transmitting a pre-established cosmic order, it comes to be seen as a way of organising experience (Stewart, *Works*, III, 178). Hegel describes analogy as

> the instinct or reason, creating an anticipation that this or that characteris-

tic, which experience has discovered, has its root in the inner nature or kind of an object, and arguing on the faith of that anticipation.[6]

This version of analogy will then tend to be vulnerable in the same way as metaphor, as a strictly 'literary' trope, had always been; open to problems of consensus and competence, with communicative potential tempered by subjective modification. The most sophisticated formulation of the analogical model, Kant's 'analogies of experience' (*Pure Reason*, p. 208ff.), can be seen as an attempt both to limit analogy to its new 'critical' role, and at the same time to face up to this threat of solipsism by implying a normative psychology governing its incidence. Kant took 'analogy' to mean

> not, as the word is commonly taken, an imperfect similarity of two things, but a perfect similarity of two relations between quite dissimilar things (*Prolegomena*, p. 125).

The locus of the perception of the similitude can then only be the mind, and the mind unsupported by any metaphysical fabric outside of the categories of pure reason themselves.[7]

To summarise, analogy has, at the end of the eighteenth century, not only been completely displaced from its traditional function as the divinely ordained mechanism of adequate perception, but it is also implicitly unstable in its new and limited rôle as a mode of seeing and relating within a basically phenomenalist epistemology. Urizen has only himself to thank for the 'similitudes' he sees around him, 'Dread terrors! delighting in blood' (Erd. 80, K. 234), and we have already argued that Wordsworth's 'sense of dim similitude' (*The Prelude*, p. 582) carries but limited conviction. Coleridge opined that analogy 'always implies a difference in kind & not merely in degree' (N 2319), and this is exactly what he says about metaphor as 'grounded on an apparent likeness of things essentially different' (*The Friend*, II, 280).[8]

I pass on now to metaphor although, as has been said, no distinction can be an absolute one. The general tenor of eighteenth-century opinion is that metaphor can function as an illustrative strategy, in which case it is appropriate and desirable, but must never be allowed to question or unsettle the stability (ontological and visual) of that which it illustrates.[9] It must be at the service of its employer, but must never raise its hand against him. This division of interest is stressed by Locke in his directive on the proper response to metaphor:

> its Beauty appears at first sight, and there is required no labour of thought, to examine what Truth or Reason there is in it. The Mind without

looking any farther, rests satisfied with the agreeableness of the Picture, and the gayety of the Fancy: And it is a kind of an affront to go about to examine it, by the severe Rules of Truth, and good Reason; whereby it appears, that it consists in something, that is not perfectly conformable to them (*Essay*, Bk. II, ch. XI, 2).

Problems arise when what should be recognised as illustrative is regarded as substantial, as 'reality'. Locke regards the incapacity to maintain this distinction as typical of the madman, who is not incapable of reason per se, but reasons from the wrong premises, having taken 'Fancies for Realities':

Hence it comes to pass, that a Man, who is very sober, and of a right Understanding in all other things, may in one particular be as frantick, as any in *Bedlam*; if either by any sudden very strong impression, or long fixing his Fancy upon one sort of Thoughts, incoherent *Ideas* have been cemented together so powerfully, as to remain united (Bk. II. ch. XI, 13).

It is worth noting that Locke's two categories of disorder correspond to two extremes of ego constitution, passivity (being subject to strong impressions) and self-concentration (fixation); though these are brought together in, for example, 'La Belle Dame'. They are, roughly speaking, the two extremes between which Wordsworth's narrative persona alternates. I shall return to the connection made between metaphor and madness later in this chapter. For the moment, it will suffice to stress that the urgency about keeping apart the metaphorical and the real occurs throughout the period. In the words of Reid,

All analogical and figurative words have a double meaning; and, if we are not very much upon our guard, we slide insensibly from the borrowed and figurative meaning into the primitive (*Works*, p. 362).

This is the context of Jeffrey's definition of the 'notional', already quoted (see p. 210), and of Stewart's warning that

the colourings and finishings of Imagination are apt to blend themselves with the recollection of realities; and often impose on the observer himself, as well as on these to whom he communicates his information (*Works*, IV, 230).

The modifying effects are both communicative and self-referring, a fact which Wordsworth recognised and dignified in making them an essential part of the poetic activity, but at a theoretical level which is itself qualified by the implicit messages of poems like 'The Thorn'.

Coleridge voices this concern over the confusion of real and metaphorical, perhaps more explicitly than any other Romantic thinker. His fascination for etymologies, for the reactivation of original meanings, and his general preoccupation with the deterioration or qualification of meaning through history and through different strata within the same society at the same time, can be rooted in his reiterated suspicion about metaphor as tending to present itself as reality. The enquirer uses etymology as a way of reading back through this mystification. The dangerous consolidation of metaphor into reality is adverted to most often in the context of the interpretation of the Scriptures (see, for example, *Lectures 1795*, p. 202; *Letters*, V, 406), but it is one of the founding concerns in Coleridge's intellectual enterprise, which can be seen in part as a campaign against the tendency of even the most intelligent minds to be convinced by mere 'impressive images in juxta-position' (*Lay Sermons*, p. 153). Luther's visions are analysed in this context (*The Friend*, I, 140), as one example of that temptation in the mind to mistake the *modes* of its apprehension of experience for the exterior (and hence tyrannical, material) imposition of particular apprehended 'realities'. Coleridge describes this process, in a passage which could well stand as an exposition of the activities of the Urizenic creator. Man is compelled to think through cause and effect:

> But, on the other hand, by the same law he is inevitably tempted to misinterpret a constant precedence into positive causation, and thus to break and scatter the one divine and invisible life of nature into countless idols of the sense; and falling prostrate before lifeless images, the creatures of his own abstraction, is himself sensualized, and becomes a slave to the things of which he was formed to be the conqueror and sovereign (*The Friend*, I, 518).

Coleridge attributes materialism to 'the propensity so common among men, to mistake distinct images for clear conceptions', to the vicious habit whereby 'the *conceivable* is reduced within the bounds of the *picturable*' (*Biographia*, I, 91, 189). We must have a relational faculty, a capacity for seeing things together; without one, there would be no perception. But this faculty must be 'methodical', governed by a '*leading Thought*', and founded in a '*staple*, or *starting-post*, in the narrator himself'. Even here there are complications:

> where the habit of Method is present and effective, things the most remote and diverse in time, place, and outward circumstance, are brought into mental contiguity and succession, the more striking as the less expected. But

while we would impress the necessity of this habit, the illustrations adduced give proof that in undue preponderance, and when the prerogative of the mind is stretched into despotism, the discourse may degenerate into the grotesque or the fantastical (*The Friend*, I, 455).

This 'going too far' would correspond to what is elsewhere described as 'making a bull':

> In a Bull there is always a *sensation* without a *sense* of connection between two incompatible thoughts . . . as when for instance, the right order of the Thoughts would be thus—a b c d e f, of which *b* and *e* are incompatible ideas, tho' b is in just connection with c, c with d, and d with *e*—Now if from any heat & hurry of mind and temper such an extreme and undue vividness is given to b and e, as to bedim and practically extinguish the consciousness of (or distract the attention from) c and d, in this case b and e will appear next door neighbors, while the actual, tho' unconscious intervention of c and d, produces a *sensation* of the connection . . . (*Letters*, VI, 632).[10]

Thus for Coleridge even the necessary relational functions of method must be handled with care, as they are prone to the same threats of slippage and excess as is metaphor. Part of the confusion which metaphor occasions for anyone who would try to describe its place in the discourse is due to the fact that, given the need to preserve it from the extremes of ossification through familiarity and overdetermined excess ('the grotesque or the fantastical'), the criterion of 'right usage' must tend to reside in some unspoken middle ground, and must then involve reliance upon a consensus which might have been blandly assumed by a Dr Johnson, but must pose a problem for any generation conscious of the uncertainties of communication and of intersubjective verification. Thus Coleridge is committed to keeping 'metaphor' within its limited role as illustrator, at the same time as insisting on the relational activity as the prime mover in the theory of knowledge and being. 'Metaphor' is kept apart from the formulations of the copula, the symbol, and the will, as a means of isolating the wrong use of relational apprehension from its proper use. In *The Friend*, for example, the will is theorised, in close accordance with the Kantian paradigm of the practical reason, as a process *in itself*, quite divorced from any contingent *ends* to which our investment in the utilitarian world might incline us. For the Hebrews, the 'common and ultimate object of the will and of the reason was purely *spiritual*, and to be present in the mind of the disciple . . . in the idea alone, and never as an image or imagination' (I, 501). This discrimination is the root of the distinction between 'trade' and 'literature', between 'commerce' and 'science'. In both cases 'there must be a mental antecedent', but for the lower pairing (trade and commerce)

> it may be an image or conception received through the senses, and originating from without, the inspiriting passion or desire being alone the immediate and proper offspring of the mind; while in the other the initiative thought, the intellectual seed, must itself have its birth-place within, whatever excitement from without may be necessary for its germination (I, 513).

And the same distinction is used to describe the phenomenon of Sophism within the Athenian state as coming about when

> the pure will . . . is ranked among the *means* to an alien end, instead of being itself the one absolute end, in the participation of which all other things are worthy to be called good (I, 444).

What is at stake here is the necessity of separating or distinguishing the activity itself from the vehicle, and Coleridge places metaphor on the negative side of this distinction. In its habitual fallen state of pseudo-reality, metaphor calls for attention as material content, as image, rather than as high spiritual activity, or idea. Conversely, the 'copula' remains purely relational and idealist, being at the same time much more difficult to recognise:

> Consequently a system that supplies image after image to the senses, however little connected they may be by any necessary copular (sic), will be a formidable rival for another which can pretend only to a logical adherence of conceptions, and which demands from men the most difficult effort in nature, that of truly and earnestly thinking (*Philosophical Lectures*, p. 343).[11]

Coleridge says that 'in all pure phenomena we behold only the copula, the balance or indifference of opposite energies'; we cannot consider 'matter as *real* otherwise than as the copula of these energies, consequently no matter without Spirit' (*Letters*, IV, 760, 775). Here, he is very close, both in spirit and in letter, to Hegel, who is also concerned to educate self-consciousness away from being exclusively 'figurative or pictorial in its thinking' (*Phenomenology*, p. 778). Even the verb 'to be' causes problem for this aspiration:

> The difficulty people find in these conceptions is due solely to sticking to the term 'is' and forgetting the character of thought, where the moments

as much *are* as they *are not*,—are only the process which is Spirit (p. 777).

The copula must be this process, not its content: 'In copulation the immediacy of the living individuality perishes; the death of this life is the procession of spirit' (*Science of Logic*, p. 774). It is not therefore surprising to find in Hegel a polemic against the metaphor which is very close to that of Coleridge. In the *Aesthetics*, he describes metaphor as 'an entirely compressed and abbreviated comparison' which 'does not oppose image and meaning to one another but presents the image alone' (pp. 403–4). Once again, the problem is that with familiarity the mind ceases to be conscious of any potential distinction here. Either it lapses into materialism, image-fixation, or, as with a word like *begreifen* (= to grasp or apprehend), it completely forgets the concrete origin of the term, so that 'the image directly affords only the abstract meaning itself of a concrete picture' (p. 404). Materialism stands at one extreme; at the other, and coming to much the same thing, is the unfilled aspiration of the 'Ichphilosophie'. In contrast to Coleridge, it may be that Hegel regarded the latter possibility as equally or even more immediate than the former. Concerned as he is with the 'self-development of the notion (die Selbstbewegung des Begriffes)' (*Phenomenology*, p. 128; *Werke*, II, 57), and reacting to a philosophical climate which threatened an over-reaction away from materialism, the task he sets himself, in both language and method, is the reconciliation of matter and spirit, spirit in matter. If philosophy is to replace the common 'generalized images (Vorstellungen)' by 'adequate *notions* (Begriffe)' (*Logic*, p. 6; *Werke*, V, 34), then it can only be through a working through of these 'notions' as they come into being.[12] Language carries meaning as Hegel reactivates the root of the noun 'notion /concept' (Begriff) in the verb 'to grasp' (begreifen):

> for the logic of the *Notion*, a completely ready-made and solidified, one may say, ossified material is already to hand, and the problem is to render this material fluid and to re-kindle the spontaneity of the Notion in such dead matter (*Science of Logic*, p. 577).

In most cases this will involve the emancipation of the mind from image-fixation—'for common life has no Notions, but only pictorial thoughts and general ideas' (p. 708)—but for the Idealist philosopher, the error was often at the other end of the scale:

> e.g. with symbolical expressions in speech, with words like *begreifen*, *schliessen*, and so forth. When these signify spiritual activities . . . we have

immediately before our minds only their meaning of a spiritual activity without recalling at all at the same time the visible actions of touching or closing (*Aesthetics*, p. 306).

If language speaks for the principle of fallen spirit in its lapse from paradisal oneness with its world, then it also contains the seeds of a possible redemption through consciousness.[13]

The basic ambivalence of the position of metaphor is again clear; it is to be admired and employed, Hegel implies, as it contributes to process and movement, but part of its very formulation inclines it towards the deadening goal of achieved content. As such, it is very closely identifiable with the problem of perception and identity in general. The mind needs objects outside it in order to recognise itself; 'A could not be affirmed to be A but by the perception that it is *not* B . . . this again implies the perception that B *is* as well as A' (Coleridge, *Letters*, V, 97).[14] For Hegel, this is nothing less than the sanction for art in general, which responds to 'man's rational need to lift the inner and outer world into his spiritual consciousness as an object in which he recognizes again his own self' (*Aesthetics*, p. 31). The risk which always attends this movement is once again that the process will come to a halt at the moment of 'outerance' and commit the subject to the standard dualism of self and other. Hegel describes the Jewish religion in exactly these terms (see *Early Theological Writings*, pp. 163, 199–200, 247, etc.); and Wordsworth has some experience of the problem in London in finding himself bombarded with more signs and objects than he can properly process through his modifying imagination whilst keeping the balance of inner and outer. As Shelley might have put it, 'the accumulation of the materials of external life exceed the quantity of the power of assimilating them to the internal laws of human nature' (*Complete Works*, VII, 135).

The risk of becoming fixed at the pole of 'outerance' and consequently tyrannised by an oversupply of objects, or even a single unassimilable object, may help to explain why it is that metaphor, identified as it is with the production of 'images', should be held to involve great risks. It is important to note here that the visual mode, based on the geometrical models and organised spaces of optical theory, and at the same time the primary constituent of the epistemological vocabulary, was subjected to a stringent criticism by Romantic thinkers. It was held to be more open than any other of the senses to employment as the metaphor of fixity and deadness. Burke had observed that 'things do not spontaneously present themselves to the palate as they do to the sight' (*Philosophical Enquiry*, p. 15), and it is exactly this implication of the passivity of the beholder before what he 'sees' which makes the Romantics suspicious of optics as a tool of the materialist philosophy. Poetic experience was thus articulated as 'viewless' and governed by something othe than what Blake called the 'perverted & single vision' of the 'Vegetated Mortal Eye' (Erd. 200, K. 684). Coleridge explicitly links his interest in etymology with the demystification of the dominant optical metaphor:

> In disciplining the mind one of the first rules should be, to lose no opportunity of tracing words to their origin; one good consequence of which will be, that he will be able to use the *language* of sight without being enslaved by its affections. He will at least secure himself from the delusive notion, that what is not *imageable* is likewise not *conceivable*. To emancipate the mind from the despotism of the eye is the first step towards its emancipation from the influences and intrusions of the senses, sensations, and passions generally.[15]

One recalls Coleridge's comments on 'The Ancient Mariner' and the parallel arguments against 'too great definiteness of terms' as consuming 'too much of the vital and idea-creating force in distinct, clear, full-made images'. What is noticeable about other comments, however, is that the eye, far from now metaphoring the passivity of the subject, stands for exactly the opposite. This is not surprising, given the argument I have been putting forward for a general preoccuption with intentionality in Romantic aesthetics and philosophy; and indeed, the two poles are really quite closely implicated one with another. Passivity before objects produces desire for those objects, and this commits us to a return movement, equally unbalanced, of intrusion into the world in an attempt to obtain and master them. Coleridge makes this very clear in the following passage:

> We have been accustomed by all our affections, by all our wants, to seek after outward images; and by the love of association, therefore, to whole truth we attach that particular condition of truth which belongs to sensible bodies or to bodies which can be touched. The first education which we receive, that from our mothers, is given to us by touch; the whole of its process is nothing more than, to express myself boldly, an extended touch by promise. The sense itself, the sense of vision itself, is only acquired by a continued recollection of touch (*Philosophical Lectures*, p. 115).

Vision thus becomes the trope of desire, of the tyrant eye, rather than the passive receiver; two halves of the same process.[16] Wordsworth and the old sea-captain.

The homophone of eye and I, identity and eye-dentity, was all too available as an associationist temptation to the mind tied into language. Exploited with virtuoso effect in a poem like Coleridge's 'Eolian Harp' (eye /I /aye), it is common as a poetic device in Blake and Shelley, and present also in Wordsworth, often as a way of bringing to attention the dangers of allowing meaning to operate at the level of the phonetic signifier, and introducing that equation of being and seeing, ontology and epistemology, which we have already seen to be a prominent factor in philosophical speculation. Romanticism in a general way sought to counteract this identification, contributing as it did to the master /slave relation to the world.[17] Locke, as usual, was regarded as the first offender—it is not accidental that Blake rechristens him 'John Lookye' (Erd. 447, K. 52)—though in the *Essay* itself the interrelation of eye and I often stands quite consciously at the level of analogy:

> The Perception of the Mind, being most aptly explained by Words relating to the Sight, we shall best understand what is meant by *Clear*, and *Obscure* in our *Ideas*, by reflecting on what we call *Clear* and *Obscure* in the Objects of Sight (Bk. II, ch. XXIX, 2).

Locke's criterion, as so often, seems to be clarity of exposition; but the example itself serves to demonstrate the propensity within the metaphorical to insinuate itself, or be taken, as the real, so that the Romantics frequently describe their purpose as the emancipation of the imagination from its foundation in the visual image, a foundation noted by Stewart (*Works*, II, 431f.), for example, as somewhat arbitrary, though I have tried to suggest that there were determining forces at work in establishing it. Blake achieved this by rendering vision as totally phenomenalistic, as constituting a world where 'the Eye altering alters all' (Erd. 476, K. 426), and where the sun is imaged simultaneously as a golden guinea and as a host of heavenly angels. The eye is not the sum of the imagination; we see through it and not with it, as Blake was found of saying (Erd. 484, 555, 512, K. 433, 617, 753). This is one reason why Blake eschews metaphor as it was conventionally understood, a fact taken in vain by at least one critic who complains that he 'did not seem to understand that successful metaphor depends upon the visualized action which Aristotle praised in Homer's metaphor.'[18] The Grecian, indeed, is mathematic proportion. For metaphor, in its pre-Shelleyan formulation, was generally understood as image-bound and materialistic. Nor was Coleridge the first to think so. Here is Hartley:

> It is probable, that Fables, Parables, Similes, Allegory, & c. please, strike and instruct, chiefly on account of the visible Imagery, which they raise up in the Fancy . . . Image-worship seems even to have been derived in great measure from this Source (*Observations*, I, 214).

The implicit materiality of the image is at the root of Wordsworth's version of the standard polemic against metaphor as false ornamentation. Even as a strictly literary trope, metaphor had always been in an ambivalent position, regarded as necessary, but also as necessarily to be limited. The idea of language as originating in metaphor, in the sense argued by Rousseau and Herder, was not immediately incompatible with the demand for restraint; although, as one critic at least has argued, there were definite problems for the eighteenth-century theorists arising from the demand that metaphor should be both just *and* new.[19] As long as it was seen to be merely illustrative, there was always the recourse to a language of plain speaking which could be represented in unadorned language. Even Shelley, in his tract of 1812, *Proposals for an Association of Philanthropists*, could call for the telling of 'the plain truth, without the confusion and ornament of metaphor' (*Complete Works*, V, 261). The plea made by Wordsworth for a purer poetic language was paralleled for philosophy by Reid and Stewart (see *Works*, p. 220; *Works*, III 6ff). But it would be inaccurate, I think, to regard Wordsworth as arguing for the total exclusion of metaphor from poetry; he seems above all concerned to establish that, when it does occur, it should be natural and appropriate, not imported and extraneously derived from the imitation of other poets. I have already given an account of what I take Wordsworth's theory of poetic diction to imply (see above, pp. 61f.); that language is never purely denotative, but always leaves out the most important elements of its meaning. The simplicity functions to make the lacunae more honestly apparent, and poetical decoration is avoided in order that the reader shall not accede to a substitutive and secondary 'creative' activity at the level of the signifier alone, the mere words on the page. Hence there are no assonances, coruscating metaphors, and so on. Hegel makes an interesting comment in this context:

> Yet one may still hear the German language praised for its wealth—that wealth consisting in its special expression for special sounds—*Rauschen*, *Sausen*, *Knarren*, etc;—there have been collected more than a hundred

such words, perhaps: the humour of the moment creates fresh ones when it pleases. Such superabundance in the realm of sense and of triviality contributes nothing to form the real wealth of a cultivated language. The strictly raw material of language itself depends more upon an inward symbolism than a symbolism referring to external objects; it depends, i.e. upon anthropological articulation, as it were the posture in the corporeal act of oral utterance (*Philosophy of Mind*, p. 214).

This is very close in spirit to Wordsworth's polemic against the standard poetic diction; and Wordsworth too is ready to admit this 'anthropological articulation', which for him is often the activity of bringing symbols into being, implicitly the genesis of 'poetic diction' itself. He always recognised as Coleridge explains,

> the *dramatic* propriety of those figures and metaphors in the original poets, which, stripped of their justifying reasons, and converted into mere artifices of connection or ornament, constitute the characteristic falsity in the poetic style of the moderns (*Biographia*, II, 28).

But when we put his speaker or protagonist into the context of this statement, then the presentation of 'metaphor' can be seen to be conveyed as essentially 'inadequate' or vulnerable to ethical censure. Metaphor is indeed the natural mode of expression of a mind in a state of excitement, but this excitement can be radically distorting.[20] Thus the old sea captain reveals through the symbolical functions of his pseudo-'descriptive' language that he has an unconscious investment in the situation of Martha Ray, one which could be called 'excitement'. Part of the burden which the adult of 'Anecdote for Fathers' places on the child is the burden of symbolical language (the weather-cock), a language which he does not understand (based as it is on analytical choice—so figurative language is the product of *reduction*) and in which he has no spontaneous investment. From this perspective, the poem demonstrates an education in error—the error of poetic diction. The narrator of 'A Slumber Did my Spirit Seal' learns too late that he has mistaken metaphor for reality and consequently failed to apprehend that living reality; and so on. In an account of the imagination as a modifying power, Wordsworth demonstrates, consciously or otherwise, the reductive implication of the relational activity in one of his own poems:

> In these images, the conferring, the abstracting, and the modifying powers of the Imagination, immediately and mediately acting, are all brought into conjunction. The stone is endowed with something of the power of life to approximate it to the sea-beast; and the sea-beast stripped

of some of its vital qualities to assimilate it to the stone; which intermediate image is thus treated for the purpose of bringing the original image, that of the stone, to a nearer resemblance to the figure and condition of the age Man; who is divested of so much of the indications of life and motion as to bring him to the point where the two objects unite and coalesce in just comparison (*Prose*, III, 33).

All the items in this comparison lose something of their individuality in order for this 'just comparison' to be achieved. The locus of the relationship, the principle of coalescence, is an imaginative process which, for this very reason, cannot be urged without the attendant problem of guilt, which is the more complex poeticising version of the theoretical voice which speaks in the above passage, as in the discussion of the 'With Ships the Sea' sonnet with which I ended the last chapter. The problem becomes almost theological; if the creation of objects from the mind alone is a false or demonic creation, then the reduction of the many to the one, even when a part of a process of reapproaching that oneness (which always involves modification), is a misuse of what *has* been created already. Wordsworth had good cause to doubt in the mind

> That domination which she oftentimes
> Exerts upon the outward face of things,
> So moulds them, and endues, abstracts, combines,
> Or by abrupt and unhabitual influence
> Doth make one object so impress itself
> Upon all others, and pervade them so
> That even the grossest minds must see and hear
> And cannot chuse but feel (*The Prelude*, XIII, 77–84).

This is not so far from murdering by dissection,[21] and it certainly contributes to an explanation of why it is that the eye is advertised as 'The most despotic of our senses', able to hold the untrained mind 'In absolute dominion' (XI, 174–76). Wordsworth goes on to suggest that 'Nature' intervenes to thwart this 'tyranny': we have already pointed to the paradoxes of this intervention.

Schiller has this to say about man in his merely physical state:

> Either he hurls himself upon objects to devour them in an access of desire; or the objects press upon him to destroy him, and he thrusts them away in horror (*Aesthetic Education*, p. 171).

I have tried throughout this chapter to position metaphor as oscillating between these two poles. The argument brought against it as an 'image producing'function, encouraging dependence upon the visual and the external, is the simpler of the two, and I hope it is now clear enough. The argument against metaphor as an intentional tool, however, is somewhat more complicated, and perhaps calls for further comment (let me stress once more that these two poles are essentially related to the common problem of achieving a viable self-other relationship, at the level of language and of experience).

I shall try to explain how metaphor can be seen as the trope of desire. The making of metaphor serves to bind the subject into a wished-for relation to its context, in that the conjunctions which it establishes are the wished-for features of an imaginary world which the subject can then reflect back in order to constitute itself. It is the subject which 'holds together' the terms of the comparison, and it can therefore focus itself as the origin of the perception of that comparison, which thus becomes an expression of how this subject wants to be.[22] Now, it is metonymy which has been recognised as the trope of desire, involving as it does the activities of displacement and deferral, with the concentration on the part as a way of invoking or aspiring to the whole.[23] This it certainly is; the images of 'La Belle Dame' are primarily metonymic (more precisely, synecdochic), and they speak for the quester's inability to compose an identifiable and separable whole out of the image-parts oppressing and giving purpose to his silent sojourn; they characterise a state of unfulfilled desire. There is a heuristic function here, as the protagonist is tempted to try to proceed along a chain of increasingly resonant signifiers—hair, foot, eyes, and so on—which he might expect to construct into a whole, into a complete presence. But this never happens, and the pre-empting of the process of construction produces fixation and arrested motion. It is as Hartley says:

> When a Person desires to recollect a thing that has escaped him . . . he recals the visible Idea, or some other Associate, again and again, by a voluntary Power, the Desire generally magnifying all the Ideas and Associations; and thus bringing in the Association and Idea wanted, at last. However, if the desire be great, it changes the State of the Brain, and has an opposite Effect; so that the desired Idea does not recur, till all has subsided; perhaps not even then (*Observations*, I, 381).

But metaphor too, in a more occluded way, fulfils or fails to fulfil the mechanisms of desire, at the very fundamental level of the subject's place in his world. If 'La Belle Dame' embodies inhibited metonymic processes, then it must be said that it is also characterised by the

complete absence of 'fulfilled' metaphor, precisely because there is no
material for the subject to employ in its self-construction in *any* terms,
no achieved balance of innering and outering. Keats elsewhere
describes what metaphor can accomplish for the business of self-
identification:

> it is an old maxim of mine and of course must be well known that evey
> point of thought is the centre of an intellectual world – the two
> uppermost thoughts in a Man's mind are the two poles of his World he
> revolves on them and every thing is southward or northward to him
> through their means—We take but three steps from feathers to iron
> (*Letters*, I, 243).

This is beautifully described, as befits a poet who has won the right to
a positive use of metaphoric apprehension by trying to eschew the
'egotistical sublime'; but the poet to whom this was attributed,
Wordsworth, could seldom shake off the doubts attendant upon the
use of the tyrant eye. He knew of a world whose objects are modified
or even created out of nothing (as, perhaps, in 'The Thorn') by
passion, where 'reaction' is prior to 'action'—'the feeling therein
developed gives importance to the action and situation and not the
action and situation to the feeling' (*Prose*, I, 128)—and where all
perception must stand trial as intentional projection. Nature, as we
have seen several times, is presented as a mediator, both to relieve the
burden of consciousness attendant upon the possibility of exclusive
self-projection, and to provide a tentative external determinant
which might offer to signify something similar to other minds; it is
nature which chastises the 'forming hand' when it risks 'acting in a
devious mood' (*The Prelude*, II, 382–3), and it is the need to balance
intention against reception which explains the presence, in the
theoretical writings, of identfications such as those between spontaneity and habituated deep thought (*Prose*, I, 126) and between
accurate description and modifying passion (*Prose*, III, 26). Some of
Wordsworth's finest poems, however, seem to stand as examples of
the correction, by experience and reflection, of the disturbance of
what Coleridge called 'the union and reconciliation of that which is
nature with that which is exclusively human' (*Biographia*, II, 254–5)
by an act of indifference or subjective appropriation, both varieties of
interference of which the poetic act itself threatens to partake. Hazlitt
found in Wordsworth 'a repugnance to admit any thing that tells for
itself, without the interpretation of the poet' (*Works*, XIX, 12), but
this 'interpretation' is often to be seen as the very drama of the poem;

it is the implicit solipsism of interpretation, as it tends to trap the mind
within the categories deduced from past experience, which shuts it off
from the possibility of innocent receptivity. For, if our metaphors are
not at the service of some new structure of desire, then they may be
preconditioned by the categories of habitual experience as we already
have them; they are either dangerously new, or stale and deadening.
This latter implication is what seems to me to introduce an irony into
the end of 'The Idiot Boy'. We can take the point that the central
'events' of the poem, those which happen to the boy during his
midnight ramble, remain uncommunicated to us and in themselves
alinguistic; we are to understand also that Wordsworth, true to his
theory, is as much interested in the 'feelings' aroused in others as in the
'actions' which we never hear about. But it is worth noting that when
the boy himself is pressured into language, he produces metaphorical
crossings:

> And thus, to Betty's question, he
> Made answer, like a traveller bold,
> (His very words I give to you,)
> 'The cocks did crow to-whoo, to-whoo,
> And the sun did shine so cold.'
> Thus answered Johnny in all his glory,
> And that was all his travel's story. (*Poetical Works*, II, 80)

Reading his words in good faith, we notice that he apprehends the
new experience exclusively in terms of the old; the categories of
habitual familiarity, the sun and the cocks, are all that he has to
'describe' the moon and the owls. The effect is comic, of course, but
speaks also for the potentially restrictive implications of the nominalist foundation of language whereby we perceive specificities
through generalities.

But this is a very sophisticated version of implied 'culpability', pre-
empting the metacomment as it does by the boy's presumably
unconscious irony. A poem like 'Nutting' asks to be read as a more
overt parable of interference, and the wandering poet-speaker of
'Resolution and Independence' can be seen within at least one reading
to be fighting a battle with his own modifying imagination, which
carries him into flights of introspection wherein the old man's
discourse is not heard. Part of the firmness of mind which the poet
figure eventually comes to appreciate may be related to the old man's
patience in repeating his tale until such time as the poet is in a fit
condition to hear it, distracted as he is by his 'mind's eye' (*Poetical*

Works, II, 240). The various revisions of 'Old Man Travelling' (*Poetical Works*, IV, 247) seem to speak for a Wordsworth who becomes more and more embarrassed about preserving the final lines of direct speech which can, on one reading, be taken as corrective of the speaker's sentimental view of man-in-nature, a view only tenable as long as the old man does not speak for himself. The son who was 'dying in an hospital' in the 1798 version is merely 'lying' there in 1800; and the lines are turned into reported speech, eventually (in 1815) being omitted altogether. One of the most comprehensive emblems of the unseeing eye is the vicar of 'The Brothers'. Boastful of his familiarity with the locale in general, he cannot recognise the living figure before him. Ironically, he claims not to need the help of symbols (gravestone inscriptions) to assist his memory, but he cannot 'read' the deep feelings which stand beside him. Obsessed as he is with the polemic against tourists, he takes Leonard for a mere 'Son of Idleness' (*Poetical Works*, II, 1), and therefore misses the hints and leading questions which might inform him otherwise. Like the idle ramblers of the 'Point Rash-Judgment' poem, his judgements rebound upon himself, although we never witness any recognition of this. Turning aside at the moment of the fraternal confirmation. 'The Vicar did not hear the words' (l. 412); how ironic it is that Leonard should write 'with a hope to be forgiven' (l.431). We are not told of the vicar's reaction to the letter—another fine example of the occluded meaning.

Wordsworth's protagonists are prone, either 'To act the God among external things' (*Poetical Works*, III, 193), or to wallow in their own private worlds, occasionally corrected by some enforced recognition of what they are doing; these are the two extremes of the same syndrome. There is in Wordsworth little of the 'guiltless eye' which a poet like Cowper could claim, content as he is with a presence in the landscape which 'Commits no wrong, nor wastes what it enjoys.'[24] A poem like 'Stepping Westward' (*Poetical Works*, III, 76) can anatomise beautifully the fantasy that there might be an external authoritative licence for the presence of the subject in its world, and a teleological principle towards which it can rightfully aim. But the way is 'endless'; the 'dewy ground' creeps up behind with every step one takes; the sunset recedes before at the same pace. The whole fantasy is built upon the coincidence of a magnificent sunset with a chance phrase which seems to speak for some metaphorical potency. The poem is a yearning that the metaphor *might* be true, that it might bear some relation to a reality; but the 'endless way' is the final image, and it implicitly affirms the division between language and reality or 'experience', the one offering the prospect of a coherence which is not fulfilled by the other.[25]

The image of perceptual insecurity, of the 'unmetaphored' condition, also produces immobility on those occasions when there is no sunset to implant paradisal fantasies. In an unpublished fragment of *The Prelude*, Wordsworth describes exactly this:

> If, from the wantonness in which we play
> With things we love, or from a freak of power,
> Or from involuntary act of hand
> Or foot unruly with excess of life,
> It chanc'd that I ungently used a tuft
> Of meadow-lillies, or had snapp'd the stem
> Of foxglove bending o'er his native rill,
> I should be loth to pass along my way
> With unreprov'd indifference, – I would stop
> Self-question'd, asking wherefore that was done (p. 612).

The 'excess of life' is worth noting; energy itself is put at risk, embedded in a context of potential guilt. Again, Cowper offers an interesting contrast. He too censures the 'inadvertent step' which might 'crush the snail', but asserts also the primacy of man in the created world as a means of avoiding the necessity of immobility, 'A necessary act incurs no blame.' Thus

> The sum is this.—If man's convenience, health,
> Or safety, interfere, his rights and claims
> Are paramount, and must extinguish their's (*Poetical Works*, p. 232).

This unquestioning anthropocentrism is not felt by Wordsworth to be a solution. Indeed, if inarticulacy be the yardstick of innocence, which is then maligned or misunderstood by conventional language—see, for example, 'Anecdote for Fathers,' 'The Idiot Boy', 'To a Highland Girl', 'The Blind Highland Boy', and 'The Solitary Reaper'—then the act of making poetry itself asks to be questioned as yet one more strategy of interference. Hence, once again, the double effect of the 'Point Rash-Judgment' poem, with the initial crime echoed to a lesser degree in the very moment of correction. But metaphor, at least, involving selection and reduction, modification and coalescence, turns all too easily into a 'freak of power'.[26]

I pass on to Blake, who uses almost no 'metaphor' in the simplest sense of the term, though a great deal of the language of correspondence. Such metaphor is, I think, to be taken as a part of the naturalising linguistic resources of the fallen mind, often imaged as a stomach or digestive tract (Erd. 75, 246; K. 229, 735), as is appropriate to the epistemological insecurity which produces an infinite craving for the 'outside', the object-world. Simple metaphor also, as I have implied, contributes to the 'steady-state' notion of subjectivity which Blake is concerned to disrupt, in that it allows for the mind to establish itself as the focal point of the comparative activity. Its selections produce re-imposed perspectives which have the features of Urizenic solidness, plotted ratios. Peculiarly enough, we find in Blake a reintroduction of the traditional language of analogy. This is no mere historical conservatism, nor is it a recourse to 'analogy' as it was being formulated by the late eighteenth century as a mechanism of general psychology, a sort of 'metaphor in common'. Blake had considerable investment in the idea of mind and world as, in Coleridge's words, an 'eternal Identity of Allness and Oneness', wherein 'the whole Universe becomes an infinity of Concentric Circles' (*Letters*, IV, 689), but he was certainly not concerned to hand over this model as just one more consoling myth. A. W. Schlegel, for example, had used a similar argument to justify all relational predications:

> But strictly speaking a metaphor can never be too bold. All things stand in relation to one another, and every thing therefore signifies every other thing, each part of the universe mirrors the whole: these are just as much philosophic as poetic truths.[27]

Blake did indeed employ the idea of the correspondence of microcosm and macrocosm, but the correspondence is always generated through infinite particularities. The function of analogical language is that it brings out the *activity* of making connections. They cannot be 'naturalised' as easily as metaphorical connections can. This is partly because in employing analogy he is emphasising a mode which had become unfashionable and therefore difficult to assimilate, especially since the standard theological verification of analogy had become less evident. This means that analogy is in fact the appropriate mode for the preservation of the disjunction *within* the comparison. Conventional metaphor can be equated with the Urizenic creation, and its insistence upon the solid selfhood as the nexus of perception:

> combining
> He dug mountains & hills in vast strength,
> He piled them in incessant labour,
> In howlings & pangs & fierce madness (Erd. 72, K. 225).

Among other things, he is of course creating the standard 'landscape' available to descriptive poetry. Images thus formed must remain gestures of limitation and self-focussing, as the false creation turns 'the fluxile eyes / Into two stationary orbs, concentrating all things' (Erd. 62, K. 241). As Urizen puts it elsewhere: 'Here will I fix my foot & here rebuild' (Erd. 343, K. 317). It is worth remarking also that metaphor tends to deal in parts or single items, and thus has its place in a debate which goes right back to the roots of the nominalist theory of language which, it will be remembered, presupposes an indefinite number of differences which find their common nature in language, and in language alone. Thus Stewart:

> The classification of different objects supposes a power of attending to some of their qualities or attributes, without attending to the rest; for no two objects are to be found without some specific difference (*Works*, II, 161).

For Blake, with his interest in particularities, any trope which threatens to elide them must be avoided, and metaphor, as we have seen with Wordsworth, where it is often identified with 'imagination' in general, does indeed work by selecting parts or items as a means of reducing the landscape into describable order; as such, it is the tool of the nominalist conspiracy. It reduces also the *activity* of thinking to the terms of the contingent *vehicles* or emblems of thought, forcing us outside into a world of images whose spiritual causes we then forget. This is illustrated, for example, in the following passage from 'Europe':

> Thought chang'd the infinite to a serpent; that which pitieth:
> To a devouring flame; and man fled from its face and hid
> In forests of night; then all the eternal forests were divided
> Into earths rolling in circles of space, that like an ocean rush'd
> And overwhelmed all except this finite wall of flesh.
> Then was the serpent temple form'd, image of infinite
> Shut up in finite revolutions, and man became an Angel;
> Heaven a mighty circle turning; God a tyrant crown'd
>
> (Erd. 62, K. 241)

This miscreative activity of creation is exactly the metaphorical process which shuts up the infinite revolutions; and it is crucially coinstantaneous with the fashioning of the Old Testament deity. Contrasting with this activity of separation whereby the subject dynamically limits its own world, the moment of analogy *starts out* in a state of division. It always leaves a space between the related terms which must be bridged, not by the assumption of a firmly centred seltnood, but by a *going forth* from one level to another, which for Blake constitutes the *act* of identity. Analogy is thus initially more disjunctive, and at the same time ultimately more synthetic, than metaphor, in that it dramatises more completely the process of becoming in its passage from mere beholding. Instead of moving in and out of the world from a fixed point in the eye, we move wholly out of our selves, as for example in the identification of Blake, Los, Albion, and Jesus at the climax of 'Jerusalem'. Analogy works with the becoming of being rather than with the pre-established terminology of the vegetated eye and its implication in organised space.[28]

II

I have tried to show that the making of metaphor threatens the integrity of the Romantic consciousness with reification, both of itself and of the elements of its world, reciprocally. The linguistic symptom of this process is the passage from illustration to apparent 'reality', the confusion of figurative and literal. This belongs within the context of the heresy of materialism. At the same time, some gesture of self-establishment is necessary if the mind is to identify itself at all. Part of the difficulty of an analysis such as this is that the term 'metaphor' asks to be considered as a determinate and monovalent signifier which, if it is thought of as metaphor-in-use, it certainly need not be. Thus I have been obliged to stress along the way that by 'metaphor' I mean the simplest sort of relational apprehension as it is constitutive of and reciprocally controlled by a stable subject; and I have tried to argue that this is a viable way to present the trope as it is involved in Romantic attitudes to image-making language.

A different approach, or emphasis, is now called for, because there is a more complex use of metaphor where the illusion of the stable subject and the fixing of its environment is not encouraged. The use of metaphor in its overdetermined or excessive state does play a positive rôle in poetics as seen from the perspective of, above all, Shelley. I hope it will be made clear, however, that the oversupply of metaphor is as much of an onslaught on the received fabric of language as is the Wordsworthian paring down into simplicity. Shelley's hyper-articulacy poses the same threat to the mind's confidence about its position in the world; excess and vacancy can almost be seen as the two interchangeable extremes of a common polemic. The reification / through metaphor which Wordsworth fears so much is countered by Shelley with an oversupply of metaphor which prevents us ever coming to a *stop* in the production of meanings.

This ambivalence over metaphor in its two states, which we may think of as normative and excessive, context-controlled and uncontrolled, is reflected also in the eighteenth-century articulation of the relation of figurative and real. What I have argued to be, in the case of writers like Wordsworth and Coleridge, an ethically unadmirable and morally stultifying process, the confusion of literal and metaphorical, is simultaneously described and undermined by those who see in this confusion the symptom of insanity. As I have said, this is one of the features of the predicament of the speaker of 'La Belle Dame', that he cannot distinguish inner from outer, and cannot therefore 'make' metaphor. Endymion has the same experience, except that this time it is explicitly revealed to *us* as solipsistic:

> He saw her body fading gaunt and spare
> In the cold moonshine. Straight he seized her wrist;
> It melted from his grasp. Her hand he kissed,
> And, horror, kissed his own—he was alone (*Poems*, p. 266).

The poet of 'Alastor' falls into a similar posture, as he 'seeks in vain for a prototype of his conception' (*Poetical Works*, pp. 14–15), thus falling into the trap which Kant describes as

> that amphiboly which transforms our idea into a supposed representation of an object that is empirically given and therefore to be known according to the laws of experience (*Pure Reason*, p. 435).

Spurzheim explains insanity generally as a condition wherein one cannot make any distinctions between the healthy and the diseased faculties (*Observations*, pp. 71–2). Elsewhere, this was referred specifically to the distinction between the literal and the figurative, as, for example, by Monboddo (*Ancient Metaphysics*, I, 428; II, 235) and Stewart (*Works*, II, 154). For Shelley, then, who calls for a 'harmonious madness' at the end of 'To a Skylark' (*Poetical Works*, p. 603), any potential confusion of the metaphorical and the real will be very much to the purpose. It is possible to suggest something of a shift in attitudes to metaphor through the period by comparing, for example, Kames's disapproval of mixed metaphor as productive of obscurity (*Elements*, II, 285), with the views of the author of the article 'On the Use of Metaphors' (*Blackwood's Edinburgh Magazine*, 18, no.

107, December, 1825, pp. 719–23). Here, 'Broken metaphors' are admired for their function as vehicles for novelty and intensity:

> it follows that the oftener the metaphor is changed, that is to say, the more of them that can be comprised in a period, the stronger must be the effect . . . a man of genius shall pour out half a dozen fine metaphors in a sentence, combined with as little obscurity as a blunderer shall produce in drawling one over the same space (p. 722).

But even this is to miss the possibility that a poet like Shelley might be purposefully concerned to produce obscurity. Shelley makes metaphor constitutive, rather than illustrative, of reality, but in doing so tries to make sure that such 'reality' is inseparable from an infinite becoming. The succession of metaphors is therefore organised so that, more often than not, they 'interfere' with one another; hence the critics' problem of trying to establish determinate readings of Shelley's symbols. This idea of interference—and this time we are not interfering in 'the world' but in our notion of what that world *is*—is anticipated by Hartley when he argues for the virtues of the diversity of languages, putting to use the curse of Babel:

> For we think in Words . . . and invent chiefly by means of their Analogies; at the same time that a servile Adherence to those of any one Language, or the putting of Words for Things, would lead us into many Errors. Now Diversity of Languages does both enlarge the Field of Invention, and by opposing Analogy to Analogy preserve us from the Prejudices derived from mere verbal Agreements (*Observations*, I, 305–6).

Priestley took over this argument almost to the word (*Lectures on the Theory of Language*, p. 292), and it appears again as part of a conscious philosophical method for Dugald Stewart:

> finding it impossible to lay aside completely metaphorical or analogical words, I have studied to avoid such a uniformity in the employment of them, as might indicate a preference to one theory rather than another; and, by doing so, have perhaps sometimes been led to vary the metaphor oftener and more suddenly than would be proper in a composition which aimed at any degree of elegance (*Works*, II, 355; see also IV, 58–9).

This is very close to Shelley's application of metaphor to the writing of poetry. He too points out the negative consequences of approaching interpretation as a merely literal exercise, the most comprehensive statements being the famous ones in 'A Defence of Poetry' (but see also *Complete Works*, VI, 232, 247; VII, 74 etc.). The alternative to the

fixing properties of simple metaphor becomes the over-supply of
mixed metaphor, employed in a continual cycle of creation and
destruction which is always producing 'the before unapprehended
relations of things' (VII, 111). It is exactly this metaphorical vitality
which Prometheus promises for Asia and himself in their new life:

> We will entangle buds and flowers and beams
> Which twinkle on the fountain's brim, and make
> Strange combinations out of common things,
> Like human babes in their brief innocence;
> And we will search, with looks and words of love,
> For hidden thoughts, each lovelier than the last,
> Our unexhausted spirits; and like lutes
> Touched by the skill of the enamoured wind,
> Weave harmonies divine, yet ever new,
> From difference sweet where discord cannot be
>
> *(Poetical Works*, p. 246).

It is as material for this process of perpetual creation that poetry,
insofar as it is poetry, must exist: 'Veil after veil may be undrawn, and
the inmost naked beauty of the meaning never exposed' (*Complete
Works*, VII, 131). The excess of metaphor, then, where each single
relation develops out of and turns into another, becomes the proper
mode for representing a situation where 'every thing is in animation'
(*Letters*, I, 215). As long as the inmost meaning is unachieved, then
there is no stopping; and it is the very definition of poetry for Shelley
that it shall prevent such achievement. At the same time, the subject
which is accustomed to the 'outering' gesture as a means of
establishing its identity will also be in a state of becoming, the ethical
corollary of which is love, where all things 'meet and mingle' (*Poetical
Works*, p. 583). Shelley's metaphors and similes are usually over-
charged, and often impossible to 'visualise', thus avoiding the threat
of image-fixation. The eye has no opportunity to establish any
despotism.[29] Nor is there, correspondingly, much chance of making
the standard ontological investment. Shelley addresses the skylark:

> What thou art we know not;
> What is most like thee? (p. 602).

And one need only glance at the plethora of created and creating
forms which are 'like' the lark to suggest that Shelley's point is that
nothing 'is', though every thing is 'like'. This preservation of the
unfilled, and unfillable, space at the centre of the poem is crucial if we
are to see the final outburst—'The world should listen then—as I am
listening now'—as something more than mere unbridled egotism.

For the world would then be listening, not to the poet as superman, but to the unidentifiable source of pure imagination, ever becoming and ever unfocussable on worldly or material ends, poured forth through a medium which does not control or comprehend the genesis of its own inspiration—as the poet of 'A Defence of Poetry' does not.

As always, there is the other side of the argument to be considered, as we found in the general equation of madness and poetry. Very few of Shelley's contemporaries, by the evidence of the reviews, seem to have been prepared to follow him through the extremes of deconstruction demanded by the poetry. If the speaker of 'La Belle Dame' has not the necessary identity for the making of metaphor, then the reader of Shelley risks losing what identity he has to begin with through the kinetic development of the metaphors themselves. In both cases, there are signs but no sure referents. Coleridge described 'Happiness' as

> a Fountain of intellectual activity, & connects the connected [sic] a b with c, d- till z.—yea, 1 and 2 with 3—& in a few moments with 595, 876, 341 (N 2495).

Three steps from feathers to iron. But there remains the necessity of distinction, courageously placed at the centre of his theory by Wordsworth at the same time as his poems are demonstrating the ethical problems of such distinction. The undifferentiated connection of everything with everything would be, as we have seen, madness.[30] Locke had noted that

> there is *no one thing*, whether simple *Idea*, Substance, Mode, or Relation, or Name of either of them, *which is not capable of almost an infinite number of* Considerations, in reference to other things (*Essay*, Bk. II, ch. XXV, 7).

Hume locates this as part of the insecurity implicit in the metaphorical mode. Demonstrating the advantages of causality as a working model over mere 'resemblance and contiguity' (which correspond quite closely to metaphor and metonymy), he argues that

> where upon the appearance of an impression we not only feign another object, but likewise arbitrarily, and of our mere good-will and pleasure give it a particular relation to the impression, this can have but a small effect upon the mind; nor is there any reason, why, upon the return of the same impression, we shou'd be determin'd to place the same object in the same relation to it. There is no manner of necessity for the mind to feign any resembling and contiguous objects; and if it feigns such, there is as little necessity for it always to confine itself to the same, without any

difference or variation. And indeed such a fiction is founded on so little reason, that nothing but pure *caprice* can determine the mind to form it; and that principle being fluctuating and uncertain, tis impossible it can ever operate with any considerable degree of force and constancy. The mind forsees and anticipates the change; and even from the very first instant feels the looseness of its actions, and the weak hold it has of its objects . . . we compare the several instances we may remember, and form a *general rule* against the reposing any assurance in those momentary glimpses of light, which arise in the imagination from a feign'd resemblance and contiguity (*Treatise*, Bk. I, Pt. III, sect. 9, pp. 109– 10).

What Shelley is doing, then, is maximising the latent indeterminacy inherent in the use of metaphor as a means of producing an experience of reading wherein all meaning shall remain at the level of 'momentary glimpses of light'. Along with this goes the idea that all essential perception is metaphorical, and should be seen to be so. Language in this overwrought state is the only medium for the perception of identity, just as this identity can never be *in* language. I have been working with paradoxes all along, and must now try to explain why it is that 'irony' is a suitable concept to employ in their description.

6 Romantic Irony

> The romantic kind of poetry is still in the state of becoming;
> that, in fact, is its real essence: that it should forever be
> becoming and never be perfected.
> Friedrich Schlegel, *Athenaeum Fragments*, 116.

> And we must at all costs avoid over-simplification, which one
> might be tempted to call the occupational disease of philosophers
> if it were not their occupation.
> J. L. Austin, *How to do things with Words*

I

Almost everything that has been proposed so far as an account of Romantic poetics has devolved upon questions of authority; problems of meaning and saying, of freedom and closure, private and public. Only a model which takes account of over-determination seems to serve to describe the features of a 'syndrome' wherein the same phenomenon in the communicative artifact can be seen from different perspectives at the same time, and with a logicality which may be overtly paradoxical.[1] Thus, the coalescence of subject and object which is the avowed goal of so much aesthetic theory in its attempt to resolve or ignore the knowledge problem, is at the same time open to criticism or misuse as the tool of the intentionalist heresy, the digestion of circumference by centre. Similarly, the employing of what I have called the 'heuristic method', which is demanded by a context highly suspicious of authoritarian discourse, whether political or textual, involves a negative (or potentially negative) corollary in the tendency towards complete abandonment of authorial control over the limits of possible interpretation. I have said a good deal about the first of these paradoxes, whereby the artifact strives to hold centre and circumference in a perpetually self-correcting equilibrium by virtue of bringing to consciousness the necessarily perpetual trespasses tending to one side or the other of this point of balance—which is, in fact, only ever a construct, an unfulfilled aspiration. I shall now say something more about the second, as a prelude to an account of 'irony' as a means of articulating, though by definition not 'resolving', them both.[2]

Few writers are more eloquent than Coleridge about the obligation which an author must place upon his reader, that of 'kindling his own torch'. At the same time we find, in *The Friend*, a sophisticated confrontation with the problem of meaning as it is placed under strain by the personal disposition and receptivity of the reader, be it determined idiosyncratically or culturally. The reader must be free to 'create' his own meaning, but the author must not cease to exercise some level of control over the limits within which such meanings can be formulated. The question of communication is isolated from the first as the besetting preoccupation of *The Friend*, which does indeed seek to become our friend, in 'The Fable of the Madning Rain' (I, 7—9). There can be no recourse to any belief in the transparency and natural availability of the message:

> Either says the Sceptic, you are the Blind offering to lead the Blind, or you are talking the language of Sight to those who do not possess the sense of Seeing (I, 10).

It is no longer sufficient to suggest that it is the beneficence of God which explains how we understand one another; and that, given this divine sanction, we therefore do so completely and rightly. A glance at James Harris's *Hermes* will help to show forth the possibilities, for Harris preserves this model of sufficiency:

> In short ALL MINDS, that are, are SIMILAR and CONGENIAL; and so too are *their Ideas*, or *intelligible Forms*. Were it otherwise, there could be intercourse between Man and Man, or (what is more important) between Man and God (pp. 395—6).

What is interesting, however, is that in his discussion of the priority between sensible and intelligible forms, Harris employs a threefold system of terms which, *without* this divine manipulation, would set adrift any possibility of interpretability. In the relation between man and the objects of his perception, sensible are prior to intelligible forms; but this priority is reversed in the relation of God to his works, which are man's objects. Thus we have three terms in operation:

> *the first* may be called THE MAKER'S FORM; *the second*, that of THE SUBJECT; and *the third*, that of THE CONTEMPLATOR (p. 377).

Replacing the rôle of God by that of the artist or communicator, and displacing the certainty of a normative psychology, we have a model allowing for the reading of the same sign in different ways (reading, of course, 'object' for Harris' standard eighteenth-century use of 'subject').

One traditional way of overcoming this problem of communicability is the reliance upon a universal theory of mind, such as Kant held; we have in common the categories of pure reason, and they ensure the communicability of experience and the possibility of, for example, scientific method. But even if we accept this, we have still to deal with language, which Kant, notoriously, hardly talks about. Language, as we have seen, was recognised to be unstable, both in its immediate context—that in which it is uttered—and in its passage through time. A familiar recourse here was the reliance on contract and consensus, of the kind which Hobbes, for example, had called for; a formal and public agreement between language users about just what constitutes proper representation. This can be modified through time by mutual consent; but such consent must be performative, and not of a kind which would be available in any simple sense to poets and their readers, present or to come. Moreover, there had been implicit in eighteenth-century responses to this question a scepticism about ever being able to limit, in predictable ways, the relations between speakers' intended meanings and hearers' (perhaps equally intended) responses. Condillac, the populariser of Locke, commented that

> The use of words is become so familiar to us, that we do not at all doubt but our meaning must be understood, as soon as we utter them; as if there must necessarily be the same ideas in the speaker and in the hearer (*Essay on the Origin of Human Knowledge*, p. 261),

implying, of course, that there need not be. Locke had sown, or stirred up, the seeds of doubt here, both in stressing the force of association on the idiosyncratic level, and in driving the radical epistemological division between real and nominal essences, thus removing the option of a 'natural language' built upon a correspondence (in the substantial sense) between word and object. Even if it be argued that we receive the 'same' sense-perceptions, there is nothing beyond the nominal contract which demands that they be processed or expressed in the same way. The 'sameness', then, is not necessarily communicable. The category of the 'simple idea' seemed, to Condillac, to offer some hope here:

Simple ideas can never occasion any mistake. All errors proceed either from our depriving an idea of something that belongs to it, for want of seeing all its parts; or from our adding something that does not belong to it, through a precipitate judgement of the imagination that it contains something which it does not (p. 321).

But Locke also explained how we go about such adding and depriving, and can thus be thought of as contributing implicitly to a problem of communicability which was bound to become more problematic in a context as conscious as the Romantic period was of history and temporality, and of the tendency of even the contract toward continual dissolution and re-creation.[3] As Stewart puts the case:

> Hence it is evident that, according to the different habits and education of individuals; according to the liveliness of their conceptions, and according to the creative power of their imaginations, the same words will produce very different effects on different minds (*Works*, II, 441).

What has happened, in terms of the sign–referent relation, is that the sign itself (the word) has taken on an untenanted or partially 'free' status. This loosening of control does not operate simply between speaker and hearer, but between speaker and sign; Shelley's theory of poetry stresses just this in its reference to the poet as unconscious of both the source and the effect of his inspiration. The mechanism of distancing between speaker and hearer is thus a double one.

This context goes some way towards explaining why it is that Coleridge should be concerned 'not to *convey* falsehood under the pretext of *saying* truth' (*The Friend*, I, 48). Thus:

> By *verbal* truth we mean no more than the correspondence of a given fact to given words. In *moral* truth, we involve likewise the intention of the speaker, that his words should correspond to his thoughts in the sense in which he expects them to be understood by others: and in this latter import we are always supposed to use the word, whenever we speak of truth absolutely, or as a possible subject of moral merit or demerit (I, 42–3).

Even here, it is clear that there is no guarantee against being taken in a sense different from one's intentions. One of the essays 'On the Communication of Truth' begins with a statement attributed to Rudolph von Langen:

> But how are we to guard against the herd of promiscuous Readers? Can we bid our *books* be silent in the presence of the unworthy? (I, 51).

Indeed not; and, as Shelley well knew, 'truth cannot be communicated until it is perceived' (*Complete Works*, VI, 243). Coleridge has a double task: to communicate what he does want to pass over in such a fashion as the reader shall participate in finding it for himself, and to prevent other readers from taking a meaning in some sense antithetical to his (elliptically) intended one. One way of reconciling the two apparently contradictory demands of freedom and closure is to offer a system, along the lines laid down by Kant, of freedom *within* closure. To his reader, he proposes 'to kindle his own torch for him, and leave it to himself to chuse the particular objects, which he might wish to examine by its light' (*The Friend*, I, 16). The supposition is that the *faculty* so activated will, in an a priori, critical sense, bear some relation to the identical faculty in Coleridge himself (the reason), even as its objects of attention will be different (and thus to an extent irrelevant); and that that faculty is the essential source of moral identity.

Having said that the mechanism of distancing is a double one, the question of intentionality can be seen once more to obtrude itself into the relation of the artist to his signs. Wordsworth dramatises exactly this in his descriptions of 'negative' creation, and Shelley forbids it in demanding that the poet eschew all didactic ambitions (though presumably these might be latent in the 'spirit of the age'). The poet does not so much have recourse to a pre-constituted language—if he did, then his work would consist of dead metaphors, in terms of the standard Romantic attitude—as fashion one of his own; and this will tend to include his own predispositions, given that language is, as Coleridge tells us, 'framed to convey not the object alone, but likewise the character, mood and intentions of the person who is representing it' (*Biographia*, II, 115–6). The less sure we are that we all share the same responses to such objects, the more fraught, ethically *and* rhetorically, become such predispositions. This is the framework within which reader and author invent each other as subject to the difficulties attendant upon what we now call the 'hermeneutic circle'. As Paul Ricoeur has put it:

> By 'hermeneutical circle', Romanticist thinkers meant that the understanding of a text cannot be an objective procedure in the sense of scientific objectivity, but necessarily involves a precomprehension which expresses the way in which the reader has already understood himself and his world.[4]

What Ricoeur refers to as characterising the relation of reader to text also affects the formation of that text by an author. Thus Blake can offer the teasing proposition that 'Imitation is Criticism' (Erd. 632, K. 453). Not only is all production original in the sense that subjective perspectives will tend to appear, but even the exact re-creation of an artifact will have a new meaning in a new context and at a different time. This principle is evident in the larger structure of the prophetic books, which generate and include a large amount of repetition, incremental or otherwise; and in such local passages as the description of Beulah (Erd. 129–30, K. 520), which is seen as a pastoral celebration when viewed from the world of generation, whilst sounding to the eternals as a lament. For Blake, of course, the whole idea of the reader as engaged in trying to reconstruct the authorial persona 'Blake' as the controlling presence behind the text is taken up with the scope of the ironies playing back upon the reader; or at least, that is the version of 'Blake' which I find myself constructing. But this is an extreme response to a question answered in much more conventional terms by, for example, Connop Thirlwall, by a recourse to the notion of organic form, which has itself become, I think it is fair to say, the central technique of the discipline of literary criticism:

> we admit that it is a most difficult and delicate task, to determine the precise degree in which a dramatic poet is conscious of certain bearings of his works, and of the ideas which they suggest to the reader, and hence to draw an inference as to his design. The only safe method of proceeding for this purpose, so as to avoid the danger of going very far astray, and at the same time to ensure some gain, is in each particular case to institute an accurate examination of the whole and of the every part[5]

One of the most common and important airings of the communication problem was in the context of the study of the Scriptures. Locke had dodged one of the traditional philosophical hurdles, that of the question of the 'authenticity' of the sacred books, by referring the whole potential falsification to their *reception:*

> Though every thing said in the Text be infallibly true, yet the Reader may be, nay cannot chuse but be very fallible in the understanding of it (*Essay*, Bk. III, chap. IX, 23).

We see but darkly, and the darkness, the indeterminacy, is in the act of seeing, of reading out. And it is this reading out, this interpretation and in-spiration, which is of paramount importance to the Romantic generation. In Hegel's words:

It is a fact of the weightiest import that the Bible has become the basis of the Christian Church: henceforth each individual enjoys the right of deriving instruction for himself from it, and of directing his conscience in accordance with it. We see a vast change in the principle by which man's religious life is guided: the whole system of Tradition, the whole fabric of the Church becomes problematical, and its authority is subverted (*Philosophy of History*, pp. 417–18).

The reader is left to face the text and to find his own illumination, just as he is left before the poem with minimal authoritarian guidance from its elided or overtly compromised author. Coleridge, for whom 'the Scriptures once understood, every man becomes his own Teacher' (*Lectures 1795*, p. 209), regarded Christianity as the ultimate poetic communication. Consider this remark in the light of what has been said on and around 'The Ancient Mariner':

the Feelings are worked upon by Hopes & Fears purely individual, & the Imagination is kept barren in definite Forms & only in cooperation with the Understanding labours after an obscure & indefinite Vastness—/this is Christianity (*Letters*, I, 466).

As such, it can only be filled out by the performative contract, like the imagination itself, and the version of poetic 'meaning' for which I have been arguing:

In order to an efficient belief in Christanity, a man must have been a Christian, and this is the seeming argumentum in circulo, incident to all spiritual Truths, to every subject not presentable under the forms of Time and Space, as long as we attempt to master by the reflex acts of the Understanding what we can only *know* by the act of *becoming* (*Biographia*, II, 216).[6]

Meaning and being are once again inseparable. Even the Bible becomes an open text, which will be used variously by altered and alternate eyes, as Blake declared:

This sense of the Bible is equally true to all & equally plain to all. None can doubt the impression which he receives from a book of Examples. If he is good he will abhor wickedness in David or Abraham if he is wicked he will make their wickedness an excuse for his & so he would do by any other book (Erd. 607, K. 393).

This question of communicability is not simply an argument about language; it is also an argument about mind, as we should perhaps expect within a predominantly nominalistic context. How can there be said to be a common or universal mind when different individuals project different readings into the same text? And of what value is the notion of a normative psychology in standardising or controlling the limits of interpretation which the same text can give rise to?

It is not the case that Romanticism simply has no place for the idea of general nature; but it is an argument which becomes much more difficult to maintain as an explanation of how art functions. The legacy of the enlightenment was, crudely put, that 'all men are partakers of the common faculty, reason; and may be supposed to have some communication with the common instructor, truth' (Godwin, *Enquiry*, I, 215). This view, at the simplest level, condones the belief in gradualism; that the kernel of truth, once implanted into society, must grow and spread of its own accord. There is thus no call for revolution or personal exertion. As Schiller explains:

> Impart to the world you would influence a *Direction* towards the good, and the quiet rhythm of time will bring it to fulfilment (*Aesthetic Education*, p. 59).

It also allows for the supposition of a relation of direct correspondence between the good of the individual and the good of the state, rendering unnecessary any concept of a division of interest (a concept unrecognised by, for example, Adam Smith). Thirdly, it offers to overcome any tension between 'meaning' and 'saying' in the communication of truth. Even Kant's sophisticated model can be seen to rely ultimately upon the same preconception of the normative. We know nothing of objects outside our modes of perceiving them, which are 'not necessarily shared in by every being, though, certainly, by every human being' (*Pure Reason*, p. 82). Communication properly enacted is transparent; what is rightly said cannot be misunderstood. The distinction between 'conviction (Überzeugung)' and 'persuasion (Überredung)' is based on the definition of the latter as having 'only private validity, and the holding of it to be true does not allow of being communicated'; the test depends on 'the possibility of communicating it and of finding it to be valid for all human reason' (p. 645; *Werke*, III, 550). 'Conviction' is then further divided into the degrees of *'opining, believing, and knowing'* (p. 646); but the point to be made is that a philosophical discrimination can be more or less confidently made on the basis of a criterion of communicability. There is, for Kant, no problem about the status of consensus, about for whom and with whom such communication is possible. And there is no discussion of language as any uncertain mediator. I do not want to enter into an argument about whether

Kant is 'right' or 'wrong' in relying on the normaive incidence of the categories of pure reason, but it is worth pointing out that he does so, and that certain aspects of the Romantic experience challenge this recourse.[7] His method is based on something very like the traditional assumption of sufficient reason. The critical task functions to restore the mind to its perfect state of total adequacy and perfection:

> Everything that has its basis in the nature of our powers must be appropriate to, and consistent with, their right employment—if only we can guard against a certain misunderstanding and so can discover the proper direction of these powers (*Pure Reason*, p. 532).

The English version of this formulation was all too often the apotheosis of 'common sense' of which Coleridge was so scornful.

However, the Romantic generation by no means gave up the notion of a general nature, as I have said before. As poetry for Shelley 'reproduces the common Universe of which we are portions and percipients' (*Complete Works*, VII, 137), so art for Schiller is the medium of the universal mind; 'only the aesthetic mode of communication unites society, because it relates to that which is common to all' (*Aesthetic Education*, p. 215). Within the context of the obligation to the heuristic method, freedom and necessity must somehow be reconciled, as they were for Kant in the moral law. Schiller is always anxious to exclude the merely 'arbitrary' from the aesthetic, to preclude the absolutely 'free' interpretability of the sign. The mind in the aesthetic state behaves freely, but in accordance with laws, laws which 'never appear as a constraint' (p. 143). Schiller's essay *On Matthisson's Poetry* (*Über Matthissons Gedichte*) contains an extended discussion of this reconciliation of freedom and necessity (*Werke*, XXII, 265ff.). The artist must create a structure in which freedom is enacted through 'nature'; only then will the artifact allow for the reader's application of a performative response which is yet capable of general communicability. To achieve this, the artist must reach for the 'pure object (das *reine Objekt*)' (p. 267), for only then are the associative habits of the imagination making necessary rather than capricious connections among appearances (p. 268). The relation of artist to reader, and of one reader to other readers, is possible without reciprocal subjective distortions, provided that the artist has taken care to purge himself of idiosyncrasies and to project only what makes him a member of the species, a paradigm of general humanity.[8]

Wordsworth does seem to me to appeal ultimately to a level of common psychological mechanisms residing as the shared foundation of different minds. Differences are only superficial, of degree rather than kind, and his interest in chastising intentionalist deviations can be related to his concern to discourage 'wanton deviation from good sense and nature' (*Prose*, I, 161). I have already suggested that by 'the primary laws of our nature' (*ibid.*, p. 122) Wordsworth makes reference to our modes of relating ideas rather than to any theory implying necessarily common responses to the *same* object. It is the association *between* ideas which functions in a generally recognisable and communicative way, even though different ideas may be chosen to demonstrate this association. Thus he finds it necessary to punctuate his exposition with the qualifier that the addressee be 'in a healthful state of association' (p. 126). This division between the manner and the matter, the a priori and the a posteriori, is very close to the Kantian paradigm, and to Coleridge's account of the function of the reason. Reason may be 'one and the same in all men' (*Letters*, VI, 928), but it does not produce the same results *for* all men, because 'the means of exercising it, and the materials (i.e. the facts and ideas) on which it is exercised' are 'possessed in very different degrees by different persons' (*The Friend*, I, 159). The distinction between degrees and kinds thus allows Coleridge to preserve the ideal community of readers as including, *in potentia*, the whole of humanity, while recognising that the immediate and contingent level of response may be very low indeed. It must be said, I think, that the standard version of the 'hermeneutic circle' is not quite the way in which Coleridge formulates his problem. In fact he is able to maintain the 'previous act and conception of the mind' as the very source of the integrity of method rather than a threat to its efficiency:

> We have seen that a previous act and conception of the mind is indispensible even to the mere semblances of Method: that neither fashion, mode, nor orderly arrangement can be produced without a prior purpose, and 'a pre-cogitation *ad intentionem ejus quod quaeritur*' though this purpose may have been itself excited, and this 'pre-cogitation' itself abstracted from the perceived likenesses and differences of the objects to be arranged (*The Friend*, I, 475–6).

The mind's prior capacity to see things in certain ways is thus the very mechanism of ordered experience, and for Coleridge it produces not a crisis of confidence but 'a belief that the productive power, which is in nature as nature, is essentially one (i.e. of one kind) with the intelligence, which is in the human mind above nature' (1,497–8):

> In all aggregates of construction therefore, which we contemplate as

wholes, whether as integral parts or as a system, we assume an intention, as the initiative, of which the end is the correlative (1,498).

This is very close to the paradox which Hirsch, for example, formulates as that of the 'hermeneutic circle', that

> We must know the whole in a general way *before* we know a part, since the nature of a part as such is determined by its function in the larger whole. Of course, since we can know a whole only through its parts, the process of interpretation is a circle (*The Aims of Interpretation*, p. 5),

but somehow for Coleridge it is not presented as a problem. For him, the 'circle' is in fact an affirmative tautology which identifies self and object coinstantaneously, and this is possible, I think, because he does not historicise this act of 'pre-cogitation'; it is not therefore tainted with the implication of a culturally or personally determined whim or desire, in the sense that it is, so often, for modern thinkers. This recognition is for Coleridge, I think, the centre of the moral identity.

I have argued that Wordsworth did not hold to such a comforting solution to the question, and Coleridge himself well understood the limits on this model as it pertains to communication. He became, as his career progressed, committed to smaller audiences, decreasing in numbers as they increased in sophistication. And it is important to note that he recognised also that, however strenuous and exact might be his delineation of the *fact* of common humanity, there would always be those unable to agree with him because unable to perceive *with* him. The criterion is, that is to say, imperatively performative, and those who cannot or will not respond can only be pitied.[9] 'Non omnia possumus omnes' (*Biographia*, I 198). Wordsworth, in a roughly similar predicament, spent a great deal of his poetic energy removing, for his reader as for himself, those very 'wanton deviations' whose absence the efficiency of his theory presupposes.

Much more dramatic even than Coleridge's developing sense of the difficulty of communication, and the reliance upon a small enlightened clerisy which developed from it, was Shelley's passage from an author of popular pamphlets in plain language handed out on the streets of Dublin, to the creator of such esoteric visions as 'Prometheus Unbound' (quite seriously, I believe, intended for no more than a half a dozen readers in its own generation), and 'Epipsychidion', of which Shelley said that he was aware of a class of readers to whom 'it must ever remain incomprehensible, from a defect of a common organ of perception for the ideas of which it treats' (*Poetical Works*, p. 411). Such hypersensitivity to the question of audience response is not simply to be attributed to the standard insecurity of the creative artist; it is part of a widespread aesthetic and philosophical investigation of the very possibility of determinate communication, a situation which is turned to a positive purpose in the ethical endorsement of the heuristic method. The extreme response is the proffering of the 'free sign', a position towards which Shelley can be seen to be moving in 'A Defence of Poetry', wherein the word in history is metaphored as the seed in the soil, producing blossoms which are visibly (and thus, in one sense, sortally) distinct from itself by way of the period of obscurity and secret germination. Every word of poetry is instinct with future life, but different words will be so inspired at different times by different people. For Shelley, the possibility of infinite meaningfulness calls for a strategy which could be called esoteric, one which does not yield at all to most enquirers, and yields only in part, by its very definition, to the initiated. As with Coleridge, he seems to believe in the universal validity and truth of what is revealed by and creative of 'poetry', at the same time as he suggests, in the metaphor of poet as nightingale, that we can never cognitively receive that universality as a *sharable* fact of communication:

> A poet is a nightingale, who sits in darkness and sings to cheer its own solitude with sweet sounds; his auditors are as men entranced by the melody of an unseen musician, who feel that they are moved and softened, yet know not whence or why (*Complete Works*, VII, 116).

By which I mean, of course, that we can never *prove* the sharing by recourse to any language outside the primary mystery of the experience itself.

Coleridge's move from poetry to prose, to a sophisticated discourse appealing to a small enlightened class as the dispensers of knowledge and information, is closer to the more familiar solution of the problem of shared meanings, the idea of consensus based on contract and proven competence; though still proven, that is, by the *act* of reading itself. The arguments now become very familiar. Quine repeats Coleridge (and Kant, at the level of the implicit) in appealing to consensus, to the 'straightforward attribute of community-wide acceptance', as a substitute for 'the controversial notion of analyticity';[10] and it is precisely to such a contract, to 'the building of amiable communities' (*A Rhetoric of Irony*, p. 28), that Booth appeals as a way of inhibiting what he regards as the threat of uninhibited irony:

the rhetorical mode dramatizes the inescapably social nature of literary standards. We do not obtain our criteria through some private intuition or divine revelation or strictly logical deduction from known first principles: we experience something together, sense its value as we experience, and then confirm that value in discourse with other valuers (pp. 208–9).

I agree with all these observations. But it will not do for an anatomy of Romanticism. Though the Romantics had, more or less, given up on divine revelation (which they were yet compelled to rediscover after the labour of the negative), they were very interested in private intuition and its relation to a potential public, and they had not entirely dismissed epistemology and its first principles, though they were obliged to experience its shortcomings. They recognised also the difficulties besetting any recourse to shared experiences, and the sorts of closed communities which any successful application of this solution must entail. They saw, it could be said, that there might be no solution to the problem which was capable of satisfying all the objections which might be brought against it.

Heinrich Bosse has identified a tension in modern communication theory which we have seen anticipated, if only tentatively answered, by Schiller:

> To achieve any understanding, the relation between what signifies and what is signified must in some way become necessary. It will become so if the autonomous nature of the receiver is anticipated; he will then follow his nature and co-ordinate, arbitrarily, the signifier and the signified in the same way as the sender has done. What makes this argument inconclusive is that it arrives at a fundamental and double uncertainty. If it is an act of human freedom to establish the actual semiotic relation, both the speaker and the hearer will be free as to how each does it.[11]

The paradox is, then, is that the text must try to remain both open and closed; capable of being filled out by the reader's active response, and yet capable of controlling that response within limits in some sense foreseen by the author. This is meant to stand as a rough generalisation of the problem, for Blake and Shelley, at least, certainly overstep this balance point in the direction of the 'free sign'. I have already dealt with the strategies adopted to try to meet the demands of this situation. Blake's proper names, for example, can be seen to function by suggesting significations which produce, by association, other related or antithetical significations, all tied together within the scope of meaning-possibilities. This is clear in my gloss upon the various potential etymologies of 'Urizen'. Art can aspire towards an open system by including as many options as possible, relying upon the reader to provide his own coherence between them. Thus, for Schiller, beauty resides not 'in the *exclusion of certain realities*, but in the *absolute inclusion of all realities*; that it is, therefore, not limitation but infinity' (*Aesthetic Education,* p. 125). Tieck puts it thus:

> Every real poetic creation makes possible, and is worthy of, an infinite contemplation, and all these intuitions from different sides are always only as diverse rays emanating from the same centre, which the luminosity of the artist diffuses once again, so that they themselves are art.[12]

Within the balance of openness and closure, the text must fight back in order to render such closure as but partial and temporary; A. W. Schlegel sees 'Hamlet' as resembling "those irrational equations in which a fraction of unknown magnitude always remains, that will in no manner admit of solution" (trans. Black, *Lectures*, II, 193). In the same spirit Keats asked Bailey, throwing his voice:

> Do not
> "the Lovers of Poetry like to have a little Region to wander in where
> "they may pick and choose, and in which the images are so numer-
> "ous that many are forgotten and found new in a second Reading:
> "which may be food for a Week's stroll in the Summer?
> (*Letters*, I, 170).

There is no final closure with 'full Poesy or distilled Prose' (I, 231), and it never becomes 'stale'. Blake's works 'resist' perhaps more than any, partly by virtue of his employing a composite art:

> [as Poetry admits not a letter that is Insignificant so Painting admits not a Grain of Sand or a Blade of Grass [Insignificant] much less an Insignificant Blur or Mark] (Erd. 550, K. 611).

It is probably impossible to hold within any one model of significance *all* the items within any one of Blake's illuminated plates.

Closely related to this resistance is what I have described as the abolition of the 'metacomment', the language outside language which might offer the reader a stable perspective from which to look down upon the landscape of the poem. This is the function often provided by the hill in descriptive poetry, but which is no longer available to Wordsworth when he climbs Snowdon. Though he is 'outside' the perspective of what is below, he is so completely so that he cannot see anything at all. There is no knowledge, only an inversion of ends and means which indicates that he, the poet, is carrying the mystery around with him, whose solution will always remain at an irrecoverable distance beyond and behind him. The process becomes the product, as the artist dramatises his own complicity as a vehicle for the reader to do the same. Poetry must 'always be simultaneously poetry and the poetry of poetry'.[13] Shelley writes a landscape of language where the frost leaves a 'bright print' and the mist a series of 'complicating lines' (*Poetical Works*, pp. 557, 40), and 'Prometheus Unbound' is full of such examples of the interfusion of linguistic and natural terms. The world is a text, but no longer in the sense that it is the book of God; the act of reading is one of imaginative self-confrontation, setting up a framework of in-terdetermination from which there is no escape. But at the same time there is a kind of freedom within this system. Within this inclosure, where the reader is at times so isolated that he is conscious of having to 'invent' the author as his proxy, this reader can also be aware of having to make decisions about himself through his near-total responsibility for the 'meaning' of the text. If there is no sure way of articulating the degree to which the reader is forming the text and the text forming the reader, then one possible response becomes the 'leap of faith', the decision about which priorities will be adopted being taken despite the refusal of the text to satisfy them completely. This is not a stable 'metacomment' because it is incomplete in terms of the text's own demands, and because the reader will tend to find himself always passing back into the text to search again for what he thought he might find in stepping outside it; like Wordsworth on Snowdon, and, with a different emphasis, like Kant's model of the moral law, according to which we must leave experience in order to constitute a pattern of behaviour perfect in itself, but always committed to disappointment if it is applied back to experience. The tools of 'reading' will not quite fit the 'text' to which they tend to be applied.[14]

The typical structural manifestation of this situation is cyclic form, of the sort that we have seen to be operative, though with different degrees of overtness, in our two Keats poems, one demanding re-reading by explicit repetition, the other by an apparent closure so aggressive that it will not fit the demands of what has preceded it. Coleridge's theory of polarity, Hegel's use of the dialectic, and Wordsworth's simultaneous progress towards and distancing from his hidden beginnings all provide models of discovery, of one's self and of the world, which are always becoming, and can never rest in 'being': as Blake says, 'nor can the man who goes/The journey obstinate refuse to write time after time' (Erd, 342, K. 316). Poetry provides irreducible knots and empty spaces, lest we 'fall into Eternal Death' (Erd. 299, K. 267). Schiller's aesthetic state is one wherein man is 'Nought' (*Aesthetic Education*, p. 144), and one which he should, ideally, pass through as an act of cleansing every time he moves from one determinate state to another. Coleridge identified, in a passage (already quoted) which once more adds to the evidence for regarding 'The Ancient Mariner' as a dramatic allegory of imperfect appropriation and incompletion,

> a middle state of mind more strictly appropriate to the imagination than any other, when it is, as it were, hovering between images. As soon as it is fixed on one image, it becomes understanding; but while it is unfixed and wavering between them, attaching itself permanently to none, it is imagination . . . not to produce a distinct form, but a strong working of the mind, still offering what is still repelled, and again creating what is again rejected (*Shakespearean Criticism*, II, 103−4).[15]

It is the void which is the source of movement, not just in the sense that 'something can only move into an empty space, and not into an already occupied space', but in the sense of 'the profounder thought that in the negative as such there lies the ground of becoming, of the unrest of self-movement' (Hegel, *Science of Logic*, p. 166). Here is a beautiful example from Wordsworth:

> In an obscure corner of a Country Church-yard I once espied, half-overgrown with Hemlock and Nettles, a very small Stone laid upon the ground, bearing nothing more than the name of the Deceased with the date of birth and death, importing that it was an Infant which had been born one day and died the following. I know not how far the Reader may be in sympathy with me, but more awful thoughts of rights conferred, of hopes awakened, of remembrances stealing away or vanishing were imparted to my mind by that inscription there before my eyes than by any other that it has ever been my lot to meet with upon a Tomb-stone (*Prose*, II, 93).

The unwritten epitaph remains infinitely writeable, infinitely fillable by the awakened imagination of the beholder, always open to changing speculations about what might have been; it is a deep truth, and it is imageless. Rather than admitting that we can never achieve certain knowledge of first principles, and then insisting on absolute coherence and closure between the parts of any system built upon those *assumed* first principles, Romantic aesthetics insists on a recourse to emptiness, a re-founding in imperceptible beginnings, at every point of transition between the parts of its systems. The organic model itself, whilst appearing to introduce an indubitable continuity, yet locates that continuity at some level beyond or within what can be apprehended as phenomenal appearance; we can only wonder at the transition from seed to blossom.[16] Art, correspondingly, has moved full circle away from any potential identification as determinate statement, and is recognised as an enigma, as 'the outer shell of an inner mystery'.[17] I shall now try to describe the central paradigms of the artist as he operates within such a medium—figures which are, in very similar ways, all 'Romantic ironists'.

II

Kant had written, in his account of the 'synthetic unity of apperception', that

> only in so far as I can grasp the manifold of the representations in one consciousness, do I call them one and all *mine*. For otherwise I should have as many-coloured and diverse a self as I have representations of which I am conscious to myself (*Pure Reason*, p. 154).

A precise epistemological point is being made here; that the content of empirical experience is held together by the pre-formed synthetic, and synthesising, function of the consciousness. Personal identity, properly speaking, cannot be said to change every time the content of particular experiences changes. Some twenty years previously, Diderot had written *Rameau's Nephew*, where the protagonist comes very close indeed to exemplifying this, for Kant, unthinkable possibility. This novel is very close to the nerve of what I want to call 'Romantic irony', and much more so than its occult transmission through even the hands of Goethe and Hegel would suggest. Of course, Rameau's nephew does not contradict Kant philosophically, but he certainly questions what the use of such a concept of identity might be. Hegel made him into an emblem of self-consciousness at the beginning of its process of development:

> To be conscious of its own distraught and torn condition and to express itself accordingly,—this is to pour scornful laughter on existence, on the confusion pervading the whole and on itself as well: it is at the same time this whole confusion dying away and yet apprehending itself to be doing so (*Phenomenology of Mind*, p. 546).

In knowing 'its own peculiar torn and shattered condition', Hegel finds that the spirit has '*ipso facto* risen above that condition' (p. 548).

But one could be forgiven for not finding much evidence in Diderot's novel for this view of the saving value of consciousness. The protagonist has no 'self', and declares himself to have no permanent allegiances in the world; but as the conversation between narrator and nephew proceeds we come to realise that the latter's vaunted 'independence' conceals the most desperate dependence, that he is passionately committed to certain stable relationships which cause him pain (as with his daughter), and that his whole performance can be explained as an attempt to earn a dinner invitation—not extended. The spirit does not soar far on an empty stomach. The reservations which the narrator has about Rameau's nephew are very close to those expressed by a contemporary reviewer of Byron's poetry, as he complains of its tendency to bring

> qualities of a most contradictory kind into close alliance; and so shape them into seeming union as to confound sentiments, which, for the sake of sound morality and social security, should for ever be kept contrasted, and at polar extremities with respect to each other (Hayden, *Romantic Bards*, p. 238).

The nephew's intelligence, rather like Byron's, is anarchistic, but much less confidently so—he has no private income and no social status. And, unlike Byron for his reviewer, his function as an ironist plays upon his interlocutor, who comes to recognise a great deal of identity in the difference between them. But the dialectic is only partial, and the nephew is unsuccessful in his appeal to the narcissistic alter ego, the 'other', of the narrator, as a means of self-gain. He depends upon the world, not just in the context of his identity crisis, his finding of himself through reflecting negatively off others, but also for his daily bread, and it is here that Diderot's narrator is able to resist successfully. For the narrator, the nephew almost seems to exemplify Plato's polemic against rhetoric and poetry as involving a loss of self and basic confusion about moral integrity and a determinate point of view. One imagines that Keats would have transgressed the same standards in suggesting that 'Men of Genius' are those who 'have not any individuality, any determined Character' (*Letters*, I, 184).[18] Keats of all the Romantic poets is most 'addicted to passiveness' (p. 214), that state of being which even Wordsworth, it will be remembered, admired only as secondary to the higher powers of the mind. In the context of the problem of intentionality as I have described it, Keats's posture is clearly to be taken seriously:

> The only means of strengthening one's intellect is to make up ones mind

about nothing – to let the mind be a thoroughfare for all thoughts (II, 213).

The synthesis of becoming and beholding in its Keatsian version only happens when the mind is emptied of the utilitarian imperatives which characterise the sense of self. There must be a loosening of the ego's hold over the associative process, turning the subject into what Locke had felt the need to denounce as 'a very idle unactive Creature' passing his time 'only in a lazy lethargick Dream' (*Essay*, Bk. II, ch. VII, 3). The poet cannot be accused of intruding in his own person if he has no sense of selfhood upon which to base such an intrusion; the erasing of the selfhood thus becomes one way of dodging the intentionality problem, and the poet can thus avoid having to dramatise his own presence in the text. Monboddo admires Homer and Plato for never appearing in their own productions (*Origin and Progress of Language*, III, 129; V, 325), and Schiller (*Naive and Sentimental Poetry*, p. 107) relates Homer and Shakespeare in the same sense. For Keats, and for his generation, Shakespeare more than any other is the type of the 'camelion Poet' who has 'as much delight in conceiving an Iago as an Imogen' (*Letters*, I, 387).[19] He is thus, as the archetypal poet, himself 'unpoetical'—that is, unidentifiable as subject matter, as any part of a project of writing or reading, and immune, therefore, from identification as the first principle in an ever-expanding hermeneutic circle. Coleridge describes 'our *myriad-minded* Shakespeare' (*Biographia*, II, 13) as the poet who 'darts himself forth, and passes into all the forms of human character and passion, the one Proteus of the fire and the flood'; he 'becomes all things, yet for ever remaining himself' (p. 20).[20] Similarly, for Hazlitt, Shakespeare 'appears to have been all the characters, and in all the situations he describes' (*Works*, IV, 284). He was

> the least of an egotist that it was possible to be. He was nothing in himself; but he was all that others were, or that they could become . . . He was like the genius of humanity, changing places with all of us at pleasure, and playing with our purposes as with his own (*Works*, V, 47).

One can find opinions such as this all over Romantic criticism of Shakespeare. A. W. Schlegel, for example, describes him as having

> the capability of transporting himself so completely into every situation, even the most unusual, that he is enabled, as plenipotentiary of the whole human race, without particular instructions for each separate case, to act and speak in the name of every individual (trans. Black, *Lectures*, II, 128).

Shakespeare thus becomes a more confident and admired version of Rameau's nephew. Unlike Diderot's protagonist, he is wholly 'nothing', wholly absorbed into his production, with no seams left showing, no apparent commitment to the world. Like Rameau's nephew, he has the sort of mind which Friedrich Schlegel admired, that which 'contains within itself simultaneously a plurality of minds and a whole system of persons' ('*Lucinde' and the Fragments*, p. 177), but he has it without stress, without passion, without insecurity. His omnipresence is a corollary of his nothingness. It could as well be Keats speaking when we read what Diderot says of the great actor:

> Perhaps it is just because he is nothing that he is above all everything. His own special shape never interferes with the shape he assumes[21]

Hazlitt opined that Shakespeare 'never committed himself to his characters' (*Works*, IV, 225), and Coleridge pointed out 'the utter *aloofness* of the poet's own feelings, from those of which he is at once the painter and the analyst' (*Biographia*, II, 16). Very few eyes, indeed, can see the mystery of his life (Keats, *Letters*, II, 67). But this aloofness is possible because there is a corresponding elision of the question of personal identity. If the artist chooses to confront his selfhood as an issue, then he is also compelled to assess it as it intends or modifies his presentation of things outside him, objects or characters. Shakespeare represents, one might say, the ideal fusion of self and other, but he stands essentially as a fantasy figure for those poets who cannot resist showing forth the *activity* of that fusion, the 'labour of the negative' which for Hegel was the very condition of authenticity, of meaning achieved.[22] But he does, by the very extremity of his genius and the totality of his absence, create an artifact which functions on heuristic principles. He offers his audience the illusion of immediate experience, before which, for Wordsworth, the poet as simply a *describer* of events is always inferior. As Coleridge said, 'You seem to be told nothing, but to see and hear everything' (*Biographia*, II, 15). Consequently, Shakespeare has produced the infinitely writeable text, ever productive of new meanings, 'notwithstanding that we read the same Play forty times' (Keats, *Letters*, I, 133).

Shakespeare is the most successful Romantic ironist. He avoids the problems of communication which I have argued to be obsessive for these poets, and outrages none of their ethical convictions. But of course, like the child, he is 'constructed' as a paradigm of perfection, and exists as such precisely because he is irrecoverable. His art is exclusive of his own overt moral convictions, even as it is infinitely productive of them for others; he has obeyed the mandate of Shelley's 'Defence'. No other figure among the gallery of those who were accorded the status of 'honorary' Romantic artists achieved this sort of success. Two in particular demand mention, both ironists; Socrates and Jesus Christ. Indeed, they were often taken together. Coleridge, although he had reservations about the Socratic method, regarded its founder as having prepared the way for Christ (*Philosophical Lectures*, p. 140), and Shelley saw both figures as types of the political radical in his conflict with the 'thorns of life'.[23] They have in common the fact that they left no texts behind them; they never wrote, they were only 'written about'. They are pure absence, and must therefore always be approached through a refracted consciousness, an exercise of interpretation. As 'poets', they are at an indeterminate distance behind their works, and yet those 'works' are their very lives, a situation which Kierkegaard exploits to the full in the synthesis of eternity and historicity which is his *Philosophical Fragments*. Their actual 'presence' can only be constructed by an 'integral calculation',[24] be it through the various accounts of the life of Socrates, or through the Gospel narratives. And they are both proponents of the same message, that 'the truth is in the subject's transformation in himself' (*Concluding Unscientific Postscript*, p. 38). They offer, then, the most heuristic of methods as the way to meaning, that which Friedrich Schlegel (*Krit. Ausgabe*, XII, 199) called 'the free construction of self-awareness (freie Ausbildung des Selbstdenkens)'. Socratic irony, as Schlegel elsewhere defines it, 'contains and arouses a feeling of indissoluble antagonism between the absolute and the relative, between the impossibility and the necessity of complete communication' (*'Lucinde' and the Fragments*, p. 156). Socrates is a midwife (Monboddo, *Ancient Metaphysics*, II, 69), a practitioner of the maieutic art of bringing to birth in others, in the same sense as Christ's programme is the preparation for a 'kingdom of heaven' which is beyond and yet within. Both, like Shelley's Prometheus, work from within the cave, out of sight of the world for whom their 'absent presence' is a stimulant to the continual production of meaning. Like Rameau's nephew, Christ and Socrates are all things to all men, but their methods and intentions are different. The fact that they disguise the nature of their commitment becomes itself the sign that that commitment is of an absolute sort. Thus Christ's message, for the young Hegel, was in absolute tension with the law and with authority. All outer relationships being determined by law, he was obliged to locate his kingdom 'within': 'he could find freedom only in the void' (*Early Theological Writings*, p.

285),[25] the same void out of which Shelley generates the notion that 'the moral sayings of Jesus Christ' are in tension with 'the mystery and immorality which surrounds them' (*Letters*, I, 265). Were these sayings to be acted upon, then 'no political or religious institution could subsist a moment' (*Complete Works*, VI, 255; cf. VII, 8, 145), and society would return to a state of vacancy, as an unwritten text.

The lives and meanings of Christ and Socrates, like those of Shakespeare, constitute the infinitely writeable text. But the first two, unlike Shakespeare (as far as we know), paid a price for their ironical ways. Their careers were implicitly and also overtly political. Coleridge regarded the Socratic ambiguity as a potentially deceptive strategy, 'as easily, perhaps more easily, adapted to delusion than [to] sound conviction' (*Philosophical Lectures*, p. 137). They do not simply puzzle their interlocutors, they discomfort them, largely because the ironic artifact in their case is not something as detached as a text or a contained dramatic spectacle; it is their own very existences, their physical presences, which refuse incorporation into preconceived patterns of recognition whilst only 'half' providing what they would replace them by, and insisting on the absolute superiority of *what* they half provide. As Monboddo said of the Socratic method, 'the very attempting it, if we should not succeed, gives the greatest offence' (*Origin and Progress of Language*, II, 298; see also IV, 338–39).[26] Christ and Socrates offer, then, not just examples for the Romantic poets to follow in their elision of the authoritarian selfhood (which yet commands an indubitable authority) but also warnings about the implications of the 'presence' of a discourse within a society which one imagines were not lost upon a generation facing the censorship and domestic repression attendant upon England's involvement in the Revolutionary and Napoleonic wars. These warnings may be thought of as combining with the other demands we have discussed in the production of a poetics ever more sophisticated and defensive. Brougham, defending the Hunts against a libel suit, was thus described by Shelley:

> He was compelled to hesitate when truth was rising to his lips; he could utter that which he did utter only by circumlocution & irony (*Letters*, I, 346).

De Quincey complained of 'the quantity of enigmatical and unintelligible writing' which he found in Goethe, regarding it as a 'way of keeping up a system of discussion and strife upon his own meaning amongst the critics of his country' (*Works*, XV, 179).

Brougham is an ironist in the time-honoured sense, compelled to indirection as a way of getting across something of his message without the responsibility of explicit statement. If Goethe is this too, then he is much more, in that he is reacting to the ethical and aesthetical configurations of a particular historical situation; he is a Romantic ironist.

III

I must now try to gather the evidence for the utility of the term 'irony' as a description of those features of the Romantic discourse which I have emphasised in this account. I must summarise the ways in which 'irony' can operate as a model of the commitment to, and necessarily *partial* solution of, the problems implicit in poetic communication. It would not be practical to try to acknowledge all previous discussions of the subject of irony; in fact, surprisingly few of them seem to treat the concept in the way it has been treated here, though of course almost all of them have something in common with, and something to say about, what has been described as the Romantic situation. I shall try to indicate the most important connections and relations as they seem significant;[27] but it will be clear by now that I am less interested in the historical usages of a particular word than in the delineation of a concept, or series of interrelated concepts, dominant in the Romantic period even if not unique to it.[28]

It is the German, and not the English tradition which is explicit in using the term 'Ironie' to define the sorts of communicative techniques which I have been describing in English poetry. Only someone for whom the German tradition is central could suggest, as Kierkegaard suggests (*Concept of Irony*, p. 292), the self-evident synonymity of irony and Romanticism. This is a connection which even Coleridge, the arch exponent of Germanisms in England, did not feel the need to articulate; and Thirlwall, when he examines irony as a Sophoclean mode, makes no reference to the Romantic context. There is thus no *literal* reference to a concept of irony in English Romanticism, whilst among the Germans there is so much reference of so many sorts as to demand a completely separate study.[29] Hegel, notoriously, had a very low opinion of the 'irony' of his own times as but a frivolous and superficial alternative to the seriousness of the Socratic mode (*Lectures on the History of Philosophy*, I, 398f.). He regarded the irony of Friedrich Schlegel as developing from the philosophy of Fichte, and as mere caprice, whereby everything becomes 'mere appearance due to the *ego* in whose power and caprice and at whose free disposal it remains' (*Aesthetics*, p. 65). Thus it becomes an obstacle in the way of the achievement of philosophical seriousness. Only Solger is exempted from this polemic, for having, Hegel thought, pushed irony to the point where it must negate itself.[30] Irony for Solger is indeed above all serious:

> Purposelessness and caprice in and for themselves can never have a place in the activity of the beautiful. There must be a higher order recognizable, and this is only to be understood through irony.[31]

A. W. Schlegel regards 'irony' in a much more limited way as a technique for surreptitiously sharing meanings, whereby the artist 'places himself in a sort of secret understanding with the select circle of the intelligent among his readers or spectators' (trans. Black, *Lectures*, II, 140); as such, it ceases when anything as weighty as the tragic mode prevails. His brother Friedrich, conversely, locates 'irony' in many and varying ways as the central concept of his early creative life.[32] This is not the place to go into an exhaustive examination of the German tradition; Tieck and Müller would also demand attention, as would many others if we left the realms of theory and began to consider the practice of writing. It is not to this tradition that one would appeal for any sort of 'historical' or deterministic evidence for the presence of a similar 'Romantic irony' in contemporary English poetry and poetics. Although there are extraordinary correspondences, the connections do not seem to have been those of direct influence; indeed, so little was this the case, that it has been assumed that there is no place for a concept of Romantic irony in English Romantic literature.[33] I have tried to demonstrate that there is such a place, and that its features would be more accurately considered as coinstantaneous with, rather than caused by, developments in the German tradition. Even if we recognise the importance of the interchanges between the two cultures in the eighteenth century (see Blackall, *The Emergence of German*), and accord special significance to Shaftesbury and Hume as advocates of ironic detachment as a way of coping with certain problems of meaning, we are still faced with correspondences which go far beyond the influences of possible direct contacts; and we would still have to explain 'why' it is that certain items of the available material, rather than others, were taken up and felt to be significant. I have tried to limit myself to demonstrating the extent of the correspondence, rather than proffering any specific or limiting causes for it.

English Romantic irony, broadly put, consists in the studied avoidance on the artist's part of determinate meanings, even at such times as he might wish to encourage his reader to *produce* such meanings for himself; it involves the refusal of closure, the incorporation of any potentially available 'metacomment' within the primary language of the text, the provision of a linguistic sign which moves towards or verges upon a 'free' status, and the consequent raising to self-consciousness of the authoritarian element of discourse, as it effects both the author-reader relation and the intentional manipulation, from both sides, of the material through which they communicate. Brooks has defined invulnerability to irony as 'the stability of a context in which the internal pressures balance and mutually support each other' ('Irony as a Principle of Structure', pp. 732–3). Romantic poetry, in general, seems to refuse this stability by insisting upon a context which is at least in part always forcefully and evidently outside or beyond the poem. This externality provides a posited but unsupplied content which in turn creates a necessary indeterminacy, one which keeps us reading.[34] This constitutes a disturbance of the classical trope of the 'discordia concors' in the direction of movement, modification of the system in ways which are *not* contained by those parts of it already present. Shelley spoke of poetry as subduing 'to union under its light yoke, all irreconcilable things' (*Complete Works*, VII, 137), but the organic model which dominates 'A Defence of Poetry' itself incorporates radical discontinuities. Coleridge's theory of polarity is a version of the principle of balance which recognises and incorporates the necessity of a perpetual disequilibrium, a perpetual 'moving between' two extreme points:

> But observe that Poles imply a null punct or point which being both is neither, and neither only because it is the Identity of Both. The Life of Nature consists in the tendency of the Poles to re-unite, and to find themselves in the re-union; but this tendency to *find* is impossible without a repetition of the act of separation (*Letters*, IV, 771).[35]

Whereas Reynolds could write that

> The summit of excellence seems to be an assemblage of contrary qualities, but mixed, in such proportions, that no one part is found to counteract the other,[36]

Thirlwall, by the time that he begins to theorise a concept of irony, opines that

> the liveliest interest arises when by inevitable circumstances, characters, motives, and principles are brought into hostile collision, in which good and evil are so inextricably blended on each side, that we are compelled to give an equal share of our sympathy to each, while we perceive that no earthly power can reconcile them ('On the Irony of Sophocles', p. 490).

The discord has come to be more noticeable than the concord, and this discord pervades all points in the system of communication. We cannot 'regain' meanings dormant in the past without active effort, without a performative in-spiration; and this 'pastness' characterises also the 'contemporary' text, and indeed, in terms of the gap between 'sensation and reflection' and 'inspiration and composition', the very creative act itself. The obligatory recognition of temporality is also a recognition of the impossibility of historical accuracy; almost as if 'history' comes into being as a discipline at exactly the moment when it must prove impossible that it shall ever satisfy its own demands. This is exactly what we would expect as part of a movement away from recourse to any idea of the transparency of meanings. It relates to that double movement around the problem of selfhood, whereby the artist is persuaded to either a cumbersome incorporation or a complete elision of his creative ego; in both cases, the *division* between author and reader is communicated, a division which yet speaks for a mutual 'recognition'—or a mutual invention. The result is that we are left with no 'author' in the affirmative sense. As Culler has commented, 'the process of reading is especially troubled when we cannot construct a subject who would serve as a source of the poetic utterance' (*Structuralist Poetics*, p. 170). Keats bravely announces his adoption of the Shakespearean unidentifiability as a gesture of self-confidence:

> every one thinks he sees my weak side against my will; when in truth it is with my will—I am content to be thought all this because I have in my own breast so great a resource (*Letters*, I, 404).

But this can also, as we have seen, be related to a profound lack of confidence, an uncertainty about what that resource might be as it is expressed in communicative terms, and about what it might effect if it were so expressed. 'No wonder', says Coleridge, 'if the philosophers felt themselves bound, in the strict sense, to be prudent and reserved, if it was only to spare their countrymen the guilt of repeating the murder of a Socrates' (*Philosophical Lectures*, p. 159). At the other extreme, as I have said, irony involves the incorporation of the creative ego into the artifact, and in this sense it functions as a public and voiced response to the presence of the hermeneutic circle as it was pointed out by Goethe:

> and so it may be said that we are already theorising at the moment of each attentive glance into the world.[37]

The division between 'poet' and 'speaker' of which I have made a great deal, is the vehicle of this incorporation;[38] like God in Kierkegaard's description, the artist 'communicates in creating, so as by creating to *give* independence over against Himself' (*Concluding Unscientific Postscript*, p. 232). This is not quite the same as the sort of 'irony' defined by Monboddo as occurring 'when the speaker assumes a character and sentiments different from his own' (*Origin and Progress of Language*, III, 136). This assumes absolute control of the 'deception' by the artist, and does not threaten or qualify the pre-established ego which fashions it. Romantic 'speakers', I have argued, are there to dramatise the poet's presence or complicity, as no sure sense of distinction between self and other is offered. There is always the option of an alternative language, of course, but this will obtain beyond the 'poem' at the same time as it may be performatively demanded by it. Thus the implied proper homage to the Grecian urn would seem to be that of silent contemplation.

The very use of the notion of a 'speaker' points to a feature of the ironic mode which I have already identified; the implied tension between the written and the spoken word, the status of tonality. I have already quoted Rousseau's arguments about the spoken and the written word (see p. 218), whereby the latter is seen to have 'an equivocation which would be eliminated by a vocative mark.' Language is, as Coleridge declared, 'framed to convey not the object alone, but likewise the character, mood and intentions of the person who is representing it' (*Biographia*, II, 115–6). It was Shakespeare's commitment to performance which prompted him to work into *Venus and Adonis* 'a substitute for that visual language, that constant intervention and running comment by tone, look and gesture, which in his dramatic works he was entitled to expect from the players' (*ibid.*, p. 15). When the strictly written discourse insists upon implying a tonality which, could we but be sure what it is, would specify the meaning of that discourse, then we can hardly avoid confronting the interplay of these two sorts of communication. We are teased with the prospect of a tonal (spoken) qualifier, but the written word will not 'speak' it for us. Could it do so, then we would confirm a 'meaning'. As Blair puts it:

> for tones, looks, and gestures, are natural interpreters of the sentiments of the mind. They remove ambiguities; they enforce impressions; they operate on us by means of sympathy (*Lectures*, I, 172).

And in the words of Priestley:

> By the tone of the voice we can vary, and modify our ideas in a manner that no power of letters can ever equal. In *Irony* the meaning of words is quite reversed (*Lectures*, p. 23).[39]

The qualification is, of course, that, in the specific case of Romantic irony, the meaning is not simply 'reversed' in any determinate and identifiable sense; it is unsettled in such a way that we can never verify the suggested tonality as belonging to an authoritatively 'present' persona; and we must, if we are to establish such a presence, assume the ultimate responsibility for it ourselves. The critical debate upon and around the last lines of the 'Ode on a Grecian Urn', involving as it does a reconstruction of the whole poem up to that point of decision, is simply one among the more dramatic examples of this strategy.

Further, irony is closely identifiable with the function of metaphor in the Romantic context.[40] I have given some account of the ambivalent position of metaphor, as poised uneasily between a 'usage' (by, e.g., Coleridge) in its stable sense as merely an illustrative trope, and an implicit place in a fundamentally phenomenalist discourse as the constitutive and limiting feature of all perception and judgement—limiting, that is, in terms of reference to 'things in themselves', and in its pre-empting of the possibility of transparent or automatic communication. As soon as it is recognised that there is no metaphor which can be described other than metaphorically, then we have once again eroded the potential gap between comment and metacomment, and between subject and predicate, which is the *sine qua non* of authoritarian discourse. So that the connection between irony and metaphor in Romantic aesthetics is not simply the traditional one, that we use metaphorical expressions to avoid the responsibility for direct statements; it is that the recognition of the metaphorical status of language itself, both as it is created and as it is received (i.e. at all points along the author-reader axis), involves the simultaneous commitment to a system of meaning-production which is ever expanding and proliferating, and yet ever evasive, ever digesting itself as the means of its ongoing progress—a commitment, in other words, to Romantic Irony.

Coda
'And this is why I sojourn here'

Sojourn, so remain, so journey whilst remaining . . . It will not be necessary, I hope, to do more than indicate summarily the centrality of this pun, and of the elided poem from which it is taken. Keats certainly read *The Spectator* (*Letters*, II, 188), and the similarity between his wretched wight/knight-at-arms and the knight of no. 413 has been pointed out.[41] But the real logic of articulation which governs this poem is not to be found, I think, in its sources, which are probably capable of infinite expansion, so much as in the way its parts relate. From this perspective also, it is almost an 'open' signifier for a great many patterns of thought developing through the period roughly covered by the creative lifetime of Blake. The fusion of protagonists, author-speaker-wight-reader, begs comparison with the other fusions of extremes elsewhere in Romantic discourse. Pain and pleasure, for example, are for Hartley (*Observations*, I, 35) simply the two ends of a continuous system; the one can turn into the other 'by frequent Repetition' (p. 39). Similarly, mania and melancholy, the two categories between which the phenomenon of madness tended to be subdivided, are brought together by Spurzheim (*Observations*, p. 90) as interchangeable.[42] The *Encyclopédie* identifies mania as characterised by repetition and loss of memory, often caused by sexual excess (X, 32); melancholy, on the other hand, is related to abstinence and frustration, and is signified by a disposition towards solitude (X, 307). The real and the imaginary are out of joint, and it is most prevalent during spring and autumn, at the changing of the seasons. The symptoms imaged in Keats's poem are unspecifically specific enough to supply both of these categories; the dry, cold, autumnal landscape and the overall atmosphere of unfulfilled longing go hand in hand with repetition, both desired and enacted (in the cyclic form), and with the hints of some sort of achieved consummation.[43]

Roughly speaking, these coalescences of taxonomical categories can be related to the erosion of the 'metacomment' which I have argued to be an important feature of poetics. What has been 'kept apart' now comes together, just as the alerted reader must become what he beholds. The pattern is one which De Quincey describes in his account of (Coleridge's account of) a set of plates by Piranesi:

Creeping along the sides of the walls, you perceived a staircase; and upon this, groping his way upwards, was Piranesi himself. Follow the stairs a little farther, and you perceive them reaching an abrupt termination, without any balustrade, and allowing no step onwards to him who should reach the extremity, except into the depths below. Whatever is to become of poor Piranesi, at least you suppose that his labours must now in some way terminate. But raise your eyes, and behold a second flight of stairs still higher, on which again Piranesi is perceived, by this time standing on the very brink of the abyss. Once again elevate your eye, and a still more aerial flight of stairs is described; and there, again, is the delirious Piranesi, busy on his aspiring labours: and so on, until the unfinished stairs and the hopeless Piranesi both are lost in the upper gloom of the hall. With the same power of endless growth and self-reproduction did my architecture proceed in dreams (*Works*, I, 263-4).

Schelling, probably unknown to De Quincey and certainly so to Keats, describes a similar model in his account of philosophical method:

Two contraries *a* and *b* (subject and object) become united through the action *x*, but in *x* there is a new antithesis, *c* and *d* (the sensing and the thing sensed). The action *x* therefore becomes itself an object; it is itself only articulable through a new activity = *z*, which again perhaps involves an antithesis, and so on.[44]

Hegel adopted just this as 'the *infinite progress of mediation*' (*Science of Logic*, p. 749), at the same time as poetry begins to speak forth 'longing and aspiration (*Sehnsucht* und *Streben*)' (*ibid.*, p. 233; *Werke*, III, 230). 'Endymion', 'Alastor', 'The Triumph of Life', and any number of other poems dramatise this longing; Shelley's images of mists, shadows, caves, and thresholds, are always held at the *point* of apparency, without ever settling into determinate form. In 'La Belle Dame' the 'I' cannot be posited (that is to say, successfully limited) because there is no certain apprehension of an inner-outer polarity, only a sliding scale of possibilities; and this refusal of fixity has obvious ethical as well as epistemological corollaries. The 'I' for Schelling must be 'infinite activity (*unendliche Thätigkeit*)' (*Werke*, II, 380), albeit that it discovers itself as an unlimitable concept through its being temporarily limited, this being the only condition under which it can be thought at all (pp. 383-4):

Every original antithesis can only be overcome moment by moment in an infinite synthesis and through a finite, particular object. The antithesis occurs afresh at each moment, and is again on each occasion overcome.[45]

Hence the burden of the mystery, the seeing by glimpses, which Burke had previously identified as precisely the posture of terror:

> But a light now appearing, and now leaving us, and so off and on, is even more terrible than total darkness; and a sort of uncertain sounds are, when the necessary dispositions concur, more alarming than a total silence (*Philosophical Enquiry*, p. 84).

However disappointing its consequences may be for the moment of near-perception, in the immediate sense, this limited apprehension is demanded by the ethical imperatives operating within Romanticism. This paradox must be maintained as a paradox, just as the dismissal of the criteria of contingent experience which Kant demands in the constitution of the moral law is ultimately a way of trying to reinforce the mind against the fluctuations of that experience, fluctuations which it *cannot* contain. But Keats's poem, so far as I can see, does not offer any internal pointers to a way of perceiving which would resolve its problems by directing our energies to a new level or mode of decision. It offers repetition and transference, and the prospect of meanings, as in Shelley's 'The Triumph of Life', 'for ever sought, for ever lost' (*Poetical Works*, p. 517). We awake, like Adam from his dream, but find nothing—or everything—to be 'true'. The commitment to language only dramatises the inability to express; utterance articulates absence, experience which can be 'spoken around' but never contained. Geraldine casts a similar spell over Christabel:

> Thou knowest to-night and wilt know to-morrow,
> This mark of my shame, this seal of my sorrow;
> But vainly thou warrest,
> For this is alone in
> Thy power to declare,
> That in the dim forest
> Thou heard'st a low moaning,
> And found'st a bright lady, surpassingly fair;
> And didst bring her home with thee in love and charity,
> To shield her and shelter her from the damp air
>
> (*Poetical Works*, p. 225).

There is 'knowledge' but no speech; all that can be 'spoken' is the bare framework of apparent events held together by no syntax of 'meaning', not even the syntax of intentional projection whose operations Wordsworth so feared. There is nothing of 'the balance or reconciliation of opposite or discordant qualities', but simply their presentation; and nothing of that 'consolatory feeling that accompanies the sense of a proportion between antecedents and consequents' (*Biographia*, II, 12, 207). The metonyms upon which 'La Belle Dame' is built do not, as I have said, allow for that desired passage from part to whole which would permit us to identify an 'object' corresponding to the title of the poem, and consequently a stable investigative 'I' reflected back from it. The speaker/reader is almost in the position of Spurzheim's 'partial idiots', those who can 'pronounce single words very well; but they cannot maintain any discourse, they cannot keep up their attention, nor combine their expressions' (*Observations*, p. 124).[46] The composite protagonist of the poem is fixated, trapped within the artifact and the experience, which is a typical feature of madness as described by, for example, Burke:

> they remain whole days and nights, sometimes whole years, in the constant repetition of some remark, some complaint, or song; which having struck powerfully on their disordered imagination, in the beginning of their phrensy, every repetition reinforces it with new strength; and the hurry of their spirits, unrestrained by the curb of reason, continues it to the end of their lives (*Philosophical Enquiry*, p. 74).[47]

Unable to achieve a metacomment, we are trapped in a perpetual present, where causality and temporality are completely suspended. The imagery of immobility and thraldom was one which appealed to Keats (see, for example, *Complete Poems*, pp. 199, 281, 348), and it is worth relating this to another common preoccupation of the period, the so-called 'animal magnetism' or somnambulism.

Animal magnetism never achieved the popularity in England which it enjoyed in France and Germany; but this is to say very little, given the interest which it gave rise to on the continent.[48] Here, it was a subject of widespread fascination; Coleridge in particular was drawn to it, though he remained sceptical as late as 1817.[49] One very specific feature of the phenomenon, which we now tend to call 'hypnotism', was the passage of the patient into thraldom and passivity—for which Hegel, not surprisingly, criticised it (*Philosophy of Mind*, p. 116). Viewed positively, this can be an experience of symbiosis, as described by Schubert:

> Every constraint which physicality maintains between two different individuals is overcome in this condition; the soul of each, being opened inwardly, becomes one and the same with the soul of the magnetizer.[50]

But, viewed otherwise, the same posture can be seen to embody loss of will, of consciousness, and of control; complete subservience to the magnetiser (Kluge, *Versuch*, p. 83), 'And nothing else saw all day long.' The somnambulist condition is marked by the fusion and confusion of pleasure and pain (p. 82), of inner and outer (pp. 83–4), and by the loss of the ability, if not of the urge, to speak (p. 83). 'With horrid warning gapèd wide'. Most significantly, then, animal magnetism seems to relate to poetic communication in its stress upon transference and seizure (which may of course appear in its more generous manifestation as the offer of a performative contract). Its effects rely upon and encourage a weakening of the ego and a declension from the reliance upon determinate identity, and in this it resembles the relations prevailing between author and reader through the literary text. I have argued for incidences of such transference at work, in such poems as 'The Two April Mornings' and 'The Ancient Mariner', for example, and implicitly in others such as 'Tintern Abbey' and 'Frost at Midnight', where the possibility for meaning involves a 'handing on',[51] just as it does in *The Prelude*. Beholding is becoming. What is more complicated, however, is, as we have seen, the variety of motives which seem to reinforce this articulation, varying as they do from ethical compulsion and the refusal of authoritarianism to a desperate uncertainty about the modes of expressing, and even of perceiving, 'knowledge'. Virtue and necessity seem to go hand in hand:

> But follow thou, and from spectator turn
> Actor or victim in this wretchedness,
>
> And what thou wouldst be taught I then may learn
> From thee (Shelley, *Poetical Works*, p. 514).

There are of course alternatives to what I have been describing as a world where 'infinite blindness supplies the place of sight' (*Biographia*, I, 181), though I have chosen to indicate rather than delineate them; love and faith, the acceptance of half-knowledge without paradox (some versions of 'imagination' belong here), and the categorical imperative in its emphasis upon stoical self-reliance. But all of these positions place strains upon communicability. Political commitment, which partakes of something of each of these, is another option, and it is in this context that we would have to take account of the possibility that the insistence upon the impossibility of a 'metacomment' is nothing more than a conspiracy to pre-empt the opportunity for any sort of determinate action.[52] But the poets of this generation were not, by and large, 'activists', and the alternatives I have indicated here all involve a 'stepping over' of the terms of the discourse I have described, rather than, in the strictest sense, emerging from *within* it; that is to say, that the 'way beyond' does not so much involve the assimilation of our leading problems as the refusal of them. Such an option consorts awkwardly with the Romantic emphasis upon the 'labour of the negative', upon working through; but it must always remain.

The paradox of Keats seems to me to be that, whilst standing as the poet perhaps least affected or defeated by these predicaments, he should yet be able to write what I believe to be a paradigm poem. There is, it seems, a historical situation which invades and determines, or exists in correspondence with, the most private, unpublished utterances of a young poet to his mistress:

I cry your mercy, pity, love—aye love!
Merciful love that tantalizes not,
One-thoughted, never-wandering, guileless love,
Unmasked, and being seen—without a blot!
Oh, let me have thee whole—all, all, be mine!
The shape, that fairness, that sweet minor zest
Of love, your kiss—those hands, those eyes divine,
That warm, white, lucent, million-pleasured breast;
Yourself—your soul—in pity give me all,
Withhold no atom's atom or I die;
Or living on perhaps, your wretched thrall,
Forget, in the mist of idle misery,
Life's purposes—the palate of my mind
Losing its gust, and my ambition blind! (*Poems*, p. 689–90).

All the features of the paradigm are there; the desire for wholeness through the perception of parts, the passive activeness, the appeal for mercy—this time less ambiguous, in English—and the threat of thraldom. A 'natural' experience, perhaps. But behind the private agony there is, it seems, a historical force which shapes, or waits to speak out, even the most spontaneous of voices, but in such a way that its pre-established or coinstantaneous features can only ever be apprehended in recollection and re-perusal, after a lapse of time, after that 'spontaneity' has held sway for the moment of passing into form. This lapse, be it half a lifetime, as for the narrator of *The Prelude*, or the few seconds or parts of seconds between inspiration and composition, sensation and reflection, ensures the absolute inviolability of the artifact in its intrinsic, inmost, or ultimate meaning; it simultaneously provides for its eternal availability for the *making* of meaning through history, beyond the lapse, for the ever-renewing tillage of the fallow mind; and it ensures also that the appropriate mode for the apprehension of this paradox should be an 'ironic' one.

> And this is why I sojourn here
> Alone and palely loitering
> Though the sedge is withered from the lake,
> And no birds sing.

Notes

CHAPTER I

1. *The Letters of John Keats*, ed. H. E. Rollins, 2 vols, II, 98. This synthesis of the images from the two poems occurs in the long letter Keats wrote to his brother and sister-in-law (February to April, 1819), immediately after the first draft of 'La Belle Dame Sans Merci'.

   Miriam Allott, *The Poems of John Keats*, rev. ed., gives the holograph variant 'sedge-buried urn' (p. 508).

2. It would be more accurate to say that the poem is 'in process of' receiving critical attention. Earl R. Wasserman, *The Finer Tone: Keats' Major Poems*, devotes an entire chapter to it (pp. 63–83) in what I take to be the 'breakthrough', and the poem has recently been dealt with in some detail by François Matthey, *The Evolution of Keats's Structural Imagery*, pp. 174–81. The almost unanimous preference for the earlier version need not be documented in detail. Of the critics I have read, only Matthey seems to favour the '*Indicator*' version, for reasons which seem quite close to my own, as will be seen.

3. A survey, which is at least a temporary landing-place amidst the flood, can be found in Harvey T. Lyon, *Keats' Well-Read Urn: An Introduction to Literary Method*. I shall try to incorporate at least the major developments in the case since the appearance of this book.

4. I use 'dramatic' in the sense defined by Coleridge as 'suited to the narrator'; see *The Complete Poetical Works of Samuel Taylor Coleridge*, ed. Ernest Hartley Coleridge, 2 vols. (Oxford. Clarendon Press, 1912), p. 267. This edition is cited throughout. Several critics have touched upon a distinction between poet and speaker, without developing the point in quite the way I have chosen. Among them are Leo Spitzer, 'The "Ode on a Grecian Urn", or Content vs. Metagrammar', *Comparative Literature*, 7 (1955), 203–25; Cleanth Brooks, *The Well-Wrought Urn*, pp. 139–52; Stuart Sperry, *Keats the Poet*, p. 270f.; Morris Dickstein, *Keats and his Poetry*, p. 196f. Douglas Bush and M. H. Abrams make some brief but provocative remarks in *Twentieth Century Interpretations of Keats's Odes*, ed. Jack Stillinger, pp. 108–11. Dickstein sees the poem as intelligible 'only as a series of movements within a single (though divided) consciousness' (p. 196), whereas Jacob Wigod, 'Keats's Ideal in the "Ode on a Grecian Urn"' (in *Twentieth Century Interpretations*) describes the protagonist as 'Keats or the speaker' (p. 58). Brooks wants to introduce a dramatic speaker for the last lines, rather than for everything but the last lines, seeing there 'a consciously riddling paradox, put in the mouth of a particular character, and modified by the total context of the poem' (p. 142). Sperry notes a 'pattern of imaginative engagement and disengagement' (p. 270), and sees 'not a poet repeating earlier assertions, but rather discovering in them difficulties he had formerly ignored'

(p. 277). Harold Bloom, *The Ringers in the Tower*, comes closest to what I am getting at when he remarks that 'Part of this poem's strength is in the deliberate vulnerability of its speaker, who contemplates a world of values he cannot appropriate for his own, although nothing in that world is antithetical to his own nature as an aspiring poet' (p. 137).

5. See my 'Keats's Lady, Metaphor, and the Rhetoric of Neurosis', *Studies in Romanticism*, 15 (1976), 265–88. Much of what follows is dealt with in this paper, though from the specific perspective of Freud's analysis of the dream process. Further, I have made changes and modifications in the argument where they seemed necessary.

6. See, for example, Roland Barthes, *Critical Essays*, trans. Richard Howard, p. 97:

> Logic teaches us to distinguish the language object from meta-language. The language object is the very matter subject to logical investigation; meta-language is the necessarily artificial language in which we conduct this investigation.

For Barthes, this phenomenon arose when 'literature began to regard itself as double: at once object and scrutiny of that object, utterance and utterance of that utterance, literature object and metaliterature' (p. 97). He is concerned to relate this specifically to a crisis within Modernism, and therefore tends to regard the late nineteenth-century novel as the historical originator of that heuristic or participatory genre he calls the 'scriptible'. I do not find this assumption at all convincing, but do take the point that a metalanguage 'is conducted not from outside but within literature itself, or more exactly at its extreme verge' (p. 98). In other words the metacomment offers no stable, external positioning of the primary material, but is itself implicated within the same context and the same problems.

7. *OED* gives a seventeenth-century origin for 'flowery' as 'florid', and a Miltonic spelling of 'brede' as 'breade', along with some indication of the word as an obsolete form for *breed*.

8. H. W. Garrod, *Keats*, 2nd ed., p. 101, complains about line 41 in these terms, as does William Empson *The Structure of Complex Words*, p. 374.

9. Most accounts of the poem vary between these two extremes; it is in the account of Newell F. Ford, *The Prefigurative Imagination of John Keats: A Study of the Beauty-Truth Identification and its Implications*, that the hypothesis of a poet-speaker distinction seems most called for, when he notes that the third stanza 'rings over and over the theme of unfading happiness . . . A less empathic poet would have remembered the irony implicit in his theme . . .' (p. 137).

10. *Biographia Literaria*, ed. J. Shawcross, 2 vols. (Oxford: Clarendon Press, 1907), II, 65–6. Subsequent references will be to this edition. See also *The Poetical Works of Edward Young*, 2 vols., II, 148–9; and *Collected Works of Oliver Goldsmith*, ed. Arthur Friedman, 5 vols., I, 113–14, for similar remarks on the generic features of the ode. A modern critic has noted much the same thing of Keats. Bruce E. Miller, 'Form and Substance in "Ode on a Grecian Urn"', *Keats-Shelley Journal*, 20 (1971), 62–70, observes thus:

> Considered dynamically, the Keatsian ode consists of an unstable vehicle that works towards resolution. As it throws off imbalances and rights itself, it produces tensions and ambivalences (p. 63).

Walter Jackson Bate, *The Stylistic Development of Keats*, p. 135, notes of 'Ode on a Grecian Urn' that the 'use of consonantal syzygy occasionally assumes a kind of balance . . . but such balance is rough and infrequent enough to appear coincidental.' Marianne Thalmann, in *The Literary Sign Language of German Romanticism*, trans. Harold A. Basilius, observes that:

> The early romantic structures are built on an eccentric base, which can no longer be comprehended from a center but which is animated by the double resonance of elliptic focuses (p. 122).

Thalmann's wider purpose is to relate this, and other phenomena, to a crisis in the experience of the urban environment, which is not to the point here; but the coincidence of the structural dislocation is worth noting.

11. I shall have more to say about this later, most specifically in the discussion of metaphor in Chapter 5.

12. Why the distinction works, I think, is because the poet has the self-consciousness throughout his *writing* of the poem necessary to present the speaker ironically. This would allow for the speaker becoming one with the poet, as I shall later argue. See also n. 25.

13. Thus the one reading which I do seem to exclude, for the moment, is that which makes the last line and a half an expression of grim resentment on the speaker's part at the indifference of the urn and its refusal to expand on the tautology. This is, roughly, the interpretation of Walter H. Evert, *Aesthetic and Myth in the Poetry of Keats*, p. 317. There may be a deep credibility to this explanation, as will become apparent later in the argument. Brooks, as might be expected, sees the last lines as 'consciously riddling paradox' (p. 142), open to modification in the dramatic context of the whole poem. He is followed by Dickstein, who regards the urn's statement as 'self-limiting, a piece of dramatic irony' (p. 228, note). Wasserman, *The Finer Tone*, p. 59, sees the antecedent to the 'that' (l. 49) as the whole of the preceding passage from l. 46 onwards—not just the aphorism itself. A summary of the options, intrinsically tied up as they are with any editorial decision about which of the six versions to adopt as a 'standard' text, and of the most important accounts through which the argument has developed, is Jack Stillinger's 'Who Says What to Whom at the End of "Ode on a Grecian Urn"' in Stillinger, ed., *Twentieth Century Interpretations*, pp. 113–14. This is reprinted and expanded in his book, *The Hoodwinking of Madeline, and Other Essays on Keats's Poems*, pp. 167–73. See also the same author's *The Texts of Keats's Poems*, pp. 245–7.

It seems to me that no decision about textual and even grammatical priority can solve the question of 'meaning' with any finality; it could be argued that the meaning is properly conveyed by the very variation between the six versions.

In the context of the accusation of philosophical thinness which has been levelled at the aphorism itself, it is worth noting that the relationship of truth to beauty was a central preoccupation of eighteenth-century thinkers. See, for example, Schiller, *On the Aesthetic Education of Man*, trans. Elizabeth M. Wilkinson and L. A. Willoughby, p. 189, and Ernst Cassirer, *The Philosophy of the Enlightenment*, trans. F. C. A. Koelln & J. P. Pettegrove, p. 314. James Burnett, Lord Monboddo, in his *Ancient Metaphysics*, 6 vols. (London: 1779–99), identifies the highest achievement of the mind as the making of each of beauty and truth into the other (I, 489–90; see also II, 104). For some of Keats's famous formulations, see *Letters*, I, 184, 192; II, 19.

14. See Dwight E. Robinson, 'Ode on a "New Etrurian" Urn: A Reflection of Wedgwood Ware in the Poetic Imagery of John Keats', *Keats-Shelley Journal*, 12 (1963), 11–35. A copious bibliography of the subject can be found in Ian Jack, *Keats and the Mirror of Art*, rev. ed., pp. 214–24.

15. Matthey announces himself as having made the choice between cyclic and linear structures in the interpretation of Keats, when he says that he sees the imagery to be producing 'an architectural framework allowing progress along an ascending or descending line' (p.v.). His actual readings, however, are more subtle than this would imply, as when he describes two contrapuntal patterns running through 'The Eve of St Agnes' (pp. 169–73).

16. In something of the same spirit, Coleridge had maintained that even 'sensation itself is but vision nascent, not the cause of intelligence, but intelligence itself revealed as an earlier power in the process of self-construction' (*Biographia*, I, 187–8); so that the urn must take its life from the process of self-construction?

17. It might reasonably be queried why, after having so painstakingly separated out the two personae, I should then try to bring them together again. Firstly, I hope it will be clear that the effort to 'make sense'—coherent sense—sends us in this direction, and that the explanation does seem to do this; secondly, Keats himself gave us no evidence for the reidentification of the personae, outside that suggested by the faltering or ambiguous tone of the last lines, so that the process seems worth describing in some detail. I leave aside for the moment the numerous analogues throughout Romantic poetry which could be suggested here.

18. Jane Rabb Cohen, 'Keats's Humor in "La Belle Dame Sans Merci"', *Keats-Shelley Journal*, 17 (1968), 10–13, has tried to make a case for comedy in the poem.

19. I should say 'might have wished', since the hypothesis of a normative reading must be a troubled one, and I have come across readers who construe the poem from the first as the utterance of a single voice.

20. I came across Matthey's account too late to acknowledge it in my earlier paper. He does notice (p. 176) the way in which the repeated 'I' seems to disrupt the apparent organisation of the stanzas, though without developing the point. Evert poses the right question—'One may ask how, *precisely*, are the poet and the dreamer distinct' (p. 244)—and goes on to point out another sort of 'gap' in the poem, wherein the 'truncation of each stanza's closing line impels the reader into a repeatedly opening metrical void in which something is going unsaid' (p. 245). Wasserman, *The Finer Tone*, p. 67, notes a coalescence of human and natural images in the early stanzas, but does not apply the model to the personae themselves. At the end he does notice the importance of the cyclic form, and 'the gradual transfer of grammatical control from one actor to another' (p. 81).

21. Needless to say, no such complications are to be found in Dr Johnson's dictionary. *OED* gives *Mete*, Pa. pple. 3–4 *met* as 'to dream', with a selection of examples from Middle English poetry, as well as a specialised usage meaning 'to paint, design'. Keats could have found the word in Chaucer, but not, apparently, in his beloved Chatterton. Donald S. Taylor, ed., *The Complete Works of Thomas Chatterton*, 2 vols., glosses only one use of *meeten* = 'to meet' (I, 214, l. 1072). But, more prosaically, the usage is cited in that rag-bag of popular philology,

John Horne Tooke's ΕΠΕΑ ΠΤΕΡΟΕΝΤΑ, *or the Diversions of Purely*, 2nd ed.,
2 vols., II, 341–2.

22. See, for example, Peter Rickard, *Chrestomathie de la langue française au quinzième siècle*, pp. 73, 98 etc.

23. Huguet, *Dictionnaire du seizième siècle*, gives both usages, as do Hatzfeld and Darmesteter, *Dictionnaire général de la langue française*, for the eighteenth century. Could it be that Keats, or somebody, in allowing an English or old French rather than a modern French spelling to slip through in line 39 of the '*Indicator*' version, is surreptitiously fronting the familiar usage of the English word as masking an ambivalence in the French? It would seem that we are bound to set it against the alternative spelling in the title of the poem. Barbara Fass, *La Belle Dame Sans Merci and the Aesthetics of Romanticism*, p. 27, relates the ambiguity to the belle dame's 'own deprivation, since she exists without the hope of divine grace. The demonic creature who is excluded from God's mercy is herself to be pitied.'

24. That is, if the theory of repression be accepted. My earlier paper specifically discusses elision, displacement, and teleological inversion in this context.

25. Michael Ragussis, 'Narrative Structure and the Problem of the Divided Reader in "The Eve of St Agnes"', *ELH*, 42 (1975), 378–94, offers a fine account of the same process at work in this other major poem. Ragussis sees its speaker as 'obsessed by his own fiction' (p. 382), and standing in the same relation to the romance represented by the poem as a poem as Madeline does to her dream. The reader tends to follow the speaker, so that he 'participates in the limitations of the story's characters and narrator, and curiously learns only by sharing these limitations. The writer ironically involves the reader in a partial fiction to make him see, at last, a truth' (p. 390). The argument is well achieved, I think. We seem to understand 'objectively' Madeline's position, and the way in which she is 'exploited' by Porphyro, who plays upon her imaginative credulity and her tendency toward mystification. It is her belief in the myth which commits her to reality. At the same time, we read through the poem as though we are at a comfortable distance away from any participation in what goes on; we think we are seeing things from the perspective of a metacommentary. Thus we are woken up with a start at the very end, when we are lifted out of the past of the romance into the present, with its harsh message of extinction. That is to say, we have been trapped into indulging in the material of the poem as a sort of distraction or contemplation, believing ourselves immune from the mistakes of its protagonists, only to be ourselves thrust into the same state of shock and disorientation which Madeline feels on waking from her dream. This is a masterly example of the expanding circle of inclusion. The dice are loaded against us from the start, however. 'The Fall of Hyperion' opens with a preamble in the voice of the poet *as* poet, placing the narrative which follows in a given context. 'Endymion' does the same thing, even announcing the prospective timetable of its own composition. In these cases, we are given an external perspective from which to move into the events of the poems; a prior distancing is established and apparent. In 'The Eve of St Agnes', however, the poem opens with a voice which is already within the same perspective as the events which it will describe; we are given no warning, no hint that we must be on our guard. The last stanza therefore throws us into a present which has never yet been invoked in the poem. Ragussis does find a clue in the fluctuations of past and present tenses (p. 382), but these are all too easy to miss.

The early work on the exegesis of this poem was done by Jack Stillinger, *The Hoodwinking of Madeline*, pp. 67–93. Ragussis has shown that this involves also the hoodwinking of the reader—at the very moment in which he is fooled into thinking that he has not been hoodwinked, but has been a spectator of someone else's folly or credulity.

Any reader who is already irritated by my use of the figure of the 'naive reader' may find it useful (allowing myself a Coleridgean habit) to refer forward to Chap. 4, n. 21 (p. 228) (it *does* exist).

26. The invitation to participation extended to the reader is thus a sort of trap. Rousseau's remarks in *Émile*, trans. Barbara Foxley, on the proper conduct of a master to his pupil, are worth quoting here:

> . . . let him always think he is master while you are really master. There is no subjection so complete as that which preserves the forms of freedom; it is thus that the will itself is taken captive (p. 84).

27. Douglas Bush, *John Keats: Selected Poems and Letters*, is the only 'honest' editor I know of, in that he gives the two versions of the poem side by side. Allott gives the *'Indicator'* text in full as an appendix (pp. 757–8). See also Stillinger, *The Texts of Keats's Poems*, pp. 232–4. Stillinger does seem to think that Keats had at least a hand in the preparation of the second version.

Some confirmation of parts of my argument for this poem can be gathered from J. M. Sinclair, 'When is a Poem like a sunset?', in *Ballad Studies*, ed. E. B. Lyle, pp. 153–69. This is a summary of the results of an experiment in oral transmission, using the *'Indicator'* version. It is particularly interesting for what it has to suggest about the habits of normalisation which go on in such a transmission. Tenses and prepositions are particularly vulnerable to 'rewriting', with a resulting simplification of the spatial and temporal indeterminacies in the poem. The apparent gap between the speakers of the third and fourth stanzas is stressed by the removal of the parallelism of the 'I' clauses: 'I see a lily on . . .' becomes 'A lily sits upon . . .' (p. 163). This goes along with the attempted strong differentiation of personae in the last stanza: ' . . . I sojourn here' becomes ' . . . you see me here' (p. 162), and this also speaks for an attempt to impose strong closure on the poem. Indeterminate words like 'met' and 'sure' also disappear, and the 'belle dame' is made the agent of the bewitching of the protagonist (p. 164).

28. Quoted in *Romantic Bards and British Reviewers*, ed. John O. Hayden, p. 144. The review, printed in *The Examiner*, 2 June 1816, is also to be found in *The Complete Works of William Hazlitt*, ed. P. P. Howe, XIX, 32f.

29. If I may be allowed a moment of pedantry, at the same time as contributing something to the argument for seeing the 'Ode on a Grecian Urn' as a system of tensions; could it be that Coleridge's poem 'Human Life: On the Denial of Immortality' (*Poetical Works*, pp. 425–6) contributes to the source material behind it? Far from dealing in intimations of eternity, Coleridge apostrophises man as a 'vessel purposeless' (l. 8), a 'nigh-finished vase' (l. 11) who goes through happiness and mourning (ll. 17–21) only to be left with the ultimate enigma of his selfhood. This poem also was published in *Sibylline Leaves*, for a copy of which Keats sent to the Dilkes in November, 1817 (*Letters*, I, 183).

30. *The Archaeology of Knowledge*, trans. A. M. Sheridan Smith, p. 130.

31. See also *The Rhetoric of Fiction*, especially Part III (p. 271f), and *Now Don't Try to*

Reason with Me: Essays and Ironies for a Credulous Age.
A much wider ranging and more systematic polemic along the same lines is Anthony Wilden's *System and Structure: Essays in Communication and Exchange.* Tracking between psychoanalysis, philosophy, and systems theory, he notes that 'the double bind depends on the deliberate confusion between referent language and metalanguage, on the refusal to allow contextual definition' (p. 445). This itself he describes as 'one of the most powerful weapons used against the individual members of our society to prevent metacommunication about its Imaginary values' (p. 108). Thus Wilden would regard my version of Keats as purporting to represent in a purely epistemological sense an argument which should properly be placed in the fallen social values of the percipient. While accepting this, I would argue that both the problem I have located *and* Wilden's preferred solution of it are contained within Romantic speculation. It is in the nature of the subject that I must appear to have more to do with the former than the latter.

32. The German is as follows:

> Literarische Ironie ist um so ironischer, je vollständiger sie auf Ironiesignale zu verzichten weiß—ohne Preisgabe ihrer Transparenz. Diese Feststellung besagt zugleich, daß es eine zureichende, rein formale Ironiedefinition für die Literatur gar nicht geben kann. Wo die Signale fehlen, ja das Fehlen der Signale zur conditio sine qua non der höchsten Ironie-stufen wird, muß die reine Formanalyse notwendigerweise versagen, denn ein reines Null-Signal kann man nicht mehr weiter formal differenzieren.

I shall try to give the German, or whatever, in all cases where I have to use my own translations, as above. Otherwise, accepted or authoritative translations will be cited where available, with the original language being given where it seems particularly irreducible, or crucial to the meaning.

CHAPTER 2

1. The prose is deliberately garbled and eclectic here, in an attempt to work the phrases and concepts to be used into some sort of equivalence with the definitions offered by *Chambers Twentieth Century Dictionary* (New Edition, 1972 & 1973) of the much used word 'heuristic'.
2. *The Prose Works of William Wordsworth*, ed. W. J. B. Owen and Jane W. Smyser, 3 vols. (Oxford: Clarendon Press, 1974), I, 154. All subsequent references to the prose will be to this edition.
3. 'The Prelude' (1805), III, 189. Quotations from the poem will be taken from *The Prelude*, ed. E. de Selincourt, 2nd ed. rev. Helen Darbishire (Oxford: Clarendon Press, 1959).
4. *The Letters of William and Dorothy Wordsworth: The Middle Years, Part 1, 1806–11*, ed. E. de Selincourt, 2nd ed. rev. Mary Moorman, p. 150.
5. J. L. Lowes's *The Road to Xanadu: A Study in the Ways of the Imagination*, 2nd rev. ed., shows a fine sense of the integrity and density of these fragments, though his account does not argue for the existence of a coherent 'method'; and in a much more negative way, Norman Fruman's *Coleridge, The Damaged Archangel*, while it locates an enormous amount of possible source material, refuses any insight

into the possible systems of meaning which Coleridge might be making out of it. Another negative view is that of J. A. Appleyard, *Coleridge's Philosophy of Literature: The Development of a Concept of Poetry, 1791–1819*, pp. 169–208, which discusses the central chapters of the *Biographia* through an attempted paraphrase. Thomas McFarland, *Coleridge and the Pantheist Tradition*, does seem to me to go some way towards arguing for the lateral connections Coleridge might be demanding of his reader, as does George Whalley, 'On Reading Coleridge', in *Writers and their Background: S. T. Coleridge*, ed. R. L. Brett, pp. 1–44. As Whalley puts it, 'the principle of unity in multeity obtains—not ideally, to be sure, or in every instance, but as a constant dynamic interanimation that makes every fragment at least potentially reverberant . . . the separate items are facets rather than fragments, germs implying growth rather than broken pieces that bespeak disorder or death' (p. 24). See also the doctoral dissertation, under way, of Kathleen M. Wheeler, Girton College, Cambridge.

6. It does not seem to me to matter much whether the artist's doings are entirely conscious or not, nor does it ever seem possible to be sure. Overdetermination is the feature of an enquiry into causes, and we can usually find more, and sometimes many more than one reason why things should be as they are. Personally, as will become clear, I do find evidence for thinking Coleridge much more self-conscious than is often argued, and much more able to make artistic virtue of necessity.

7. *Collected Letters of Samuel Taylor Coleridge*, ed. Earl Leslie Griggs, 6 vols. (Oxford: Clarendon Press, 1956–71), IV, 768. Future references will be to this edition. One of the best demonstrations of the performative imperative in Coleridge's arguments is that of I. A. Richards, *Coleridge on Imagination*, 3rd ed., pp. 46–67.

   Where I use the word 'performative', I mean it as used by J. L. Austin, *How to do things with Words*, to describe the situation where 'to utter the sentence . . . is to do it'; as Austin says, 'I am not reporting on . . . I am indulging in' (p. 6). Within a written rather than a spoken (acted) discourse such as a poem, the performative will tend to stand as an imperative, an invitation to do (or indeed to refrain from) the action which belongs with the utterance. As with Wordsworth 'perceiving' old beggars and leech gatherers, it demands belief or disbelief, endorsement or disapproval, according to the contexts we create. Thus the reader must re-perform, one way or another. In terms of this assimilation of the 'objective' into the subjective, Coleridge was fascinated by the metaphor of the Brockenspectre, wherein the beholder sees his own image enhanced and externalised before him; the reassimilation of what seems 'outer' as 'inner'. There is a discussion of this by Stephen Prickett, *Coleridge and Wordsworth, The Poetry of Growth*, pp. 22–45.

8. Compare Diderot on the relation of reader to text, where he comments that 'you almost have to be in the condition of creating it in order to feel it strongly (il faut être presque en état de le créer pour le sentir fortement).' See the 'Lettre sur les sourds et muets' in *Oeuvres Complètes de Diderot*, ed. J. Assézat, 20 vols., I, 374. The connection between the creative writer and God becomes absolutely central for Kierkegaard in, for example, *Concluding Unscientific Postscript*, trans. David F. Swenson & Walter Lowrie, p. 218:

   For no anonymous author can more cunningly conceal himself, no practitioner if the maieutic art can more carefully withdraw himself from the direct relationship, than God.

9. Compare pp. 104–5. For other Coleridgean discussions of the difficulties of wooing the reader's thought and attention, see *Aids to Reflection in the Formation of a Manly Character on the Several Grounds of Prudence, Morality, and Religion*, pp. 8, 220–1. See also *The Notebooks of Samuel Taylor Coleridge*, ed. Kathleen Coburn, 3 vols. so far, I, N 155. Subsequent citations from the notebooks will simply cite the number of the note, in the form 'N 155'.

10. *The Complete Works of Shelley*, ed. Roger Ingpen and Walter E. Peck, 10 vols. (1926; rpt. New York and London: Gordian Press and Ernest Benn Ltd., 1965), VI, 243. References to Shelley's prose will be to this edition. Compare Coleridge, *Biographia*, I, 100:

> Veracity does not consist in *saying*, but in the intention of *communicating*, truth; and the philosopher who cannot utter the whole truth without conveying falsehood, and at the same time, perhaps, exciting the most malignant passions, is constrained to express himself either *mythically* or equivocally.

11. *The Complete Poetical Works of Percy Bysshe Shelley*, ed. Neville Rogers, 2 vols. so far (Oxford: Clarendon Press, 1972 and 1975), II, 106. I shall not generally cite this edition, partly because it is incomplete, and partly because it is controversial, as I shall later suggest. Where possible, references will be to *Poetical Works*, ed. Thomas Hutchinson, corrected ed. G. M. Matthews (London, Oxford, New York: Oxford University Press, 1970).

12. *On Christianity: Early Theological Writings*, trans. T. M. Knox, pp. 256–7. For a general account of the movement in scriptural exegesis towards the heuristic, see Hans W. Frei, *The Eclipse of Biblical Narrative: A Study in Eighteenth and Nineteenth Century Hermeneutics*.

13. *Enquiry Concerning Political Justice and its Influence on Morals and Happiness*, 3rd ed., ed. F.E.L. Priestley, 3 vols., I, 168; II, 501. There is a problem, of course, for the social contract, when we stress the need for every individual to endorse it from within himself. Godwin's proffered solution argues for the universality of the faculty of reason and the inevitable progress of any truth planted within it. This explanation, I shall be arguing, did not satisfy the Romantic Poets.

14. *Immanuel Kant's Critique of Pure Reason*, trans. Norman Kemp Smith, p. 436. Compare *Kant: Selected Pre-Critical Writings and Correspondence with Beck*, trans. G. B. Kerferd and D. E. Walford, p. xxxv; *Prolegomena to any Future Metaphysics that will be able to present itself as a Science*, trans. Peter G. Lucas, p. 135; and Coleridge, *Letters*, VI, 635; *Biographia*, II, 63.

15. *Coleridge: The Philosophical Lectures, 1818–19*, ed. Kathleen Coburn, p. 176. With reference to Kant, see also pp. 388–90, 426. Kant describes himself as 'clearing, as it were, and levelling what has hitherto been wasteground', and as denying '*Knowledge*, in order to make room for *faith*' (*Pure Reason*, pp. 14, 29). For explicit references to a heuristic method in German Romantic philosophy, see *Schellings Werke*, II, 532; *Kritische-Friedrich-Schlegel-Ausgabe*, XVIII, 63. It would be very interesting, and very much to the point, to question the evidence for the suggestion of a consciously indirect method in Kant. Coleridge certainly believed in such a strategy (see *Biographia*, I, 99–100). One would have to distinguish, of course, between indirection as a protective device, and 'irony' as a

response to strictly philosophical problems which can be presented in no other way. On the question of a Kantian 'irony', see *Goethes Werke*, XIII, 30; William Drummond, *Academical Questions, Vol. One*, p. 366; P. F. Strawson, *The Bounds of Sense*, pp. 22, 35; Jonathan Bennett, *Kant's Dialectic*, p. 110; David W. Tarbet, 'The Fabric of Metaphor in Kant's "Critique of Pure Reason" ', *Journal of the History of Philosophy*, 6 (1968), 257-70.

16. *Hegel's Science of Logic*, trans. A. V. Miller, p. 62n. See also pp. 40—41.

17. *Ibid.*, p. 575. It seems unfortunate that Hegel's translators usually render 'Begriff', with its apparent and active root in the verb 'begreifen' (a sense which Hegel himself, as we shall see, would have wished to transcend), by 'notion', a term which often had suspicious connotations in its English usage. Take, for example, Francis Jeffrey, *Contributions to the Edinburgh Review*, 4 vols., III, 334:

> There is a species of insanity known among medical men by the epiphet *notional*, in which, as well as in *delirium tremens*, there is frequently no general depravation of the reasoning and judging faculties, but where the disease consists entirely in the patient mistaking the objects of his thought or imagination for real and present existences.

Thomas Brown, *Lectures on the Philosophy of the Human Mind*, 4 vols., II, 514, does try to introduce a more positive usage, choosing to call himself 'a Notionist, or Relationist', by which he means a conceptualist in the style of Locke and Reid.

18. Unless, of course, one accepts at face value the idea of the Prussian state as the achieved result of the historical process. Against this, one might ask for a consideration of the end of *The Phenomenology of Mind*, trans. J. B. Baillie, p. 807, where it is suggested that any potential forward and upward movement of the Spirit compels it simultaneously to a re-working through its own past, 'as if, for it, all that preceded were lost, and as if it had learned nothing from the experience of the spirits that preceded.' I shall merely mention, for the moment, the implicitly Wordsworthian paradox of a movement of mind which is committed to an infinite regression through its own past as a means of pursuing or establishing a 'present' which is itself moving ever further and further from its origins.

19. *A Philosophical Enquiry into the Origin of our Ideas of the Sublime and the Beautiful*, ed. J. T. Boulton, pp. 12—13; see also *The Collected Works of Dugald Stewart*, ed. Sir William Hamilton, 11 vols., II, 442, 439; V, 156.

20. Alexander Gerard, *An Essay on Taste*, 2nd ed., p. 3—4; Brown, *Lectures*, II, 255—6.

21. For an account of the Molyneux problem, see Cassirer, *The Philosophy of the Enlightenment*, pp. 108—20. See also Stewart, *Works*, IV, 300f., and C. M. Turbayne, *The Myth of Metaphor*, rev. ed., pp. 106—12.

22. *The Poetry and Prose of William Blake*, ed. David V. Erdman, 4th printing, with revisions (Garden City, N. Y.: Doubleday & Co., 1970), p. 690. Where possible, references to Blake, except to *Songs of Innocence and of Experience* (see below), will be to this edition, which is the most exact on matters of punctuation. For convenience, however, I shall also give references to the 'standard' Blake, ed. Sir Geoffrey Keynes, *Blake: Complete Writings*, corr. ed. (London, Oxford, New York: Oxford University Press, 1974). This letter is on p. 815. Subsequent citations will take the form 'Erd. 690, K. 815'.

23. Compare p. 217:

> In the kingdom of taste even the mightiest genius must divest itself of its
> majesty, and stoop in all humility to the mind of a little child.

Schiller's treatise *On Naive and Sentimental Poetry*, in '*Naive and Sentimental
Poetry*' and '*On the Sublime*', trans. Julius A. Elias, emphasises very strongly this
notion of 'reading back' as part of the phenomenon of the 'naive'. As we realise
that our apparent superiority over the child is ill-founded, we experience
reflexive guilt:

> We are touched not because we look down upon the child from the height of
> our strength and perfection, but rather because we *look upward* from the
> *limitation* of our condition, which is inseparable from the *determination* which
> we have attained, to the unlimited *determinacy* of the child and to its pure
> innocence . . . (p. 87).

See also Peter Coveney, *The Image of Childhood. The Individual and Society: a
Study of the Theme in English Literature*, rev. ed., and David Newsome, *Two
Classes of Men: Platonism and English Romantic Thought*, pp. 25–40.

24. In works such as Locke's *An Essay Concerning Human Understanding*, which is
neatly divided up by established editorial convention, I shall give book, chapter,
and section numbers, which will work for various editions. Quotations will be
taken from the edition of Peter H. Nidditch, in the series *The Clarendon Edition of
the Works of John Locke* (Oxford: Clarendon Press, 1975). For Locke's account of
children in this context, see Bk. I, ch. IV, 2ff.

25. Also in *Poetical Works*, pp. 153–4. But see *Letters*, I, 278.

26. For example, James Beattie, *Works*, 10 vols., I, 60:

> No man is ashamed of having been once an infant; that being a state of
> imperfection, which is common and necessary.

27. *Schriften*, hrsg. R. Samuel and P. Kluckhohn, 4 vols., III, 97;

> Ein Kind ist weit klüger und weiser als ein Erwachsener—das Kind muß
> durchaus *ironisches* Kind sein.

28. A pun is intended on the artist's function in 'künstliche Welt'; for the German,
see *Schillers Werke*, XX, 462.

29. Wordsworth's 'Answer to Mathetes' in *The Friend*, ed. Barbara E. Rooke, *The
Collected Works of Samuel Taylor Coleridge*, Bollingen Series LXXV, I, 397.

30. Frank D. McConnell, *The Confessional Imagination: A Reading of Wordsworth's
'Prelude'*, p. 165, notes the 'pronomial displacement', and offers a good analysis
of the tense confusions in this passage.

31. Herbert Lindenberger, *On Wordsworth's 'Prelude'*, sees the poem as modelled
around repetition, 'saying essentially the same thing again and again' (p. 188),
and coming to 'no real conclusion' (p. 191).

32. In *The Poetical Works of William Wordsworth*, ed. E. de Selincourt, 5 vols.
(Oxford: Clarendon Press, 1940–9), II, 216. References to the poetry other
than *The Prelude* will be to this edition. The basic account, pointing out the
irreducible ambivalence of this little lyric, is by Cleanth Brooks, 'Irony as a
Principle of Structure', in *Literary Opinion in America*, ed. Morton Dauwen
Zabel 3rd (rev.) ed., II, 729–41, esp. pp. 735–7. See also A. P. Rossiter, *Angel*

With Horns: Fifteen Lectures on Shakespeare, ed. Graham Storey, pp. 48–51. Among other discussions I would pick out those of Carl Woodring, *Wordsworth*, p. 47; and David Ferry, *The Limits of Mortality: An Essay on Wordsworth's Major Poems*, p. 77. Paul de Man, in his essay 'The Rhetoric of Temporality', in *Interpretation: Theory and Practice*, ed. Charles S. Singleton, pp. 173–209, discusses the poem in terms of temporality and irony, and the passage from self-deception to self-consciousness (p. 205). Geoffrey H. Hartman, *Wordsworth's Poetry, 1787–1814* pp. 158–9, sees the poem as moving beyond irony, the experience having already been absorbed into the healing consciousness. This cuts both ways, it seems to me.

33. Ferry, *The Limits of Mortality*, p. 64, thinks that Matthew turns away because not to do so 'would be taking up again the burden of human relationships with their joy and attendant sorrow'. See also Frederick Garber, *Wordsworth and the Poetry of Encounter*, p. 165; and E. D. Hirsch Jnr., *Wordsworth and Schelling: A Typological Study of Romanticism*, p. 85. For a view different from my own, see Anne Kostelanetz, 'Wordsworth's "Conversations"; A reading of "The Two April Mornings" and "The Fountain"', *ELH*, 33 (1966), 43–52. Here the end of the poem is taken to speak for 'the narrator's transcendent vision of nature as the eternal cycle of joy and vitality' (p. 48).

34. *Concluding Unscientific Postscript*, p. 526 n. Compare *Either/Or*, trans. David F. Swenson and Lillian Marvin Swenson, 2 vols., II, 88:

> There is something sad in the feeling that one is growing old, but it is a far deeper sadness which grips one when one cannot grow old.

35. The first version of the poem is slightly different, and is worth consulting. De Selincourt gives the variants in footnotes.

36. See Robert Langbaum, *The Poetry of Experience: the Dramatic Monologue in Modern Literary Tradition*, ch. 1. Coleridge, *Biographia*, II, 31, speaks of a group of poems 'in which the author is more or less dramatic'.

37. I say 'familiar', since Coleridge, for one, had a higher use for the term. I mean it in the sense employed by Shelley, *Complete Works*, VII, 109:

> Reason respects the differences, and imagination the similitudes of things.

38. I cannot agree with Donald Davie on the child's motives here. In *Wordsworth's Mind and Art*, ed. A. W. Thomson, p. 117, he finds that 'the boy, like the man, is enjoying himself so much that he can afford, and deliberately seeks out, some regret for which there is no objective reason.' This seems to me to repeat the adult's mistake in trying to predicate what the child is feeling. The choice of a symbol may equally well be a gesture prompted by terror.

39. Thus Srikumar Banerjee, *Critical Theories and Poetic Practice in the 'Lyrical Ballads'*, p. 159, is dissatisfied with the poem precisely because 'the psychological truth embodied in it . . . is not, in any way, imaginatively transformed.'

40. M. H. Abrams, *Natural Supernaturalism: Tradition and Revolution in Romantic Literature*, pp. 225–37, has discussed this work as a literary phenomenon. His account is very close to my own at several points, not the least so when he describes it as a 'self-implicative puzzle-book, which is enigmatic in the whole and deliberately equivocal in all its parts and passing allusions' (p. 236).

41. Compare pp. 102–5.

42. Compare *Prose*, I, 10:

Human Life is like the [plate] of a dial, hope brightens the future, Reflection the hour that is past—but the present is always marked with a shadow.

I do not wish to undertake a detailed exposition of 'Tintern Abbey', but it seems worth pointing to one way in which this poem can be read as a prelude to *The Prelude*. The 'present' in which the narrator is speaking only appears to exist as it is constructed out of the past and the hypothetical future (though the expression of 'oneness' can, and has been, read in good faith; I tend to see it as dramatically compromised), and it may be that it is the tension of this posture which explains the poet's transference to Dorothy of the responsibility for the ultimate gathering of meaning from what has happened. Wordsworth's reader bears a similar burden at the end of *The Prelude*. See Mary Warnock, *Imagination*, pp. 113–19.

43. Compare pp. 43, 748; see also *The Phenomenology of Mind*, pp. 80–81.

44. It is interesting that Coleridge offers a similar formulation of giving and receiving in 'Dejection: An Ode', where the same sort of ambivalent relation between mind and nature is embodied in the unanswered question of whether the rise of the storm is causally related to the deepening of the poet's introspection, as he begs that it should be.

45. Two interesting essays in *Bicentenary Wordsworth Studies in Memory of John Alban Finch*, ed. Jonathan Wordsworth, may be consulted on the question of Wordsworth's uncertainty about the insights of his poem. See Ford T. Swetman Jnr., 'The Satiric Voices of "The Prelude"', pp. 92–110; and Mark Reed, 'The Speaker of "The Prelude"', pp. 276–93. For a more positive view, arguing that Wordsworth learns to trust even the negative elements of his experience of nature, see Charles Altieri, 'Wordsworth's Wavering Balance: The Thematic Rhythm of *The Prelude*', *Wordsworth Circle*, 4 (1973), 226–40. I should not leave the subject without mention of Empson's fine observation, *The Structure of Complex Words*, p. 294, that *The Prelude* begins with 'two distinct quotations from the throwing out from Paradise of Adam and Eve'.

46. David V. Erdman, *Prophet Against Empire*, p. 118, thinks that 'Blake had both contraries in mind all along'. See also E. D. Hirsch Jnr., *Innocence and Experience: An Introduction to Blake*, pp. 14–20.

47. References to *Songs of Innocence and of Experience* will follow a different form, since I shall quote from the superb and easily available facsimile, ed. Sir Geoffrey Keynes (London: Oxford University Press, 1970), giving plate numbers. Thus, for the above, *Songs* 1.

48. Donald D. Ault, *Visionary Physics, Blake's Response to Newton*, p. 51, puts the case very well when he opines that 'Blake's poetry requires the reader to be constantly shifting his perspective and never to be willing to settle on a finite solution to a problem.' See also p. 168. It is hard to understand Coleridge's complaint (*Letters*, IV, 836) about Blake's 'despotism in symbols', though his grumble about 'the ambiguity of the Drapery. Is it a garment—or the body incised and scored out?' seems to ask the right question. For comments on the relation of text to design, see Northrop Frye, 'Poetry and Design in William Blake', in *Blake: A Collection of Critical Essays*, ed. Northrop Frye, pp. 119–26; Anne Kostelanetz Mellor, *Blake's Human Form Divine*; Karl Kroeber, 'Graphic-Poetic Structuring in Blake's "Book of Urizen"', *Blake Studies*, 3 (1970), 7–18; and, most succinct and suggestive of all, W. J. T. Mitchell, 'Blake's Composite

Art', in *Blake's Visionary Forms Dramatic*, ed. David V. Erdman and John E. Grant, pp. 57–81. Mitchell regards the relation as habitually disjunctive (p. 62), and Kroeber finds that Blake's visual perspective forces us 'to reconsider how and why we attribute to our perceptions characteristics which are not "objectively" in what we see' (p. 15). It seems worth pointing out that great caution is appropriate in using David V. Erdman's *The Illuminated Blake*, which describes definitively items in the designs which might be thought to be deliberately ambiguous.

49. Ronald L. Grimes, 'Time and Space in Blake's major Prophecies', in *Blake's Sublime Allegory: Essays on 'The Four Zoas', 'Milton', 'Jerusalem'* ed. Stuart Curran and Joseph Anthony Wittreich Jnr., pp. 59–81, has this to say of 'The Four Zoas':

> We do not see Tharmas fall. He has already fallen, so we never see an Edenic beginning into which division intrudes . . . Blake does not begin his poem at the beginning, nor does the image of an undifferentiated or primordial unity ever occur . . . There is no Innocence—Experience—Return-to-Innocence sequence. Instead the sequence is Experience—(Remembrance of Innocence)—Brotherhood (pp. 72, 73, 75).

This is exactly the scheme which I would wish to apply to the lyrics.

50. Kathleen Raine, *Blake and Tradition*, Bollingen Series, 2 vols., I, 14–19, finds that the poem demonstrates the Swedenborgian doctrine that God can only be known in human form. Compare Erdman, *Prophet Against Empire*, p. 115; S. Foster Damon, *William Blake: His Philosophy and Symbols*, p. 271; and Stanley Gardner, *Blake*, p. 80. D. C. Gillham, in his *Blake's Contrary States: The 'Songs of Innocence and of Experience' as Dramatic Poems*, pp. 91–1, and also in his later *William Blake*, p. 101, regards the poems as properly more 'simple' than they tend to appear to us, as does John Holloway, *Blake: the Lyric Poetry*, pp. 27–8. This latter sort of argument, that any complications we discover are to be at once discounted as the results of our fallen minds, seems to me the most inhibiting of all. It cuts out the working through of pluralities and possibilities which always bears fruit with Blake's poetry. The complexities are specific and foreseen, and have a purpose, involving what Hegel called "the seriousness, the suffering, the patience, and the labour of the negative" (*Phenomenology of Mind*, p. 81). E. D. Hirsch Jnr., at least (*Innocence and Experience*, p. 187), has puzzled over a possible causal connection between the child's weeping and the disappearance of the vapour, and Robert F. Gleckner, *The Piper and the Bard: A Study of William Blake*, pp. 99–100, finds it to be crucial to the boy's chances of salvation that he does not find the father.

51. Some evidence for the 'antithetical' reading of the plates is provided by the treatment of copy W, the Jebb-Forster copy, in the library of King's College, Cambridge. In the first plate there is noticeable overpainting in the text, and in the first stanza, reading the words marked out by overpainting produces the sequence 'Father father . . . O do not w . . . Speak . . . or else I shall be lost.' I am attracted by the notion that Blake might have seen the chance to speak forth a negative reading by the use of this technique. The explanation will not fit the second stanza, however, where the selection of words, or parts of words, for such overpainting, seems to be random, and where certain letters are picked out by shadowing rather than overpainting effects. The second plate has no overpaint-

ing, but the use of gold striations emanating from *behind* the hat /halo /solar form around the adult's head does seem to indicate that the figures are leaving the source of light behind them. All the plates in this copy are contained within 'frames' painted around their edges; the frame on the first 'Little Boy' plate is very 'open', whilst that around the second is firmly 'closed' and contained, with no breaks in its borders. Copy W was Blake's personal copy.

52. I am being slightly dogmatic here, but error may be productive of truth. I tend to see the design dialectically, with the adult restraining the child, and the child fathering, or giving birth to, the man. Gillham, *Blake's Contrary States*, p. 150, argues that the earlier plate speaks for a generous relationship of adult to child, wherein the piper 'does not have to contend with a clumsy, grasping self' (i.e. in himself). In his *William Blake*, p. 43, he sees the first plate as an emblem of free communication, and the second representing contact with no communication. Erdman, *The Illuminated Blake*, pp. 70– 1, notes that the two figures are looking at each other in the first plate, and at us in the second. This would fit my argument for the two 'Little Boy' poems as descriptive of the passage out of potential innocence into experience.

53. Blake does inscribe his own name directly under this figure; indeed, the strangely solid background to the legend 'The Author & Printer W. Blake' might be seen as a coffin or sepulchre, upon which the group of figures is seated (to prevent, or try to prevent, resurrection?). It certainly invites contrast with the more common image of water running along the bottoms of many of the 'Innocence' plates (materialism perhaps, but also movement—into or out of?—Innocence). Of course, Blake being Blake, we are not allowed to hypostatise self-images every time we see the author's name on a title plate, but they can be suggested from time to time. The point is, of course, that the eye altering alters all, and must be seen to do so. The 'bound figure', it must be said, does not appear in all copies.

54. Analogous to this whole question of loss and confusion, and its potentially positive implication (the reader in the text?), is Milton's 'Comus', which Blake illustrated. For some suggestions about Blake's possible interpretation of this masque, see Irene Tayler, 'Say First! What Mov'd Blake? Blake's "Comus" Designs and "Milton"', in ·*Blake's Sublime Allegory*, pp. 233– 58.

55. Thus Holloway, *Blake: The Lyric Poetry*, p. 15.

56. See Brian Wilkie, 'Blake's "Innocence and Experience", An Approach', *Blake Studies*, 6, ii (1975), 126; Gillham, *Blake's Contrary States*, p. 181, and *William Blake*, pp. 2– 5; and Hirsch, *Innocence and Experience*, p. 201.

57. Thus Wilden, *System and Structure*, p. 26:

As a sign or an icon exchanged in his parent's phantasies, the child becomes the equivalent of a WORD in somebody else's conversation . . . The child . . . is SPOKEN rather than allowed to speak.

Compare M. Merleau-Ponty, *The Prose of the World*, ed. Claude Lefort, trans. John O'Neill, p. 7:

. . . we never find among other people's words any that we have not put there ourselves. Communication is an appearance; it never brings us anything truly new.

We have already hinted at, and will discuss again, the idea that this insight was felt as a problem by Wordsworth. The point about a heuristic method is that it makes us aware of this implication in communication

58. This is noticed by Hirsch, *Innocence and Experience*, p. 201, when he mentions that the last line conveys 'the mother's foreknowledge of the sorrow of life'.

59. *The Works of Thomas Reid*, ed. Sir William Hamilton, 6th ed., p. 383. But Coleridge, in the context of this poem, protested (*Letters*, IV, 837) that 'a Babe two days old does not, cannot *smile*—and innocence and the very truth of Nature must go together.'

60. Compare Shelley's 'Queen Mab', *Poetical Works*, p. 776, on the fate of the child:

> It is bound
> Ere it has life: yea, all the chains are forged
> Long ere its being: all liberty and love
> And peace is torn from its defencelessness;
> Cursed from its birth, even from its cradle doomed
> To abjectness and bondage!

61. Jean H. Hagstrum, *William Blake, Poet and Painter. An Introduction to the Illuminated Verse*, p. 6, notes the 'dramatic ambiguity' added by this figure, connecting it to an annunciation. But it could be renunciation.

62. This must be what Martin K. Nurmi has in mind in his *William Blake*, p. 59:

> To end in the state of Experience would be to end in cynicism and perhaps despair. But in Blake's scheme there is a third state, that of wise Innocence, which synthesizes the first two. This is to be achieved only after the suffering that is an essential aspect of Experience . . . It is a state of 'organized' Innocence . . . a state in which the bitterness of Experience has been met, absorbed, and transcended.

63. Roger R. Easson, in his fine essay, 'William Blake and His Reader in "Jerusalem"' in *Blake's Sublime Allegory*, pp. 309–27, comments on the poet's offering of 'the end of a golden string' (Erd. 229, K. 716):

> Traditionally, the guide gives the end of the ball of string to the adventurer as he enters the confusion of the labyrinth. Here, however, Blake hands the reader the end of the string, which is unwound, indicating that the reader is in the depths of the labyrinth already (p. 314).

64. Compare Shelley again, in 'The Cloud', expressing a message which is often that of Blake's natural forms (lilies, clods of clay etc.):

> I am the daughter of Earth and Water,
> And the nursling of the Sky;
> I pass through the pores of the ocean and shores;
> I change, but I cannot die (*Poetical Works*, p. 600).

65. Compare *Samuel Taylor Coleridge: Shakespearean Criticism*, ed. T. M. Raysor, 2nd ed., 2 vols., II, 112.

CHAPTER 3

1. For general summaries, see Stephen K. Land, *From Signs to Propositions: The*

Concept of Form in Eighteenth Century Semantic Theory, and Hans Aarsleff, *The Study of Language in England, 1780–1860.*

2. For an account of the background to the nominalist/realist argument, see *The Encyclopaedia of Philosophy*, ed. Paul Edwards, entries on Hobbes, Roscelin, Ockham etc. The conceptualist alternative opines that the mind comes to its conceptual intuitions prior to any expression *in* language; but, as Stewart (*Works*, II, 202–3) says, 'in every case in which we extend our speculations beyond individuals, language is not only a useful auxiliary, but is the sole instrument by which they are carried on.' See also II, 161, 185ff.; III, 96f.; Brown, *Lectures*, II, 495f.

3. See also *Letters*, II, 698; V, 228; *Aids to Reflection*, p. xi; and Appleyard, pp. 80–2. For other discussions, see Henry Home, Lord Kames, *Elements of Criticism*, 6th ed., 2 vols., I, 426; Beattie, *Works*, VI, 3–4; Reid, *Works*, p. 117f. See also Locke, *Essay*, Bk. III, ch. IX, 21; and John Fearn, *An Essay on Consciousness*, 2nd ed., p. 97. The Neoplatonic approach, of course, accepted and utilised the gap between word and object; see James Harris, *Hermes: or, a Philosophical Enquiry Concerning Language and Universal Grammar*, pp. 314, 333, 336–7, etc. As Shelley comments (*Complete Works*, VII, 109), there is 'a principle within the human being, and perhaps within all sentient beings, which acts otherwise than in the lyre, and produces not melody, alone, but harmony, by an internal adjustment of the sounds or motions thus excited to the impressions which excite them.'

4. *A Course of Lectures on Dramatic Art and Literature*, trans. John Black, 2 vols., II, 135. This lapse was regarded as something of a fortunate fall, and the Chinese language, conceived as exactly one which seeks to identify word and object, was usually seen as the emblem of sterility, conservatism, and confusion. See, e.g., Shelley, *Complete Works*, VII, 54; and *Poetical Works*, p. 447; William Warburton, *Works*, 7 vols., II, 399; Joseph Priestley, *A Course of Lectures on the Theory of Language and Universal Grammar*, p. 31f.; Lord Monboddo, *Of the Origin and Progress of Language*, 6 vols., II, 426f.; Hegel, *The Philosophy of History*, trans. J. Sibree, pp. 135–6; *Hegel's Philosophy of Mind*, trans. William Wallace and A. V. Miller, p. 216.

5. *Lectures 1795 On Politics and Religion*, ed. Lewis Patton and Peter Mann, *The Collected Works of Samuel Taylor Coleridge*, Bollingen Series LXXV, p. 94.

6. See my account of metaphor, below. It should be said, however, that there is a very important aspect of Romantic aesthetics which insists on our beholding 'at once the sign and the thing signified' (Shelley, *Poetical Works*, p. 492). Thus the 'symbol' for Coleridge functions as the perfect communicative mechanism wherein the sign *is* intrinsically a whole-in-part of the thing it signifies or instantiates. As he puts it in *Lay Sermons*, ed. R. J. White, *The Collected Works of Samuel Taylor Coleridge*, Bollingen Series, LXXV, p. 29, symbols are 'consubstantial with the truths, of which they are the *conductors*'. The symbol 'always partakes of the Reality which it renders intelligible; and while it enunciates the whole, abides itself as a living part in that Unity, of which it is the representative' (p. 30). The appeal of this model, which appears to contradict the common Coleridgean discrimination between means and ends, illustration and actuality, is based on its facility for *determinate* communication, on which he depends for his most deeply held ideas; see, e.g., the remarks on Christian ritual (*Aids to Reflection*, p. 17). As the symbol is within what it represents, so to understand the

symbol is to stand within what is represented; to behold is to become. Thinking of Blake's use of the same image, it is worth pointing out that Coleridge *must* reserve the symbol for those ideas he endorses absolutely. The same mechanism applied to habitual perception would produce image-worship, or materialism (again, see the account of metaphor, below). For an account of the symbol in the Romantic context, see Hans-Georg Gadamer, *Truth and Method*, pp. 63–80. For Coleridge on the 'symbol', see Appleyard, pp. 236–8; and J. Robert Barth, S. J., *Coleridge and Christian Doctrine*, pp. 20–2.

7. *The Letters of William and Dorothy Wordsworth: The Early Years, 1787–1805*, ed. E. de Selincourt, 2nd ed., rev. Chester L. Shaver, p. 684. The letter is printed also in Coleridge, *Letters*, II, 666. Compare Coleridge, *Biographia*, II, 39–40:

> The best part of human language, properly so called, is derived from reflection on the acts of the mind itself.

For Shelley, the independence of language from things is precisely its virtue as an expressive medium, it being 'arbitrarily produced by the imagination', having 'relation to thoughts alone', and therefore obtruding less material distraction 'between conception and expression' (*Complete Works*, VII, 113).

8. See Stephen K. Land, 'The Silent Poet: An Aspect of Wordsworth's Semantic Theory', *Univ. of Toronto Quarterly*, 42 (1973), 157–69. Compare David Perkins, *Wordsworth and the Poetry of Sincerity*, pp. 84–107; and *The Prelude*, XII, 270f.

9. See Land, *From Signs to Propositions*, p. 38; Burke, *Philosophical Enquiry*, p. 172.

10. Compare Diderot, *Oeuvres Complètes*, I, 369.

11. Thus Rousseau, in *Jean-Jacques Rousseau, 'Essay on the Origin of Languages', Johann Gottfried Herder, 'Essay on the Origin of Language'*, trans. John H. Moran and Alexander Gode, pp. 21–2:

> Writing, which would seem to crystallize language, is precisely what alters it. It changes not the words but the spirit, substituting exactitude for expressiveness. Feelings are expressed in speaking, ideas in writing. In writing, one is forced to use all the words according to their conventional meaning. But in speaking, one varies the meaning by varying one's tone of voice . . .

He goes on to specify the vagueness of written language: (p.22n.)

> There really is an equivocation which would be eliminated by a vocative mark. The same equivocation is found in irony, when it is not made manifest by accent.

It is exactly this equivocation which, I would argue, is brought to the front in Romantic poetics with the stress upon the dramatic form, and the division of the poet and the speaker; this is discussed in my next chapter.

Compare Hegel on the symbolic status of the sacrament, *Early Theological Writings*, p. 251:

> This return may perhaps in this respect be compared with the thought which in the written word becomes a thing and which recaptures its subjectivity out of an object, out of something lifeless, when we read. The simile would be more striking if the written word were read away, as if by being understood it vanished as a thing.

Hegel, in at least one of his voices, that expressed in *Lectures on the History of Philosophy*, trans. E. S. Haldane, 3 vols., III, 204, felt that

> speech is the pure existence of spirit; it is a thing which when once heard goes back within itself.

For an account of Hegel on speech, see Daniel J. Cook, *Language in the Philosophy of Hegel*, esp. pp. 122–·4, 131–4, 180–1.

12. Citations of the German, which I have made only when they seemed necessary, are from *Sämtliche Werke*, hrsg. G. Lasson (-J. Hoffmeister), 30 vols., incomplete (Leipzig, 1928–). This reference is to II, 363.

13. Trans. Michael Bullock, in *The True Voice of Feeling: Studies in English Romantic Poetry*, ed. Herbrt Read, pp. 335, 336, 342. For the German, see *Werke*, supp. vol. III, 404, 405, 410. Compare Schiller, *Aesthetic Education*, p. 129:

> Thus it is only through limits that we attain to reality, only through *negation* or exclusion that we arrive at *position* or real affirmation, only through the surrender of our unconditional determinability that we achieve determination.

See also Robert Gleckner, 'Romanticism and the Self-Annihilation of Language', *Criticism*, 18 (1976), 173–89.

14. Thus Coleridge, *Letters*, V, 48:

> Christ must become Man—but he cannot become *us*, except as far as we become *him*—& this we cannot do but by *assimilation*: and assimilation is a *vital real* act, not a notional or merely intellective one.

In Blake's myth, becoming what one beholds is an essential stage on the road to redemption, albeit a painful one when experienced from within the fallen world which is based on division (see, e.g., Erd. 215, K. 701). It is also a gesture against the tyrant eye, which tries to hold things at a distance within the trap of perspective. The Furies in Shelley's 'Prometheus Unbound' take their shape from the beholder's eye else they are nothing, and it is through them that Prometheus begins to discover community:

> Methinks I grow like what I contemplate,
> And laugh and stare in loathsome sympathy (*Poetical Works*, p. 218).

One of the major theoretical articulations of this assimilation was the sense of the importance of love, in the broadest sense, which for Coleridge 'transforms the souls into a conformity with the object loved' (N 189). For a full discussion, see Anthony John Harding, *Coleridge and the Idea of Love*.

15. As noted by C. A. F. Kluge, *Versuch einer Darstellung des animalischen Magnetismus als Heilsmittel*, 2nd ed., p. 276.

16. Noted by Michael Kirkham, 'Innocence and Experience in Wordsworth's "The Thorn"', *Ariel*, 5, i (1974), 66–80; p. 71.

17. For the latter, see Coleridge, *Aids to Reflection*, p. 223; Hegel, *Phenomenology of Mind*, p. 533.

18. See J. H. Muirhead, 'How Hegel Came to England', *Mind*, 36 (1927), 423–7, according to whom the first English translation was not until 1855.

19. See also Monboddo, *Origin and Progress of Language*, III, 41; Harris, *Hermes*, pp. 281–82.

20. *Oeuvres Complètes*, I, 350:

> Peu à peu on s'est accoutumé à croire que ces noms représentaient des êtres réels; on a regardé les qualités sensibles comme de simples accidents, et l'on s'est imaginé que l'adjectif était réellement subordonné au substantif, quoique le substantif ne soit proprement rien, et que *l'adjectif soit tout.*

21. *J. G. Hamann, Sämtliche Werke*, hrsg. J. Nadler, 6 vols. II, 59:

> Du führst einen Namen, und brauchst keinen Beweis *Deines* Daseyns.

Priestley (*Lectures,* p. 50), Stewart (*Works*, IV, 32) and Blair (*Lectures*, I, 176– 77) were all of the opinion that nouns were formed before verbs in the origin of language. Herder, however, *Herders Sämmtliche Werke*, hrsg. B. Suphan, 33 vols., XI, 227, opined that verbs, as the active principle within language, were prior to nouns:

> A noun only ever represents the thing as dead: the verb sets it in action, and excites feeling, for the thing is indeed itself inspired with spirit
> (Ein Nomen stellt immer nur die Sache todt dar: das Verbum setzt sie in Handlung, diese erregt Empfindung, denn sie ist selbst gleichsam mit Geist beseelet).

See also *J. G. Herder: Sprachphilosophische Schriften*, hrsg. E. Heintel, p. 199. There are other discussions by A. W. Schlegel, *Kritische Schriften und Briefe*, hrsg. E. Lohner, 7 vols., II, 242; and by Adam Smith, 'Considerations Concerning the First Formation of Languages', appended to *The Theory of Moral Sentiments*, 4th ed., p.460. For general critical accounts of the debate, see Eric A. Blackall, *The Emergence of German as a Literary Language, 1700–75*, esp. pp. 451–81; and Michel Foucault, *The Order of Things*, pp. 92–6.

22. Thus I cannot agree with Geoffrey H. Hartman, 'Wordsworth, Inscription, and Romantic Nature Poetry', in *From Sensibility to Romanticism: Essays Presented to Frederick A. Pottle*, ed. Harold Bloom and Frederick W. Hilles, p. 412 n. 13, that this poem belongs to a genre 'in which naming is a joyfully spontaneous act that almost escapes elegiac implications'. My own reading is more in line with his opinions as expressed in other contexts; in, for example, *Wordsworth's Poetry*, pp. 125–35, 149, etc.

23. Compare also the first poem of this series, 'It was an April Morning' (*Poetical Works*, II, 111–12), which beautifully balances the paradigm of continual creation and the implied displacement of the memory, 'Alive to all things and forgetting all' (l. 19), with the antithetical desire towards naming and commemoration. This poem again enacts the tendency to possession and its informed withdrawal, with its speaker modifying also the potential fixity of the name; he settles for the hope or fantasy that two or three among the local shepherds *might* remember the name 'EMMA'S DELL' after he has departed this life. The recourse, be it noted, is strictly to the oral rather than the written tradition, which of course offers us a paradox in the writing of the poem itself.

24. Leslie Tannenbaum, 'Blake's Art of Crypsis: "The Book of Urizen" and Genesis', *Blake Studies*, 5, i (1972), 158. See also Robert F. Gleckner, 'Most Holy Forms of Thought: Some Observations on Blake and Language', *ELH*, 41 (1974) 555–77, esp. pp. 556–7. Some hints about Blake's attitude to the word

can be gleaned from J. Walter Nelson, 'Blake's Diction—An Amendatory Note', *Blake Studies*, 7, ii (1974), 167–75.

25. Norman Nathan, *Prince William B.: The Philosophical Conceptions of William Blake*, pp. 44–5, suggests 'Ur-reason' meaning 'original reason'; Warren Stevenson, *Divine Analogy: A Study of the Creation Motif in Blake and Coleridge*, p. 90, notes 'a possible pun with "your eyes on" ' . I do not find that the conclusions of Francis Wood Metcalf, 'Reason and "Urizen": The Pronunciation of Blakean Names', *Blake Newsletter*, 21 (1972), 17–18, which try to establish a definitive pronunciation from the evidence of metrical patternings, are in any way definitive.

26. See, especially, Morris Eaves, 'The Title Page of "The Book of Urizen"', in *William Blake: Essays in Honour of Sir Geoffrey Keynes*, ed. Morton D. Paley and Michael Phillips, pp. 225–30; also Erdman, *The Illuminated Blake*, p. 183.

27. Erdman, *Prophet Against Empire*, p. viii, suggests that the 'choice of the name Los (loss) fo his visionary prophet (profit) in a world of Paradise *Lost*' might not be accidental; Northrop Frye, in *The Divine Vision: Studies in the Poetry and Art of William Blake*, ed. Vivian de Sola Pinto, p. 100–1, suggests a synonym with the mediaeval usage 'loos' = 'fame'.

28. See Raymond Lister, *Infernal Methods: A Study of William Blake's Art Techniques*; Anthony Blunt, 'The First Illuminated Books', in *Blake*, ed. Frye, pp. 127–41; Robert N. Essick, 'Blake and the Traditions of Reproductive Engraving', *Blake Studies*, 5, i (1972), 59–103; John Wright, 'Toward Recovering Blake's Relief-Etching Process', *Blake Newsletter*, 26 (1974), 32–9, and 'Blake's Relief-Etching Method', *ibid.*, 36 (1976), 94–114.

29. For a recent and interesting discussion of this now familiar insight, see Mollyanne Marks, 'Structure and Irony in Blake's "The Book of Urizen"', *Studies in English Literature*, 15 (1975), 579–90, who finds that the 'putting together' is but a dubious possibility in this work. There is another ironic version of diety in Enion's lament

> I have chosen the serpent for a councellor & the dog
> for a schoolmaster to my children (Erd. 318, K. 290).

30. For the same use of 'confusion', see Shelley, *Poetical Works*, pp. 423, 479. For some thoughts on the names 'Adonais' and 'Demogorgon' see, respectively, Earl R. Wasserman, *Shelley: A Critical Reading*, p. 464f.; Lawrence John Zillman, *Shelley's 'Prometheus Unbound': A Variorum Edition*, p. 309f.

31. See also Erd. 343, K. 317.

32. Thus Wasserman, *Shelley*, p. 220, contends that 'the poem attains its final cause, although not its final effect, simply by coming into existence; and the poetic transaction involves only the poet and his poem, not an audience'.

33. *Thomas Taylor the Platonist: Selected Writings*, ed. Kathleen Raine and George Mills Harper, p. 460. For Coleridge on the 'word', see Owen Barfield, 'Coleridge's Enjoyment of Words', in *Coleridge's Variety*, ed. J. B. Beer, pp. 204–18, and Prickett's account, *The Poetry Growth*, p. 109f., of the double uses of key words in 'Dejection'.

Taylor's comment hints at a very familiar connection in the period, that between poetry and hieroglyph. See Hamann, *Werke*, II, 74; Diderot, *Oeuvres Complètes*, I, 374; and, most comprehensively of all, G. H. von Schubert, *Die Symbolik des Traumes*, pp. 6, 14, 15, 24, etc. For the hieroglyph as demanding a heuristic response, see Warburton, *Works*, II, 387ff.; Kames, *Elements*, II, 279; and for a general account, see Liselotte Dieckmann, *Hieroglyphics: The History of a Literary Symbol*. This metaphor of the poem as hieroglyph, well expressed by Francis Jeffrey in his review of Alison for the *Edinburgh Review*, 18, no. 35 (May, 1811), p. 30, as demanding that meaning be 'eked out by the fancy and the knowledge of the reader' and serving rather to 'rouse the imagination to a discovery, than enlighten it by a revelation', tended to emphasise the gap between poetic and conventional statement. Eighteenth-century opinion had tended to regard the alphabet as a successor to and improvement upon the hieroglyph; see. e.g., David Hartley, *Observations on Man, His Frame, His Duty, and His Expectations*, 2 vols. in 1, I, 297f.; Monboddo, *Origin and Progress of Language*, II, 253f.; Godwin, *Enquiry*, I, 116f.; and Blair, *Lectures*, I, 158f. On the other side, see Hartley, *Observations*, I, 308; and Beattie, *Works*, II, 115. One of the most sophisticated versions of the argument is that of Hegel, *Philosophy of Mind*, pp. 215−17. Though committed enough to a concept of philosophy as active participation, Hegel is suspicious of the chaotic variability of analysis which the hieroglyph is able to produce, and he sees it as the symptom of a stationary, unprogressive civilisation; this is another instance of the problems which a totally 'heuristic' communication must cause for the social contact, and for the communication of even partially determinate messages.

34. See, e.g., George Campbell, *The Philosophy of Rhetoric*, 2 vols., II, 23; Blair, *Lectures*, I, 281−3; Kames, *Elements*, I, 19−20; and Monboddo, *Origin and Progress of Language*, II, 354.

35. See also *Letters*, VI, 638. For other discussions, see Richard Payne Knight, *An Analytical Enquiry into the Principles of Taste*, 4th ed., p. 130; Condillac, *An Essay on the Origin of Human Knowledge*, trans. Thomas Nugent, p. 264f.; Bonnet, *Essai de Psychologie*, p. 41; Diderot, *Oeuvres*, I, 364f.; Kames, *Elements*, II, 49f.; Stewart, *Works*, IV, 43f.; Herder, *Werke*, I, 191; and A. W. Schlegel, *Krit. Schriften*, II, 268.

36. I shall not therefore spend any time demonstrating the more overt and well documented cases of syntactic ambiguities in the major poets. Wordsworth's uncertainty about whether he is taking things 'from within or from without' (*Letters: Middle Years*, Pt. I, p. 145) is often dramatised by omitting specifying punctuation; see, e.g., *The Prelude*, V, 44−46. Coleridge (*Biographia*, II, 111), indeed, complained of 'faulty and equivocal syntax' in Wordsworth. See, especially, F. R. Leavis, *Revaluation: Tradition and Development in English Poetry*, pp. 156−8; Donald Davie, *Articulate Energy: An Inquiry into the Syntax of English Poetry*, p. 106f.; Colin C. Clarke, *Romantic Paradox: An Essay on the Poetry of Wordsworth*; Empson, *The Structure of Complex Words*, pp. 289−305; Lindenberger, *On Wordsworth's 'Prelude'*, pp. 295−9; and Perkins, *Wordsworth and the Poetry of Sincerity*, p. 209f. There is a recent critical exchange which bears upon the subject; see Michael Riffaterre, 'Interpretation and Descriptive Poetry: A Reading of Wordsworth's "Yew Trees"', *New Literary History*, 4 (1973), 229−56, and Geoffrey Hartman, 'The Use and Abuse of Structural Analysis: Riffaterre's Interpretation of Wordsworth's "Yew Trees"', *New Literary History*, 7 (1975), 165−89.

For negative valuations of the Shelleyan syntax, which speak clearly of their own values, see Donald Davie, *Purity of Diction in English Verse*, pp. 133−59; and Leavis, *Revaluation* p. 203f. The beginnings of a reply may be found in Richard

Harter Fogle's 'The Abstractness of Shelley', in *Shelley: A Collection of Critical Essays*, ed. George M. Ridenour, pp. 13—29. Earl R. Wasserman, *The Subtler Language: Critical Readings of Neo-Classic and Romantic Poems*, p. 188, puts the case for Shelley's poetry that

> our failure to find coherent meaning in it and the resulting conspicuous contempt in which it is held by modern critics are the result of a failure to recognize that it is internally constitutive not only of its own reality, but also of the vocabulary and syntax of that reality.

See also Hayden, *Romantic Bards*, p. 400.

For an account of the powerful disjunctions in Coleridge's poetic style, see Davie, *Purity of Diction*, pp. 122—32. See also L. M. Grow, *The Prose Style of Samuel Taylor Coleridge*, esp. ch. 3, 'The Syntactic Labyrinth', pp. 50—69; and Hayden, *Romantic Bards*, p. 131.

37. At risk of being pedantic, a note on the question of editions seems called for here, as it bears upon my choice of a 'standard' edition, a decision which can now be put into the context of the argument. There are undoubtedly cases where an editor must face, as Mrs Shelley faced in the material which became *Posthumous Poems*, 'so confused a mass, interlined and broken into fragments, so that the sense could only be deciphered and joined by guesses which might seem rather intuitive than founded on reasoning' (*Poetical Works*, p. 676). But to launch into the texture of a 'breath-suspending song' armed with full stops, commas, and a red pen does not seem the best way to do justice to this poet. Donald H. Reiman, 'Editing Shelley', in *Editing Texts of the Romantic Period*, ed. John D. Baird, pp. 27—45, has taken F. L. Jones to task for failing to recognise on occasions that Shelley makes sense, albeit difficult sense. Such warnings seem much more apt when directed at the new Oxford edition, two volumes of which have so far appeared. Those better qualified than myself have passed opinions on this enterprise; see, for example, Timothy Webb, *TLS* 3867, p. 493. To add one small voice to the chorus of dissent, what can we make of an editorial opinion which finds that the poet of 'Alastor' has 'simply allowed grammatical logic to be carried away by the sound of words' (Rogers, *Complete Poetical Works*, II, 336), or which implies that the textual decisions about 'Hymn to Intellectual Beauty' should be left to 'anybody who can intelligently read a poem aloud', involving as it does the removal of 'a series of false syntactical parallelisms' (p. 344)? Shelley was concerned, I think, that his readers should 'recreate' his poems; but the next generation of readers may not be faced with his poems, but those of his editor. Thus I have decided to use the Hutchinson edition, that scholar being, in the words of Charles H. Taylor Jnr., *The Early Collected Editions of Shelley's Poems: A Study in the History and Transmission of the Printed Text*, p. 45, 'the most conservative of the Shelley editors', who 'depends the least upon the secondary editions and therefore makes the fewest mistakes'.

38. I need say nothing about one of my favourite examples, since the case has been very well put by Jim S. Borck, 'Blake's "The Lamb": The Punctuation of Innocence', *Tennessee Studies in Literature*, 19 (1974), 163—75.

39. I cannot agree with Holloway here, when he says (p. 62), that the sort of 'verbal ingenuity' which this concern reflects 'is what the whole diction and rhythm and narrative line of the poem reject'. Rejection usually means repression, and any meanings to be excluded must be actively excluded, not simply ignored.

40. Gillham's readings seem to be substantially in agreement with my own here; see *Blake's Contrary States*, pp. 226—7; and *William Blake*, p. 99. Harold Bloom, *Blake's Apocalypse: A Study in Poetic Argument* pp. 32—3, sees a dark hint in that 'the Shepherd inspires a confidence in his flock which is entirely dependent upon his actual presence'.It has been pointed out to me that shepherds 'really do' follow their sheep, since the sheep always know how to find the best pastures; but even if this be admitted into the scope of the poem it does not preclude Blake's play on the metaphor of supervision. Perhaps it is the metaphor which is out of key with the actual practice of shepherds.

41. Taylor, *The Early Collected Editions*, p. 47, argues that it was customary for matters of punctuation and spelling to be left to the printer; but Blake handled his own production from start to finish, and Shelley operates as often through the oversupply of punctuation as through its absence. Borck, 'Blake's "The Lamb"', p. 165, regards Romantic punctuation as being part of a heuristic function:

> Eighteenth-century punctuation theory . . . was modified by the awareness that the system of notation was inherently not precise and that the notation's primary function was to assist a reader's interpretive understanding; the reader of a work would himself interpret the points in a manner relative to his own perception of the artist's intention.

Wicksteed, *Blake's Innocence and Experience*, p. 68, is somewhere near this point of view when he argues that 'a full stop means a pause and has nothing to do with grammatical construction'. Clearly, the question is a crucial one. Donald Davie, *Articulate Energy*, pp. 80—4, constructs a careful argument showing that 'Blake makes great play with the difference between colon and semi-colon' (p. 84) in his poem 'The Human Abstract', but unfortunately quotes a normalised version of the text which differs from that in the Keynes facsimile edition (*Songs*, 47). For some remarks on spasmodic punctuation in German prose, see Thalmann, p. 63; and Blackall, p. 460.

42. See M. H. Abrams, 'Structure and Style in the Greater Romantic Lyric', in *From Sensibility to Romanticism*, ed. Bloom and Hilles, pp. 527—60; and Colin C. Clarke, *Romantic Paradox*.

43. See, especially, W. J. T. Mitchell, 'Poetic and Pictorial Imagination in Blake's "The Book of Urizen"', *Eighteenth-Century Studies*, 3 (1969), 83—107; Gleckner, 'Most Holy Forms of Thought'; and Marks, 'Structure and Irony'. Marks has an interesting perspective on the issue when she argues that a change in the syntax occurs within the work itself at the moment of Los/Blake's own implication in the fall; at this point synthesised complexity is seen to turn into simple narrative. (p. 585)

44. So Diderot, as a gesture of disturbance at the opening of his short dialogue 'Ceci n'est pas un Conte' (*Oeuvres*, V, 311), catches us out by not locating the first statement in the authoritative voice which seems to be indicated. Only after a page or so does it become apparent that the initial 'I begin' does not mark the point *after* which we should be paying critical attention, but is itself part of the dialogue and spoken by a persona whose authority is not indubitable. In much the same style, *The Paradox of Acting*, trans. W. H. Pollock, also begins with a rejoinder (followed by a question) to a statement which is outside the text (for the French, see *Oeuvres*, VIII, 361).

45. *Omniana*, ed. Robert Gittings, p. 29.
46. As, for example, by Elisabeth Schneider, *Coleridge, Opium, and 'Kubla Khan'*, p. 4.
47. Marshall Suther, *Visions of Xanadu*, p. 196, notes that

> Before finishing the first five-line section, we shall have encountered all but one of the elemental images of the poem as well as the predominating personal image, that of Kubla, and shall, in a sense, have read the whole poem.

48. I follow the text as printed in *Poetical Works*, pp. 295–8, but adopt the observation of J. B. Beer, *Coleridge the Visionary*, p. 206, that the 1816 edition prints, as the sense demands, a break after line 30.
49. Schneider, p. 287, notes that 'deprivation haunts the language . . . The whole poem oscillates between giving and taking away, bright affirmation and sunless negation.'
50. This is to depart from Schneider's bipartite reading, when she argues that the poem

> reads like a fragment with a postscript added at some later time when it has become obvious to the poet that he cannot finish the piece (p. 247).

The reading of George Watson, *Coleridge the Poet*, p. 124, also divides the poem into two parts, but in a more subtle way which seems not incompatible with my own reading. He sees the first 36 lines as expressive of one sort of poetry, which we do have before us, and the rest of the poem as suggestive of a species of poetry which we do not have, but whose effects are explained to us—madness and visionary exactitude.

51. The case is too well-known to need more than the briefest indication. Beer, in *Coleridge the Visionary*, pp. 207–10, gives a fascinating assortment of clues, including the use, in the *Zohars*, of 'Beth' for 'cavern'; hence Alph-Beth, river-cavern. Warren Stevenson, *Divine Analogy*, p. 308, cites an interesting entry in William Holwell's *A Mythological, Etymological, and Historical Dictionary* (London, 1793), under the heading 'Alphi':

> An Oracle was so termed by the Amonians: and Alpha, the voice of God.

See also G. Wilson Knight, *The Starlit Dome: Studies in the Poetry of Vision*, p. 97. Coleridge himself was under the misapprehension that Kublai 'ordered letters to be invented for his people' (N 1281). Adding a pebble to the shoreline, how about 'Aleph' as 'ox' in Hebrew (N 2450), hence Oxus, eastern river, Alph?
52. On the processes of revision from the Crewe manuscript, see Fruman, pp. 342, 400; Beer, p. 210, notes 'ABBA' as a favourite Coleridgean palindrome, and builds a case for suggesting that

> The change from Amara to Abora thus adds to the Abyssinian paradise the further symbolism of the sun, the descending dove, and the revelation of divine Truth (p. 256).

It also adds the suggestion of a Latin pun, *Ab ore* = 'from the mouth', much of this poem being written in images of incantation; the Latin verb *orare* means 'to pray', and the noun *oratio* translates as 'speech' or 'language'.
53. Compare the famous metaphor of the 'rivers of the vale', *Biographia*, I, 166.

54. Edward E. Bostetter, *The Romantic Ventriloquists: Wordsworth, Coleridge, Shelley, Keats, Byron*, p. 84.

55. Owen Barfield, *What Coleridge Thought*, p. 36, argues in the same spirit that 'the apprehension of polarity is itself *the basic act of imagination*, . . . the reader must be called on, not to think about imagination, but to use it'.

CHAPTER 4

1. *Characteristicks of Men, Manners, Opinions, Times*, 3 vols., I, 201.

2. For the influence of the dialogue model on Shelley, see Wasserman, *Shelley*, p. 15, and Norman Thurston, 'Author, Narrator, and Hero in Shelley's "Alastor"', *Studies in Romanticism*, 14 (1975), 119–31. One of the most sophisticated examples of the dialogue operating in the cause of an author's elision of his own presence—and it is to be regretted that I have not the space to analyse it—is Fichte's *Die Bestimmung des Menschen*, trans. by Roderick M. Chisholm as *The Vocation of Man*.

   For an account of the presence in later eighteenth-century theories of language of theoretical analogues to the 'dramatic' mode in poetic writing, see Murray Cohen, *Sensible Words: Linguistic Practice in England, 1640–1785*, pp. 105–36.

3. Calvin E. Young, *A Critical Explication of Irony as a Thematic Structure*, defines as 'ironic' the gap which the reader of the modern novel is encouraged to establish between himself and the characters, in order that he shall not repeat their egotistic appropriations of meanings from their world, in mistaking the part for the whole. This model, roughly transferred, would be of use in describing Wordsworth's irony.

4. The most famous critical reading of the poem is probably still that of Robert Penn Warren, 'A Poem of Pure Imagination: An Experiment in Reading', in *Selected Essays*, pp. 198–305. The case against such a rigid approach to the 'symbol' has been well put by Edward E. Bostetter, 'The Nightmare World of "The Ancient Mariner"', in *The Ancient Mariner and Other Poems, A Casebook*, ed. Alun R. Jones and William Tydeman, pp. 184–99, and by Humphry House, *Coleridge: The Clark Lectures, 1951–52*, pp. 84–113.

5. *Specimens of the Table Talk*, ed. H. N. Coleridge, 2 vols., 31 May 1830.

6. *Anima Poetae: From the Unpublished Note-Books of Samuel Taylor Coleridge*, ed. E. H. Coleridge, p. 19. There is an almost identical formulation at N 1016; see also N 383, 902. It is worth recalling Burke's arguments about the 'reasons in nature why the obscure idea, when properly conveyed, should be more affecting than the clear' (*A Philosophical Enquiry*, p. 61). See also Appleyard, pp. 86–93. I find myself wondering whether the famous passage at *Biographia*, I, 202, referring to a 'critical essay' which 'the reader will find prefixed to the poem of "The Ancient Mariner"', which is usually taken as an example of a promise left unfulfilled, might not rather be an ironical reference to the pseudo-objective marginal comments which have indeed been provided. The message being, then, that the reader who seeks for more than what has already been given can only be inviting the lapse into the doctrinaire and the language of description.

7. For what it is worth, Geoffrey Yarlott, *Coleridge and the Abyssinian Maid*, pp. 307–9, states that he can find no evidence of the excessive orthodoxy of Sara Fricker, and presents the passage as a deliberate posing on the poet's part.

8. In fact, these lines first appear, albeit rather esoterically, among the 'errata' to *Sibylline Leaves* (1817), whilst the poem as printed in that volume includes a much milder version (see *Poetical Works*, p. 101n.). The most careful account of this poem known to me, that of Albert S. Gérard, *English Romantic Poetry: Ethos, Structure, and Symbol in Coleridge, Wordsworth, Shelley, and Keats*, pp. 20–53, notes the disjunctive effect of these lines (p. 48), but I am unable to confirm his assertion that they first appear published with *Satyrane's Letters* in 1817; perhaps we may assume this as a misprint (p. 42). For an interesting manuscript version of lines 44–8, see H. W. Piper, *The Active Universe: Pantheism and the Concept of Imagination in the English Romantic Poets*, p. 43.

9. Harold Bloom, *Shelley's Mythmaking*, pp. 11–35, deals with this poem in the context of Shelley's companion piece, and seems to share my misgivings.

10. These are exactly the terms of the heuristic imperative in Friedrich Schlegel as understood by Victor Lange, 'Friedrich Schlegel's Literary Criticism', *Comparative Literature*, 7 (1955), 294:

> the ironic attitude which qualifies the *poet* to produce a construct of specific aesthetic validity enables the *critic*, not merely to recognize and judge this construct, but to perform a function that comprises and indeed transcends that of the poet. The critic illuminates the original exercise of the poet in a re-creative process and on a level where, as Schlegel says, he has brought himself to an understanding of understanding.

See also the accounts of 'The Thorn' by Gérard, *English Romantic Poetry*, p. 64f.; Carl Woodring, *Wordsworth*, p. 28; John F. Danby, *The Simple Wordsworth: Studies in the Poems, 1797–1807*, pp. 57–72; and, best of all, Stephen Maxfield Parrish, *The Art of the 'Lyrical Ballads'*, p. 97f., who makes the crucial observation that the 'events' of the poem might well exist only in the narrator's heightened imagination. For the sea captain as the apostle of the tyrant eye, see Hartman, *Wordsworth's Poetry*, p. 148. A discussion of the function of the narrator in *Lyrical Ballads* which is very close to my own argument is by Paul D. Sheats, *The Making of Wordsworth's Poetry, 1785–1798*, pp. 188–204.

11. Cf. *Prose*, III, 63, on the poet as treating things 'as they *seem* to exist to the *senses*, and to the *passions*'.

12. For an analogous process, see 'To Joanna' (*Poetical Works*, II, 112–14); in a note to this poem (p. 487), Wordsworth actually describes being unable to preserve his 'speaking' persona, and being 'caught in the trap of my own imagination'. See also Parrish, p. 29.

13. A view of Keats first endorsed by Woodhouse (see *Letters*, I, 389–90), and often since.

14. Jonathan Culler, *Structuralist Poetics: Structuralism, Linguistics, and the Study of Literature*, p. 200.

15. See, e.g., Schelling, *Werke*, II, 506, 508; Friedrich Schlegel, *Krit. Ausgabe*, XII, 288–89; Hegel, *Aesthetics: Lectures on Fine Art*, trans. T. M. Knox, p. 56.

16. See also Stewart, *Works*, II, 48, III, 23; Brown, *Lectures*, I, 193; and Hazlitt, *Works*, I, 71–2. On 'experience' as a necessary synthesis of concept and intuition, see Kant, *Pure Reason*, p. 193; Hazlitt, *Works*, II, 114; and Coleridge, *Letters*, IV, 875.

17. Coleridge, *Biographia*, I, 94; Friedrich Schlegel, *Krit. Ausgabe*, XVIII, 20–21; Kant, *Pure Reason*, p. 223. For a short general account of the epistemological

dimension in Romantic poetry, see Earl R. Wasserman, 'The English Romantics: The Grounds of Knowledge', *Studies in Romanticism*, 4 (1964), 17–34.

18. This comes to a head with Kant's inclusion of causality among the analogies of experience (*Pure Reason*, pp. 218–9), but the roots are deep in the eighteenth-century tradition. Locke had insisted on a distinction between ideas and things as they might be in themselves, thus locating causality as relational rather than essential (*Essay*, Bk. II, ch. VIII, 1–3, 7; ch. XXVI, 1), and Hume had defined the workings of cause and effect as 'beyond the reach of human understanding'; see *A Treatise of Human Nature*, ed. L. A. Selby-Bigge, Bk. I, pt. II, sect. 5, p. 64. See also pt. IV, sect. 5, p. 247.

19. Shelley, *Complete Works*, VII, 151; *Reid*, Works, pp. 158–9; Drummond, *Academical Questions*, pp. 185–6; Payne Knight, *Analytical Enquiry*, p. 264; Coleridge, *Biographia*, I, 85.

20. To do so would be to determine nothing less than a theory of creativity, and would involve a specification of the causal model whose disestablishment is here noted. It would be the assumption of a metacomment, a critical privilege which may yet in one way be a necessity; see p. 198 below.

21. Again, this is to anticipate, but it is perhaps necessary to point out that I am aware of the slippage whereby I have tended to describe the 'poet' as brought within the same frame of reference as the 'reader' and the 'characters' of the text. To be absolutely scrupulous, this would need rephrasing along these lines: the reader is led to posit this shared predicament as a way of dramatising his own involved isolation. The 'poet' is only ever, for the reader, the proxy of his own highest consciousness, the emblem cum ally of a metacomment which he is trying to preserve uncontaminated by primary level participation. The arguments I have put forward for the presence of poet/speaker distinctions which are not fully enacted, so that the personae come together again, *must* therefore involve the re-entry of the 'poet' with that of his reader into participation, since they are never properly separate. As I have said before, the subsuming of distanciation into participation coincides *exactly* with the descriptive problems faced by the critic, who, unless he opts for contextualist arguments of the 'constant conjunction' type, is allowed (can allow himself) no privileged standpoint outside his participation in the reading act. 'Poet' and reader, therefore, are engaged in mutually inventing one another, but always through the reader's consciousness. As Culler, *Structuralist Poetics*, p. 170, has put it, the 'poetic persona is a construct, a function of the language of the poem, but it none the less fulfils the unifying role of the individual subject, and even poems which make it difficult to construct a poetic persona rely for their effects on the fact that the reader will try to construct an enunciative posture.' Hence the irony whereby the exposition of an ethic of indeterminacy is continually involving me in the hypostatisation of a negatively 'wise' author—at the same time as, in Kierkegaardian fashion, I know that I cannot ever 'prove' him. See Paul de Man, *Blindness and Insight: Essays in the Rhetoric of Contemporary Criticism*, p. 141; and Walker Gibson, 'Authors, Speakers, and Mock Readers', *College English*, 11 (1950), 265–9.

22. As it does for Keats on top of Ben Nevis (*Complete Poems*, pp. 375–6), and, within a slightly different metaphor, for Byron's Manfred in his pact with the infernal powers; *Byron: Poetical Works*, ed. Frederick Page, 3rd ed. corrected by John Jump, p. 400.

23. For general accounts, see Cassirer, *Philosophy of the Enlightenment*, pp. 328–31; W. J. Hipple, *The Beautiful, the Sublime, and the Picturesque in Eighteenth Century British Aesthetic Theory*; and Samuel H. Monk, *The Sublime: A Study of Critical Theories in Eighteenth Century England*.

24. *The Critique of Judgement*, trans. James Creed Meredith, 2 vols. in one, I, 115. See also II, 89–93.

25. *The Letters of Percy Bysshe Shelley*, ed. F. L. Jones, 2 vols., I, 497.

26. Cf. the description of Vesuvius, *Letters*, II, 62f., and of the Apennines, wherein 'the imagination cannot find a home' (II, 18).

27. See also *Aids to Reflection*, pp. 165–6, 197, 228–9, and N 2509.

28. Cf. Schiller, *Aesthetic Education*, p. 77; Coleridge, *Biographia*, II, 258, and *Letters*, V, 388, 399.

29. See Schelling, *Werke*, II, 356; Coleridge, *Biographia*, I, 180.

30. See Reid, *Works*, pp. 111, 344; Beattie, *Works*, IV, 87.

31. See also *Aids to Reflection*, p. 136. For the distinction between will and volition, see *Letters*, VI, 986; *Philosophical Lectures*, p. 362; *Biographia*, I, 193–4: also Hazlitt, *Works*, I, 9f. Kant makes this discrimination central to his deduction of the moral law; see *Foundations of the Metaphysics of Morals*, trans. Lewis White Beck, pp. 7, 18; and the same translator's *Critique of Practical Reason*, p. 57. Coleridge, having questioned the identification of the will with the practical reason (N 1717), later comes to accept it (*Biographia*, I, 193). For the place of the will in Coleridge's theology, see the numerous comments by Barth (e.g. pp. 35–7, 86–9, 108f.); and James D. Boulger, *Coleridge as Religious Thinker*, pp. 127–40.

32. This is clearly enough an analogue of the reading process, which supposes, like the act of redemption,

> an Agent who can at once act *on* the Will as an exciting cause, *quasi ab extra*: and *in* the will, as the *condition* of its potential, and the *ground* of its actual, Being (*Aids to Reflection*, p. 329).

33. On the intangible origins of the will, see Hume, *Enquiries Concerning Human Understanding and Concerning the Principles of Morals*, ed. L. A. Selby-Bigge, 3rd ed. rev. P. H. Nidditch, I, sect. VII, pt. 1, par. 52; *Treatise*, Bk. II, pt. III, sect. 3, p. 413f. For other discussions, see Locke, *Essay*, Bk. II, ch. XXI, 16, 21, 31f.; Hartley, *Observations*, I, 371; Drummond, *Academical Questions*, pp. 11–20. The whole subject of the place of the will in Romantic thought has been dealt with by Michael G. Cooke, *The Romantic Will*; see esp. pp. 8–9, 13–29, 52–6, 76–144. Cooke's chapter on 'The Extremes of Self and System' (pp. 52–144) endorses my argument for the interdetermination of mind and world.

34. It is worth pointing out that, for Keats and Shelley, the vocabulary of 'will' is almost always employed in a derogatory sense, although of course they do not share the higher, Coleridgean formulation. I have argued for Keats's great 'Ode' as a rebuke to will-cum-wilfulness (see also Cooke, *The Romantic Will*, pp. 145–82), and Shelley also is adamant that poetry is outside the control of this faculty (*Complete Works*, VII, 135, 138). Whether 'Alastor' be read as a dramatised critique of Wordsworth, Coleridge, Shelley's own ego, or all three at once, it is certainly an investigation of solipsism, of reading oneself into nature. This may perhaps be related to the experience of the French Revolution and the gradual emergence of tyranny and empire, of which the villain of 'The Borderers' may

be reflective, as the anti-hero of Byron's 'Sardanapalus' is a retrospective alternative.

35. For memory as a basic ingredient in personal identity, see Diderot, *Oeuvres*, IX, 370; Brown, *Lectures*, I, 383; Locke, *Essay*, Bk. II, ch. X, 8; Rousseau, *Émile*, p. 246; Reid, *Works*, p. 345f.; Stewart, *Works*, II, 13; Coleridge, *Letters*, VI, 599.

36. See Prickett, *The Poetry of Growth*, ch. 5, 'Memory and Perception', pp. 120–46. Hartleian psychology, notoriously, explained the mind as a register wherein one idea is perpetually effacing another, thus challenging the memory from another angle, as simply inadequate for storing past experience. See *Observations*, I, 376, and Godwin, *Enquiry*, I, 411. Compare Locke, *Essay*, Bk. II, ch. X, 5, in a passage strangely prophetic of *The Prelude*:

> The Memory in some Men, 'tis true, is very tenacious, even to a Miracle: but yet there seems to be a constant decay of all our *Ideas*, even of those which are struck deepest, and in Minds the most retentive; so that if they be not sometimes renewed by repeated Exercise of the Senses, or Reflection on those kind of Objects, which at first occasions them, the Print wears out, and at last there remains nothing to be seen. Thus the *Ideas*, as well as Children, of our Youth, often die before us: And our Minds represent to us those Tombs, to which we are approaching; where though the Brass and Marble remain, yet the Inscriptions are effaced by time, and the Imagery moulders away.

37. For some account of Wordsworth's treatment of memory, see Christopher Salvesen, *The Landscape of Memory: A Study of Wordsworth's Poetry*, especially ch. 2, 'Self, Memory, and Sensuous Continuity', pp. 76–107. See also Lindenberger, *On Wordsworth's 'Prelude'*, p. 141f., who stresses the positive side of the case, which he sees as best expressed by 'such images as the dynamo and the powerhouse' (p. 182).

38. See also Erd. 107, 201, K. 496, 685.

39. See Peter F. Fisher, ed. Northrop Frye, *The Valley of Vision: Blake as Prophet and Revolutionary*, pp. 102–5, for other comments on the subject.

40. For Blake on the will, see Erd. 591, K. 89.

41. For a brief account, see Michel Foucault, *Madness and Civilization: A History of Insanity in the Age of Reason*, trans. Richard Howard, pp. 101–5. See also Hume, *Enquiries*, I, sect. XII, pt. 1, par. 119; Kant, *Pure Reason*, p. 139.

42. See Monboddo, *Ancient Metaphysics*, I, 427–28, II, 244; Beattie, *Works*, I, 17; Stewart, *Works*, II, 289f.; Coleridge, *Letters*, IV, 641; Erasmus Darwin, *Zoonomia: or, the Laws of Organic Life*, 3rd ed., 4 vols., I, 288f.; J. C. Spurzheim, *Observations on the Deranged Manifestations of the Mind, or Insanity*, p. 243.

43. *Encyclopédie, ou Dictionnaire Raisonné des Sciences, des Arts, et des Métiers*, 17 vols., XV, 355.

> L'imagination de la veille est une république policiée, où la voix du magistrat remet tout en ordre; l'imagination des *songes* est la même république dans l'état d'anarchie.

Cf. Godwin's formulation of anarchy as a transitional state, *Enquiry*, II, 367f. See also Hegel, *Philosophy of Mind*, p. 70; Hume, *Treatise*, Bk. I, pt. II, sect. 3, p. 35; Hartley, *Observations*, I, 378; Coleridge, *Letters*, II, 974; De Quincey, *The Works of Thomas De Quincey*, 3rd ed., 16 vols., I, 259.

44. The narrator of *The Prelude* finds that he has 'A little space of intermediate time' (VII, 65), only to turn it towards London, ironically the very environment which will, through its overdetermination of organisational motifs, convert an apparently ordered humanity into chaos. For an account of space and time as the co-ordinates which poetry must transgress, see Angus Fletcher, '"Positive Negation": Threshold, Sequence, and Personification in Coleridge', in *New Perspectives on Coleridge and Wordsworth: Selected Papers from the English Institute*, ed. Geoffrey Hartman, esp. pp. 137–41. See again Ronald L. Grimes, 'Time and Space in Blake's Major Prophecies', in *Blake's Sublime Allegory*, pp. 59–81.

45. See Hazlitt, *Works*, V, 3; Bonnet, *Essai de Psychologie*, pp. 362–3; Hartley, *Observations*, I, 383f.; Hegel, *Philosophy of Mind*, p. 125; Monboddo, *Ancient Metaphysics*, II, 235; Spurzheim, *Observations*, p. 72.

46. As it is, perhaps, for Nathan Drake, *Literary Hours*, p. 29; see also Payne Knight, *Analytical Enquiry*, pp. 137–8.

47. 'eine permanente Parekbase' (*Krit. Ausgabe*, XVIII, 85). For Coleridge's 'imagination' as a mediating faculty, see J. R. de J. Jackson, *Method and Imagination in Coleridge's Criticism*, pp. 109–21.

48. Kant's model of the mind does of course rely upon a basic division, but it is one which is turned into a 'fortunate fall':

> the antinomy of pure reason, which becomes obvious in its dialectic, is, in fact, the most fortunate perplexity in which human reason could ever have become involved, since it finally compels us to seek the key to escape from this labyrinth (*Practical Reason*, p. 111).

This is one 'way out' of the ironic paradigm; but in Kierkegaardian terms, of course, this itself demands 'irony' as the symptom of a relation to a world from which one is cut off.

49. Cf. Schiller, *Aesthetic Education*, pp. 41, 73, 79, etc.

50. *Werke*, VII, 367; trans. James Gutman, *Of Human Freedom*, p. 43. See also the almost identical formulations of Hegel, *Phenomenology of Mind*, p. 796, *Science of Logic*, p. 172. Cf. Coleridge, N 3154:

> ? Every finite Being or only some that have the temptation to become intensely & wholly conscious of its distinctness, thence tempted to division— thence wretched . . .

51. Cf. *Poetical Works*, p. 263; Stewart, *Works*, III, 174; and Coleridge on the synthetic function of 'joy', *Philosophical Lectures*, p. 179. See also Prickett, *The Poetry of Growth*, p. 103.

52. It is only fair to consider also Coleridge's own analysis of this predilection, discussed, e.g., at N 1772, 2495.

53. This letter is discussed by Woodring, *Wordsworth*, pp. 158–60; Wasserman, *The Subtler Language*, p. 186; and by Geoffrey Hartman, *The Unmediated Vision: An Interpretation of Wordsworth, Hopkins, Rilke, and Valéry*, p. 179.

CHAPTER 5

1. R. A. Foakes, *The Romantic Assertion: A Study in the Language of Nineteenth Century Poetry*, p. 22, identifies Romantic poetry as 'not committed to

metaphor'. For remarks on the scarcity of metaphor in Wordsworth, see Roger
N. Murray, *Wordsworth's Style: Figures and Themes in the 'Lyrical Ballads' of 1800*,
p. 138; and F. A. Pottle, in *Romanticism: Vistas, Instances, Continuities* ed. David
Thorburn & Geoffrey Hartman, p. 117. There is an important discussion of
Coleridge on metaphor in Barfield, *What Coleridge Thought*, pp. 112–4. For a
more specialised overview, and an emphasis rather different from my own, see
Cyrus Hamlin, 'The Temporality of Selfhood: Metaphor and Romantic
Poetry', *New Literary History*, 6 (1974), 169–93.

2. See, for example, Dorothy Mack, 'Metaphoring As Speech Act: Some
   Happiness Conditions for Implicit Similes and Simple Metaphors', *Poetics*, 4, no.
   2–3 (1975), 221–56. Arguing that metaphor involves comparison and
   deletion, she comments that

   > Deletion enhances the power of the hearer; as the speaker is less explicit, the
   > hearer must be more active . . . With metaphoring, the hearer may choose—
   > to interpret or block interpretation; to interpret literally or nonliterally; to
   > select one or several possible metaphorical interpretations (p. 242).

3. We may cite Crabbe as a late example of the reliance upon the unspoken subject,
   implicitly a part of the world he describes, and at the same time a judge upon it in
   the act of description. Right reason and general nature preclude any problem of
   interference. How out of place seems the incursion of apparent irony into the
   heightened account of Peter Grimes' sojourn:

   > Here dull and hopeless he'd lie down and trace
   > How sidelong crabs had scrawl'd their crooked race.

   Nothing prefigures this, and nothing seems to come out of it, at the level of
   methodological purpose. See *The Poetical Works of George Crabbe*, ed. A. J. and
   R. M. Carlyle, p. 198.

4. See *The Works of George Berkeley, Bishop of Cloyne*, ed. A. A. Luce and T. E.
   Jessop, 9 vols., II, 88–9. See also Hume, *Enquiries*, I, sect. IX, 82; Hartley,
   Observations, I, 343; Stewart, *Works*, III, 284f.; Campbell, *Philosophy of Rhetoric*,
   I, 145.

5. 'Les raisonnemens par *analogie* peuvent servir à expliquer et à éclaircir certaines
   choses, mais non pas à les démontrer' (I, 399).

6. *Hegel's Logic*, trans. William Wallace, p. 254.

7. See also *Critique of Judgement*, Pt. II, 136–37; *Religion Within the Limits of Reason
   Alone*, trans. T. M. Greene and H. H. Hudson, p. 58n.

8. We should note, however, the distinction made between analogical and
   metaphorical modes in *Aids to Reflection*, p. 198f.

9. For a résumé, see Alex Page, 'Faculty Psychology and Metaphor in Eighteenth-
   Century Criticism', *Modern Philology*, 66 (1968–9), 237–47.

10. For other references to the 'bull', see, for example, *Biographia*, I, 52, 181; N 1643;
    Omniana, pp. 125, 332.

11. This determined refusal of materialistic implications is parodied with some
    philosophical precision by Peacock when he has his Mr Flosky maintain that 'the
    pleasure of metaphysical investigation lies in the means, not in the end'. See *The
    Novels of Thomas Love Peacock*, ed. David Garnett, p. 381.

12. Jonathan Bennett sees this as exactly the function of Kant's use of 'Begriff'
    (concept). See *Kant's Dialectic*, p. 23; *Kant's Analytic*, p. 73.

13. For the play of Begriff/begreifen, see *Phenomenology*, pp. 144, 275 (*Werke*, II, 74, 177); *Science of Logic*, pp. 623, 755 (*Werke*, IV, 264, 407). Blackall, *The Emergence of German*, p. 36, cites Wolff as having determinedly removed the verbal sense from 'Begriff'; see also pp. 29, 312—3. See also A. W. Schlegel, *Krit. Schriften*, II, 243; Herder, in Heintel (*op. cit.*), p. 208.

14. Hence, for Coleridge, the 'calming power which all distinct images exert on the human soul' (*Biographia*, II, 254). See also p. 69, above.

15. *Coleridge on Logic and Learning*, ed. Alice D. Snyder, pp. 126—7. The homophone of 'vale' and 'veil' is significant here, in enforcing the potential obscurity of the vision of landscape. See, among many examples, Shelley, *Poetical Works*, pp. 131, 148; Wordsworth, *The Prelude*, I, 100, XII, 133; *Poetical Works*, V, 288; and the play on 'vale' and 'veil' in Blake's 'The Book of Thel' (Erd. 5, K. 130). In short, the word is one which would well suit the thesis of Colin C. Clarke, *The Romantic Paradox*; see also Perkins, *Wordsworth and the Poetry of Sincerity*, p. 107. For discussions of the symbol of the veil in Shelley, see Neville Rogers, *Shelley at Work: A Critical Enquiry*, 2nd ed., pp. 120—46; Peter Butter, *Shelley's Idols of the Cave*, pp. 109—13.

16. For Ella F. Sharpe, 'An Examination of Metaphor', in *The Psycho-Analytic Reader*, ed. Robert Fliess, pp. 273—86, language itself is entirely metaphorical in origin, in that it is a transferred form of 'outerance' which becomes available to the child at the same time as it is being taught to control its bodily orifices: 'words themselves become the substitutes for the bodily substances' (p. 276).

17. For some general remarks, see Abrams, *Natural Supernaturalism*, p. 366f.

18. Matthew Corrigan, 'Metaphor in William Blake: A Negative View', *Journal of Aesthetics and Art Criticism*, 28 (1969), 193.

19. See Scott George, 'The Eighteenth-Century Philosophy of Metaphor', pp. 134, 148f. etc.; see also Page, 'Faculty Psychology', p. 46.

20. Strong passion expresses itself in metaphor borrowed from objects alike remote or near, and casts over all the shadow of its own greatness
(Shelley, *Letters*, II, 108).

Where Shelley sees himself as borrowing, Wordsworth is worried about plundering.

21. There are some interesting arguments along this line by Paul de Man, 'Theory of Metaphor in Rousseau's "Second Discourse"', in *Romanticism*, ed. Thorburn and Hartman pp. 83—114.

22. See James Fernandez, 'The Mission of Metaphor in Expressive Culture', *Current Anthropology*, 15 (1974), 119—45. In exact correspondence with my argument, metaphor (and metonym) are here defined as 'the predication of a sign-image upon an inchoate subject' (p. 120).

23. See, for example, Anthony Wilden, *The Language of the Self* (*The Function of Language in Psycho-analysis*, by Jacques Lacan, trans. with notes and commentary by Anthony Wilden), p. 242.

24. *Cowper, Poetical Works*, ed. H. S. Milford, 4th (rev.) ed., p. 136.

25. Empson, *The Structure of Complex Words*, p. 294, has noted, as I have said already, that *The Prelude* begins with 'two distinct quotations from the throwing out from Paradise of Adam and Eve'. This poem ends with another echo of 'The earth is all before me', implying that the vision of the 'endless way' is already located within a falling off of the paradisal fantasy. There is a further version of

the image at the end of that same first book of *The Prelude*: 'The road lies plain before me' (I, 668). I would suggest that this speaks for a further narrowing of vision as the image of unorganised plenitude turns into the image of purposeful progress, the highway of potential intrusion—as tourists to the Lakes.

26. It is worth remarking here that the German Romantics, particularly Schiller and Hegel, were concerned with the problem of desire (*die Begierde*) at an explicit theoretical level. For Hegel, it is art which has the capacity to counteract 'the ferocity of desires' (*Aesthetics*, p. 48):

> From the practical interest of desire, the interest of art is distinguished by the fact that it lets its object persist freely and on its own account, while desire converts it to its own use by destroying it (p. 38).

The *Science of Logic* describes how the subject, insofar as it is related by *need* to what is outside it, 'uses *violence* on the object' (p. 771). Schiller makes similar distinctions in his attempt to differentiate art from a context in which 'material needs reign supreme and bend a degraded humanity beneath their tyrannical yoke' (*Aesthetic Education*, p. 7):

> If desire seizes directly upon its object, contemplation removes *its* object to a distance, and makes it into a true and inalienable possession by putting it beyond the reach of passion (p. 183).

This is also the function of 'dignity' (*Würde*); see *Werke*, XX, 303—5. Recalling the description of Coleridge's 'guiding Thought' (*The Friend*, I, 456) and its need for a 'pre-conception' without which 'there can be no transition with continuity' (p. 457), it is worth stressing once again the attempts made to deter this necessary methodical faculty from any concentration on determinate material ends. In the same sense, if we suggest that 'desire' is the motive force of *The Prelude*, that sense of 'something evermore about to be' (VI, 542), of having 'something to pursue' (II, 341), then it must at the same time be emphasised that such desire remains 'pure' because by definition unfulfilled, and unfulfillable. It can have no achieved content, for its goals are unregainable except as continually created recollections.

27. Sonst aber kann eigentlich eine Metapher niemals zu kühn sein. Alle dinge stehen in Beziehungen aufeinander, alles bedeutet daher alles, jeder Teil des Universums spiegelt das Ganze: dieses Sind ebensowohl philosophische als poetische Wahrheiten (*Krit. Schriften*, II, 251).

28. What I have said here seems to me very close in spirit, though not in terminology, to the account of Peter F. Fisher, *The Valley of Vision*, esp. p. 109ff. Compare again *Aids to Reflection*, p. 198.

29. Much to the regret of some of Shelley's critics, apparently. Leavis, *Revaluation*, complains that the 'images stand for nothing Shelley could have pointed to' (p. 205); that he has a 'weak grasp upon the actual' (p. 206), and is 'peculiarly weak in his hold on objects' (p. 222); in short, that he 'does not grasp and present anything' (p. 227). The best account of the constitutive function of metaphor in Shelley's aesthetics is by John W. Wright, *Shelley's Myth of Metaphor*.

30. Thus J. S. Kasanin, ed., *Language and Thought in Schizophrenia*, p. 44:

> the schizophrenic shows endless hesitancy and vacillation between various

aspects of the material. This is due to his inability to abstract one principle of the given material while he neglects the others. He takes all the possibilities into simultaneous consideration . . .

CHAPTER 6

1. For the concept of the 'syndrome', see W. T. Jones, *The Romantic Syndrome: Toward a New Method in Cultural Anthropology and History of Ideas*, 2nd ed., pp. 18−9; 'not the absolute range of variation found during the period in question: it simply defines the predominant style-preference of the period'.

2. For general accounts of the communication problem, see McKenzie, *Critical Responsiveness*, esp. chap. 5, pp. 117−79; and Land, *From Signs to Propositions*, esp. p. 41ff. It is perhaps worth pointing out that the typology or model of Romantic poetics which I have been suggesting is rather at odds with that of M. H. Abrams, *The Mirror and the Lamp: Romantic Theory and the Critical Tradition*, p. 22f., in its refusal to endorse the centrality of what he calls the 'expressive theory' of poetry, which makes the artist's own feelings and perspectives the most important 'content' of the message. My own version includes rather more of what Abrams calls the 'pragmatic theory' (p. 14), but with the proviso that what is 'told' can only be 'found', often only by a sortal break with the idea of text-sufficiency, a move outside the poem into the space left vacant by the author's self-elision, the space wherein he 'ought' to reside. See my note on p. 228.

3. Kames (*Elements of Criticism*, I, 426f.) identifies gesture and physiognomic expression as a 'natural language' capable of automatic communication, not open to the arbitrary reception which vitiates the efficiency of mere words. Another standard argument was that of Campbell (*The Philosophy of Rhetoric*, I, 186ff.), who divides language into 'sense' and 'expression'. Though failure in communication may be due to either, it is primarily the latter which occasions misunderstanding, since sense 'ought to have its source in the invariable nature of truth and right' (I, 99).

4. 'Metaphor and the Main Problem of Hermeneutics', *New Literary History*, 6 (1974), 95−110, p. 106. There is a fine résumé of issues in communication theory which relate very closely to my argument here by David E. Linge, in his translation of Hans-Georg Gadamer's *Philosophical Hermeneutics*, pp. xi−lviii. As he puts it, 'Hermeneutics has its origin in breaches in intersubjectivity' (p. xii). I would take issue, however, with the definition of 'romantic hermeneutics' as having believed that 'the one who understands abandons his own horizons and simply steps into the historical horizons of his subject matter' (p. xxxvii).

5. 'On the Irony of Sophocles', *The Philological Museum*, II, 483−537; p. 536. For a brief account of Thirlwall's ideas, see Eleanor Hutchens, 'The Identification of Irony', *ELH*, 27 (1960), 352−63.

6. For another discussion of the subject, see *Aids to Reflection*, pp. 88−90; for specific comments on the textual status of the Scriptures, see *Letters*, V, 1−9, 134−5; VI, 556, 569, 611, 683, etc.; and *Confessions of an Inquiring Spirit*, ed. Henry Nelson Coleridge. Implicit in this work is the fear of rampant literalism in interpretation, and of strictly idiosyncratic illuminations by those who 'frame oracles by private divination from each letter of each disjointed gem,

uninterpreted by the Priest, and deserted by the Spirit' (p. 62). Hence Coleridge's reliance upon an enlightened clerisy. For an account, see Barth, pp. 53–84. I am passing rather briefly over a very important field. The discipline of 'hermeneutics' rose specifically out of the exegesis of the Bible, though it was never as central to the English as it was to the German tradition. For general accounts, see Frei, *The Eclipse of Biblical Narrative*, and Elinor S. Shaffer, *'Kubla Khan' and the Fall of Jerusalem*. Both these authors stress the importance of St John's as the most performative of the Gospels; see Shaffer, pp. 71–95; Frei, p. 311.

7. Bennett has noticed the problem; see *Kant's Analytic*, p. 3, and *Kant's Dialectic*, p. 264. Strawson, *The Bounds of Sense*, p. 151, has suggested that Kant's idea of the one objective world 'must at least allow for the point that another name for the *objective* is the *public'*.

8. Jeffrey's review of Archibald Alison, *Edinburgh Review*, 18, no. 35 (May, 1811), makes a similar point about the artist's obligation:

> if he conceive of the ambition of creating beauties for the admiration of others, he must be cautious to employ only such objects as are the *natural* signs and *inseparable* concomitants of emotions, of which the greater part of mankind are susceptible (p. 45)

Schiller also tries to achieve his desired reconciliation of artistic control with freedom of audience reaction by driving a wedge between form and content; the artist supplies the 'form', the reader the 'content'. This works most neatly for music. With poetry, the artist is obliged to begin to specify content, although he should not go too far (p. 270f.).

9. See *Philosophical Lectures*, p. 153; *Aids to Reflection*, p. 132; and the comments on the reception of *The Friend* in *Letters*, III, 253f.

10. W. V. Quine, *Ontological Relativity and Other Essays*, p. 86.

11. 'The Marvellous and Romantic semiotics', *Studies in Romanticism*, 14 (1975), 211–34; p. 228.

12. *Kritische Schriften*, I, 149:

> Jedes ächte Dichterwerk macht eine unendliche Beschauung möglich und ist ihrer würdig, und alle diese Anschauungen von verschiedenen Seiten sind nur wie mancherlei Strahlen, die aus demselben Centro gehen, die den Glanz des Künstlers weiter verbreiten und dadurch selber Kunst sind.

See also A. W. Schlegel, *Krit. Schriften*, II, 96. For the modernity of this position, see James M. Edie, 'Expression and Metaphor', *Philosophy and Phenomenological Research*, 23 (1963), 538–61.

13. *Friedrich Schlegel's 'Lucinde' and the Fragments*, trans. Peter Firchow, p. 195. See p. 202 for the same comment applied to philosophy.

14. I am ignoring, of course, Kant's 'solution' of this question, whereby the moral law must never *be* applied to empirical experience.

15. Cf. Fichte, *Johann Gottlieb Fichte's Sämtliche Werke*, hrsg. J. H. Fichte, 8 vols., I, 216–7.

16. See Foucault, *The Order of Things*, p. 231.

17. 'die Hülle eines inneren Geheimnisses'; K. W. F. Solger, *Vorlesungen Über Aesthetik*, hrsg. K. W. L. Heyse, p. 243.

18. Coleridge, despite his strong sense of the need for will, reason, and judgement,

also described the 'man of genius' as one whose feelings 'have been habitually associated with thoughts and images, to the number, clearness, and vivacity of which the sensation of *self* is always in an inverse proportion' (*Biographia*, I, 30).

19. For Shelley's use of the image of the poet as chameleon, see *Poetical Works*, p. 579; *Letters*, II, 308, describes poets as those who 'take the colour not only of what they feed on, but of the very leaves under which they pass'.

20. See also *The Friend*, I, 457; *Shakespearean Criticism*, I, 187–8.

21. *Oeuvres*, VIII, 392. The English is quoted from *The Paradox of Acting*, trans. Pollock, p. 53.

22. This is not so much a problem for Keats as for those who are still concerned with the vocabulary of epistemology, which, as Gadamer (*Philosophical Hermeneutics*, p. 131) has pointed out in trying to supplant its place, 'asserts a false priority of self-consciousness. There are no representative images of objects in consciousness, whose correspondence to things themselves it is the real problem of epistemology to guarantee'.

23. See, for example, *Poetical Works*, p. 820f.; *Letters*, I, 307; *Complete Works*, V, 289f. For Christ as a political radical, see also Coleridge, *Lectures 1795*, esp. pp. 215–9; Blake, Erd. 604, K. 387.

24. *The concept of Irony, With Constant Reference to Socrates*, trans. Lee M. Capel, p. 50. See also *Philosophical Fragments or A Fragment of Philosophy*, trans. David F. Swenson, revised Howard V. Hong.

25. Cf. Kierkegaard, *The Concept of Irony*, p. 212 (on Christ's having 'neutralized the value of family life'), and Blake, *Songs*, 52.

26. For a hypothesis about Descartes' response to a similar situation, see my 'Putting One's House in Order: the Career of the Self in Descartes' Method', *New Literary History*, 9 (1977), 83–101. Shaftesbury had made the point at the beginning of the eighteenth century:

> if Men are forbid to speak their minds seriously on certain Subjects, they will do it ironically. If they are forbid to speak at all upon such Subjects, or if they find it really dangerous to do so; they will then redouble their Disguise, involve themselves in Mysteriousness, and talk so as hardly to be understood, or at least not plainly interpreted, by those who are dispos'd to do 'em a mischief (*Characteristicks*, I, 72–73).

27. In addition to books already mentioned, see J. A. K. Thomson, *Irony: An Historical Introduction*; Norman Knox, *The Word* IRONY *and its Context, 1500–1755*, which is a very useful account, both historical and generic, and contains a detailed bibliography; and D. C. Muecke, *The Compass of Irony* and *Irony*. A Kierkegaardian view is that of René Schaerer, 'Le Mécanisme de l'Ironie dans ses Rapports avec le Dialectique', *Revue de Métaphysique et de Morale*. 48 (1941), 181–209. See also Culler, *Structuralist Poetics*, pp. 152–60; the comments on 'naturalization' and 'motivation' are especially relevant.

28. There is good evidence, it seems, for suggesting a similar aesthetic configuration in the seventeenth century. Besides the case for Descartes, see Wilden, *System and Structure*, pp. 88–109 (on Montaigne); and Stanley E. Fish, *Self-Consuming Artifacts: The Experience of Seventeenth-Century Literature*.

29. The definitive account is that of Ingrid Strohschneider-Kohrs, *Die Romantische Ironie im Theorie und Gestaltung*, the first half of which is a theoretical exposition. A briefer summary is that of Helmut Prang, *Die Romantische Ironie*. See also

Ernst Behler, 'Techniques of Irony in the Light of the Romantic Theory', *Rice University Studies*, 57, no. 4 (1971), 1−17.

30. *Aesthetics*, p. 68; see also p. 1175; the review of Solger in *Werke*, XI, 155f; and *Hegel's Philosophy of Right*, trans. T. M. Knox, pp. 101−3.

31. *Solgers Nachgelassene Schriften und Briefwechsel*, hrsg. L. Tieck and F. von Raumer, 2 vols., II, 536:

> Zwecklosigkeit aber und Willkür können an und für sich niemals die Wirkung des Schönen machen. Es muß darin eine höhere Ordnung erkennbar sein, und diese wird eben nur durch Ironie darin verstanden.

For Solger's main accounts of irony, see p. 513f.; *Vorlesungen*, pp. 241−9; *Erwin*, hrsg. W. Henckmann, p. 387f.; *Tieck and Solger: The Complete Correspondence*, ed. Percy Matenko, p. 59f.

32. A useful beginning for any assessment is Raymond Immerwahr, 'The Subjectivity or Objectivity of Friedrich Schlegel's Poetic Irony', *Germanic Review*, 26 (1951), 173−91.

33. René Wellek, *Confrontations: Studies in the Intellectual and Literary Relations between Germany, England, and the United States in the Nineteenth Century*, p. 21, claims that there was no Romantic irony in England, nothing of 'the detachment of the author, the psychic distance, the irony, the playing with the material'. Morton L. Gurewitch, *European Romantic Irony*, takes Byron's *Don Juan* as the beginning of Romantic irony outside Germany.

34. Sperry, *Keats the Poet*, identifies 'irony' as consequent upon the recognition that 'the concerns and questions that matter most to us . . . cannot be brought to any final determination' (p. 245); thus it involves ' a sense of perpetual *indeterminacy*' (p. 258). See also Paul de Man, in *Interpretation*, ed. Singleton, for whom irony 'engenders a temporal sequence of acts of consciousness which is endless . . . a temporality that is definitely not organic, in that it relates to its source only in terms of distance and difference and allows for no end, for no totality' (pp. 202, 203).

35. Newsome, *Two Classes of Men*, p. 6, identifies this posture with that of the Renaissance platonists. See esp. ch. 3, 'Opposites and Contraries', pp. 41−56; also Barfield, *What Coleridge Thought*, pp. 26−40.

36. *Seven Discourses*, p. 158.

37. *Werke*, XIII, 317;

> und so kann man sagen, das wir schon bei jedem aufmerksamen Blick in die Welt theoretisieren.

Thus we must theorise with 'consciousness, self-knowledge, freedom, and, to use a precarious word, with irony (mit Bewußtsein, mit Selbstkenntnis, mit Freiheit und, um uns eines gewagten Wortes zu bedienen, mit Ironie)'.

38. It may have been worth saying such a great deal, in view of Booth's observation (*A Rhetoric of Irony*, p. ix) that 'The way irony works in uniting (or dividing) authors and readers has been relatively neglected since the latter part of the eighteenth century, and it has never been fully explored.'

39. See also Beattie, *Works*, IX, 115; *Encyclopédie*, VIII, 906, both of which connect irony with tonality. Ricoeur, 'Metaphor and the Main Problem of Hermeneutics', p. 95, puts the case well in saying that 'there are problems of interpretation because the relation writing-reading is not a particular case of the

relation speaking-hearing in the dialogical situation.' I quote also, from among many possible sources, Jay Haley, 'An Interactional Description of Schizophrenia', *Psychiatry*, 22 (1959), p. 323:

> Communication between people consists of (1) the context in which it takes place, (2) verbal messages, (3) vocal and linguistic patterns, and (4) bodily movement. As people communicate, their relationship is defined as much by the qualifications of their messages as by the presence or absence of messages.

Haley defines schizophrenia as 'a pathology centering around a disjunction between the person's messages and the qualifications of those messages' (p. 327).

40. For some remarks on this conjunction, see Cyrus Hamlin, 'The Temporality of Selfhood', p. 182.

41. As by Ernest Lee Tuveson, *The Imagination as a Means of Grace: Locke and the Aesthetics of Romanticism*, pp. 108–9. Blair, *Lectures*, II, 120–1, picks out this passage on the 'disconsolate knight' for special praise in his discussion of Addison's style.

42. It must be said that Foucault, *Madness and Civilization*, pp. 131–5, does argue that their proximity was traditionally accepted by eighteenth-century physicians.

43. To give another example from medical theory, opium was prescribed by Darwin (*Zoonomia*, II, 136–7) as a *cure* for reverie and epilepsy, at the same time as it seems to operate as a *cause* in the familiar Romantic experience. For case histories which stand in implicit relation to the predicament of Keats's protagonist, see also Alethea Hayter, *Opium and the Romantic Imagination*, pp. 36–66. The posture of the waking sleeper 'On the cold hill side' can also be related to contemporary ideas about the effects of temperature on dream content; see John Beer, *Coleridge's Poetic Intelligence*, pp. 81–8. Hartley (*Observations*, I, 49) warns of the effects of sleeping in cold conditions, and Darwin (*Zoonomia*, II, 122–3), in describing the onset of paralysis as a consequence of great exertion—volition being lost precisely after great efforts of volition—noted the exacerbating effects of low temperatures.

44. *Werke*, II, 412:

> Zwei Gegensätze *a* und *b* (Subjekt und Objekt) werden vereinigt durch die Handlung *x*, aber in *x* ist ein neuer Gegensatz, *c* und *d* (Empfindendes und Empfundenes), die Handlung *x* wird also selbst wieder zum Objekt; sie ist selbst nur erklärbar durch eine neue Handlung = *z*, welche vielleicht wieder einen Gegensatz enthält u.s.w.

45. *ibid.*, p. 488;

> Jener ursprüngliche Gegensatz kann nur in einer unendlichen Synthesis und im endlichen Objekt nur momentan aufgehoben werden. Der Gegensatz entsteht in jedem Moment aufs neue, und wird in jedem Moment wieder aufgehoben.

46. A fascinating analogue of the linguistic strategies of 'La Belle Dame' is the famous essay by Jakobson, 'Two Aspects of Language and Two Types of Aphasic Disturbances', in R. Jackobson and M. Halle, *Fundamentals of Language*. Aphasia is divided into two categories, marked respectively by selection or combination deficiencies. With the former, the aphasic finds paradigmatic

substitution difficult, and relies tenaciously upon syntax; correspondingly, he is unable to substitute verbal for pictorial signs, or vice versa. Jackobson relates this to a loss of 'metalanguage' (p. 67). Relationships are established by contiguity (context) rather than similarity; by metonymy rather than metaphor. One notices the metonymic structure of Keats's poem, with the inhibitions on substitution (i.e. on any movement 'up' the scale towards identification), and the untranslatability of the title phrase. With the opposite problem, 'contiguity disorder' (p. 71), there occurs agrammatism and chaotic ordering, with a converse reliance on the metaphoric mode.

47. See also Hartley, *Observations*, I, 397 Coleridge, *The Watchman*, ed. Lewis Patton, *The Collected Works of Samuel Taylor Coleridge*, Bollingen Series, LXXX, pp. 32–3.

48. See Henri F. Ellenberger, *The Discovery of the Unconscious: The History and Evolution of Dynamic Psychiatry*, pp. 53–83; Kluge, *Versuch einer Darstellung*, esp. pp. 15–80; and Stewart, *Works*, IV, 150ff. J. P. F. Deleuze, *Histoire Critique du Magnétisme Animal*, 2 vols., gives a whole array of case histories offering specific parallels to the symptoms of Keats's protagonist, e.g. I, 137–42, 162–201. Kluge and Deleuze give bibliographies which indicate the enormous amount of interest in the subject.

49. See *Letters*, IV, 731. For some remarks on Coleridge's attitude, see the editor's note, *The Friend*, I, 59; Beer, *Coleridge's Poetic Intelligence*, pp. 220–3, and Lane Cooper, 'The Power of the Eye in Coleridge', in his *Late Harvest*, pp. 65–95.

50. *Die Symbolik des Traumes*, p. 133:

> Jene Schranken, welche die Körperlichkeit zwischen zwei verschiedenen Individuen feststellet, sind in diesem Zustande aufgehoben, die Seele jener innerlich Eröfneten, wird mit der Seele des Magnetiseurs Eine und dieselbe.

51. As Reeve Parker, *Coleridge's Meditative Art*, p. 132, has said of 'Frost at Midnight':

> In a gesture characteristic of the meditative poems, the quest for an adequate symbology in the natural world . . . is displaced onto the poet's companion.

52. See Wilden, *System and Structure*, pp. 227, 286, 445; and Ernest Gellner, *Legitimation of Belief*, pp. 13, 21, 193–4.

Bibliography

Aarsleff, Hans. *The Study of Language in England, 1780–1860.* Princeton: Princeton University Press, 1967.

Abrams, Meyer H. *The Mirror and the Lamp: Romantic Theory and the Critical Tradition.* 1953; rpt. New York: W. W. Norton, 1958.

——'Structure and Style in the Greater Romantic Lyric'. *From Sensibility to Romanticism.* Ed. Bloom and Hilles, 1965, pp. 527–60.

——'Ode on a Grecian Urn'. *Twentieth Century Interpretations of Keats's Odes.* Ed. Stillinger, 1968, pp. 110–11.

——*Natural Supernaturalism: Tradition and Revolution in Romantic Literature.* New York: W. W. Norton, 1971.

Alembert, Jean le Rond d'. See *Encyclopédie.*

Allemann, Beda, 'Ironie als literarisches Prinzip'. *Ironie und Dichtung.* Hrsg. Albert Schaefer. Munich: C. H. Beck, 1970, pp. 11–37.

Altieri, Charles. 'Wordsworth's Wavering Balance: The Thematic Rhythm of *The Prelude'. Wordsworth Circle,* 4 (1973), 226–40.

Anon. 'On the Use of Metaphors'. *Blackwood's Edinburgh Magazine,* 18 no. 107 (Dec. 1825), 719–23.

Appleyard, J. A. *Coleridge's Philosophy of Literature: The Development of a Concept of Poetry, 1791–1819.* Cambridge, Mass.: Harvard University Press, 1965.

Ault, Donald D. *Visionary Physics, Blake's Response to Newton.* Chicago and London: University of Chicago Press, 1974.

Austin, J. L. *How to do things with Words.* 1962; rpt. Oxford: Clarendon Press, 1965.

Banerjee, Srikumar. *Critical Theories and Poetic Practice in the 'Lyrical Ballads'.* London: Williams & Norgate, 1931.

Barfield, Owen. *What Coleridge Thought.* London: Oxford University Press, 1972.

——'Coleridge's Enjoyment of Words'. *Coleridge's Variety.* Ed. J. B. Beer. London: Macmillan, 1974, pp. 204–18.

Barth, J. Robert, S. J. *Coleridge and Christian Doctrine.* Cambridge,

Mass.: Harvard University Press, 1969.

Barthes, Roland. *Critical Essays*. Trans. Richard Howard. Evanston: Northwestern University Press, 1972.

Bate, Walter Jackson. *The Stylistic Development of Keats*. New York and London: Modern Language Association and Oxford University Press, 1945.

Beattie, James. *Works*. 10 vols. Philadelphia, 1809.

Beer, John B. *Coleridge the Visionary*. London: Chatto & Windus, 1970.

——*Coleridge's Poetic Intelligence*. London: Macmillan, 1977.

Behler, Ernst. 'Techniques of Irony in the light of the Romantic Theory'. *Rice University Studies*, 57 no. 4 (1971), 1–17.

Bennett, Jonathan. *Kant's Analytic*. Cambridge: Cambridge University Press, 1966.

——*Kant's Dialectic*. Cambridge: Cambridge University Press, 1974.

Berkeley, George, Bishop of Cloyne. *The Works of George Berkeley, Bishop of Cloyne*. Ed. A. A. Luce and T. E. Jessop. London, etc.: Thomas Nelson & Sons, 1948–57.

Blackall, Eric. A. *The Emergence of German as a Literary Language, 1700–75*. Cambridge: Cambridge University Press, 1959.

Blair, Hugh. *Lectures on Rhetoric and Belles Lettres*. 4th ed., 3 vols. London, 1790.

Blake, William. *Songs of Innocence and of experience*. Copy W (Jebb-Forster). In the library of King's College, Cambridge.

——*The Poetry and Prose of William Blake*. Ed. David V. Erdman, commentary by Harold Bloom. 4th printing, with revisions. Garden City, N.Y.: Doubleday & Co., 1970.

——*Songs of Innocence and of Experience*. Facsimile reproduction with introduction and commentary by Sir Geoffrey Keynes. London: Oxford University Press, 1970.

——*Blake: Complete Writings*. Ed. Sir Geoffrey Keynes. 1966; corrected ed. London, Oxford, New York: Oxford University Press, 1974.

Bloom, Harold. *Shelley's Mythmaking*. New Haven: Yale University Press, 1959.

——*Blake's Apocalypse: A Study in Poetic Argument*. Garden City, N.Y.: Doubleday & Co., 1963, 1965.

——Ed., with F. W. Hilles, *From Sensibility to Romanticism: Essays Presented to Frederick A. Pottle*. New York: Oxford University Press, 1965.

——*The Ringers in the Tower*. Chicago and London: University of

Chicago Press, 1971.

——*Poetry and Repression: Revisionism from Blake to Stevens*. New Haven and London: Yale University Press, 1976.

Blunt, Anthony. 'The First Illuminated Books'. *Blake*. Ed. Frye, 1966, pp. 127–41.

Bonnet, Charles. *Essai de Psychologie*. London, 1755.

Booth, Wayne C. *The Rhetoric of Fiction*. Chicago and London: University of Chicago Press, 1961.

——*Now Don't Try to Reason With Me: Essays and Ironies for a Credulous Age*. Chicago and London: University of Chicago Press, 1970.

——*A Rhetoric of Irony*. Chicago and London: University of Chicago Press, 1974.

Borck, Jim S. 'Blake's "The Lamb": The Punctuation of Innocence'. *Tennessee Studies in Literature*, 19 (1974), 163–75.

Bosse, Heinrich. 'The Marvellous and Romantic Semiotics'. *Studies in Romanticism*, 14 (1975), 211–34.

Bostetter, Edward E. *The Romantic Ventriloquists: Wordsworth, Coleridge, Shelley, Keats, Byron*. Seattle: University of Washington Press, 1963.

——'The Nightmare World of "The Ancient Mariner"'. *The Ancient Mariner and Other Peoms, A Casebook*. Ed. Alun R. Jones and William Tydeman. London: Macmillan, 1973, pp. 184–99.

Boulger, James D. *Coleridge as Religious Thinker*, New Haven: Yale University Press, 1961.

Brooks, Cleanth. *The Well-Wrought Urn*. London: Denis Dobson Ltd, 1949.

——'Irony as a Principle of Structure'. *Literary Opinion in America*. Ed. Morton Dauwen Zabel. 3rd (rev.) ed., 2 vols. continuously paginated. New York and Evanston: Harper & Row, 1962, II, 729–41.

Brown, Thomas. *Lectures on the Philosophy of the Human Mind*. 4 vols. Edinburgh, 1820.

Burke, Edmund. *A Philosophical Enquiry into the Origin of our Ideas of the Sublime and the Beautiful*. Ed. J. T. Boulton. London: Routledge & Kegan Paul, 1958.

Burnett, James. See Monboddo.

Bush, Douglas. Ed. *John Keats: Selected Poems and Letters*. Cambridge, Mass.: Riverside Press, 1959.

——'Ode on a Grecian Urn'. *Twentieth Century Interpretations of Keats's Odes*. Ed. Stillinger, 1968, pp. 108–9.

Butter, Peter. *Shelley's Idols of the Cave.* Edinburgh: Edinburgh University Press, 1954.

Byron, George Gordon, Lord. *Byron: Poetical Works.* Ed. Frederick Page. 3rd ed. corrected by John Jump. London, Oxford, New York: Oxford University Press, 1970.

Campbell, George. *The Philosophy of Rhetoric.* 2 vols. London, 1776.

Cassirer, Ernst. *The Philosophy of the Enlightenment.* Trans. F.C.A. Koelln and J. P. Pettegrove. Princeton: Princeton University Press, 1951.

Chambers Twentieth Century Dictionary. New ed. 1972 and 1973.

Chatterton, Thomas. *The Complete Works of Thomas Chatterton.* Ed. Donald S., Taylor. 2 vols. Oxford: Clarendon Press, 1971.

Clarke, Colin C. *Romantic Paradox: An Essay on the Poetry of Wordsworth.* London: Routledge & Kegan Paul, 1962.

Cohen, Jane Rabb. 'Keats's Humor in "La Belle Dame Sans Merci"'. *Keats-Shelley Journal,* 17 (1968), 10–13.

Cohen, Murray. *Sensible Words: Linguistic Practice in England, 1640–1785.* Baltimore and London: The Johns Hopkins University Press, 1977.

Coleridge, Samuel Taylor. *Aids to Reflection, in the Formation of a Manly Character on the Several Grounds of Prudence, Morality, and Religion.* London: Taylor & Hessey, 1825.

——*Specimens of the Table Talk.* Ed. H. N. Coleridge. London, 1835.

——*Anima Poetae: From the Unpublished Note-Books of Samuel Taylor Coleridge.* Ed. E. H. Coleridge. London: William Heinemann, 1895.

——*Biographia Literaria.* Ed. J. Shawcross. 2 vols. Oxford: Clarendon Press, 1907.

——*The Complete Poetical Works of Samuel Taylor Coleridge.* Ed. Ernest Hartley Coleridge, 2 vols., continuously paginated. Oxford: Clarendon Press, 1912.

——*Coleridge on Logic and Learning.* Ed. Alice D. Snyder. New Haven: Yale University Press, 1929.

——Coleridge: *The Philosophical Lectures, 1818–19.* Ed. Kathleen Coburn. London: The Pilot Press, 1949.

——*Collected Letters of Samuel Taylor Coleridge.* Ed. Earl Leslie Griggs. 6 vols. Oxford: Clarendon Press, 1956–71.

——*The Notebooks of Samuel Taylor Coleridge.* Bollingen Series L, ed. Kathleen Coburn. 3 vols. so far. Vols. I and II, London and New York: Routledge & Kegan Paul and Pantheon Books, 1957 and

1961. Vol. III, London and Princeton: Routledge & Kegan Paul and Princeton University Press, 1973.

——*Samuel Taylor Coleridge: Shakespearean Criticism.* Ed. T. M. Raysor. 2nd ed. 2 vols. London and New York: Dent & Dutton, 1960.

——*The Collected Works of Samuel Taylor Coleridge.* Ed. Kathleen Coburn (with Bart Winer). Bollingen Series LXXV. 16 vols. (5 vols. so far). London and Princeton: Routledge & Kegan Paul and Princeton University Press, 1969– .

——Vol. IV. *The Friend.* Ed. Barbara E. Rooke. 2 vols. 1969.

——Vol. II. *The Watchman.* Ed. Lewis Patton, 1970.

——Vol. I. *Lectures 1795 on Politics and Religion.* Ed. Lewis Patton and Peter Mann, 1971.

——Vol. VI. *Lay Sermons.* Ed. R. J. White, 1972.

——*Omniana* (with Robert Southey). Ed. Robert Gittings. Fontwell, Sussex: Centaur Press, 1969.

——*Confessions of an Inquiring Spirit.* Ed. Henry Nelson Coleridge. 1840; Facsimile rpt. Menston: Scolar Press, 1971.

Condillac, Étienne Bonnot de Mably de. *An Essay on the Origin of Human Knowledge.* Trans. Thomas Nugent. 1756; facsimile rpt. Gainesville, Florida: Scholars' Facsimiles and Reprints, 1971.

Cook, Daniel J. *Language in the Philosophy of Hegel.* The Hague and Paris: Mouton, 1973.

Cooke, Michael G. *The Romantic Will.* New Haven and London: Yale University Press, 1976.

Cooper, Lane. 'The Power of the Eye in Coleridge'. *Late Harvest.* Ithaca: Cornell University Press, 1962, pp. 65–95.

Corrigan, Matthew. 'Metaphor in William Blake: A Negative View'. *Journal of Aesthetics and Art Criticism,* 28 (1969), 187–99.

Coveney, Peter. *The Image of Childhood. The Individual and Society: A Study of the Theme in English Literature.* Rev. ed. Harmondsworth, Middlesex: Peregrine Books, 1967.

Cowper, William. *Cowper, Poetical Works.* Ed. H. S. Milford. 4th (rev.) ed. London: Oxford University Press, 1957.

Crabbe, George. *The Poetical Works of George Crabbe.* Ed. A. J. and R. M. Carlyle. London: Oxford University Press, 1914.

Culler, Jonathan. *Structuralist Poetics: Structuralism, Linguistics, and the Study of Literature.* London: Routledge & Kegan Paul, 1975.

Curran, Stuart. Ed., with Joseph Anthony Wittreich Jnr. *Blake's Sublime Allegory: Essays on 'The Four Zoas,' 'Milton', 'Jerusalem'.* Madison: University of Wisconsin Press, 1973.

Damon, S. Foster. *William Blake: His Philosophy and Symbols*. 1924; rpt. Gloucester, Mass.: Peter Smith, 1958.

——*A Blake Dictionary*. 1965; rpt. New York: E. P. Dutton & Co., 1971.

Danby, John F. *The Simple Wordsworth: Studies in the Poems, 1797–1807*. London: Routledge & Kegan Paul, 1960.

Darmesteter, Arsène. With Hatzfeld, Adolphe. *Dictionnaire général de la langue française*. 5th ed. Paris: Delagrave, n.d.

Darwin, Erasmus. *Zoonomia; or, the Laws of Organic Life*. 3rd ed. 4 vols. London, 1801.

Davie, Donald. *Purity of Diction in English Verse*. London: Chatto & Windus, 1952.

——*Articulate Energy: An Inquiry into the Syntax of English Poetry*. 1955; rpt. London: Routledge & Kegan Paul, 1966.

——'Dionysus in "Lyrical Ballads"'. *Wordsworth's Mind and Art*. Ed. A. W. Thomson, Edinburgh: Oliver & Boyd, 1969, pp. 110–39.

Deleuze, J. P. F. *Histoire Critique du Magnétisme Animal*. 2 vols. Paris, 1813.

de Man, Paul 'The Rhetoric of Temporality'. *Interpretation: Theory and Practice*. Ed, Charles S. Singleton. Baltimore: The Johns Hopkins Press, 1969, pp. 173–209.

——*Blindness and Insight: Essays in the Rhetoric of Contemporary Criticism*. New York: Oxford University Press, 1971.

——'Theory of Metaphor in Rousseau's "Second Discourse"'. *Romanticism*. Ed. Thorburn and Hartman, 1973, pp. 83–114.

de Quincey, Thomas. *The Works of Thomas de Quincey*. 3rd ed. 16 vols. Edinburgh: Adam & Charles Black, 1862.

Dickstein, Morris. *Keats and his Poetry*. Chicago and London: University of Chicago Press, 1971.

Diderot, Denis. See *Encyclopédie*.

——*Oeuvres Complètes de Diderot*. Ed. J. Assézat. 20 vols. Paris: Garniers Frères, 1875–7.

——*The Paradox of Acting*. Trans. W. H. Pollock. London: Chatto & Windus, 1883.

Dieckmann, Liselotte. *Hieroglyphics: The History of a Literary Symbol*. St Louis: Washington University Press, 1970.

Drake, Nathan. *Literary Hours*. London, 1798.

Drummond, The Rt. Hon. William. *Academical Questions, Vol. One*. London, 1805.

Easson, Roger R. 'William Blake and his Reader in "Jerusalem"'.

Blake's Sublime Allegory. Ed. Curran and Wittreich, 1973, pp. 309–27.

Eaves, Morris. 'The Title Page of "The Book of Urizen"'. *William Blake. Essays in Honour of Sir Geoffrey Keynes* Ed. Morton D. Paley and Michael Phillips. Oxford: Clarendon Press, 1973, pp. 225–30.

Edie, James M. 'Expression and Metaphor'. *Philosophy and Phenomenological Research,* 23 (1963), 538–61.

Edwards, Paul. Ed. *The Encyclopaedia of Philosphy.* London and New York: Macmillan and The Free Press, 1967.

Ellenberger, Henri F. *The Discovery of the Unconscious: The History and Evolution of Dynamic Psychiatry.* London: Allen Lane, Penguin Press, 1970.

Empson, William. *The Structure of Complex Words.* London: Chatto & Windus, 1964.

Encyclopédie, ou Dictionnaire Raisonné des Sciences, des Arts, et des Métiers. Ed. Diderot and d'Alembert. 17 vols. Paris, 1751–7.

Erdman, David V. *Prophet Against Empire.* Princeton: Princeton University Press, 1954.

——*The Illuminated Blake.* Garden City, N.Y.: Doubleday & Co., 1974.

Essick, Robert N. 'Blake and the Traditions of Reproductive Engraving'. *Blake Studies,* 5, i (1972), 59–103.

Evert, Walter H. *Aesthetic and Myth in the Poetry of Keats.* Princeton: Princeton University Press, 1965.

Fass, Barbara. *La Belle Dame Sans Merci and the Aesthetics of Romanticism.* Detroit: Wayne State University Press, 1974.

Fearn, John. *An Essay on Consciousness.* 2nd ed. London, 1812.

Fernandez, James. 'The Mission of Metaphor in Expressive Culture'. *Current Anthropology,* 15 (1974), 119–45.

Ferry, David. *The Limits of Mortality: An Essay on Wordsworth's Major Poems.* Middletown, Conn.: Wesleyan University Press, 1959.

Fichte, J. G. *Johann Gottlieb Fichte's Sämtliche Werke.* Hrsg. J. H. Fichte. 8 vols. Berlin, 1845.

——*The Vocation of Man.* Trans. Roderick M. Chisholm. Indianapolis and New York: Bobbs-Merrill, 1956.

Fish, Stanley E. *Self-Consuming Artifacts: The Experience of Seventeenth-Century Literature.* Berkeley, Los Angeles, London: University of California Press, 1972.

Fisher, Peter F. Ed. Northrop Frye. *The Valley of Vision: Blake as Prophet and Revolutionary.* Toronto: University of Toronto Press, 1961.

Fletcher, Angus. '"Positive Negation": Threshold, Sequence, and Personification in Coleridge'. *New Perspectives on Coleridge and Wordsworth: Selected Papers from the English Institute.* Ed. Geoffrey Hartman. New York and London: Columbia University Press, 1972, pp. 133–64.

Foakes, R. A. *The Romantic Assertion: A Study in the Language of Nineteenth-Century Poetry.* London: Methuen, 1958.

Fogle,Richard Harter. 'The Abstractness of Shelley'. *Shelley: A Collection of Critical Essays.* Ed. George M. Ridenour. Englewood Cliffs, N.J.: Prentice-Hall, 1965, pp. 13–29.

Ford, Newell F. *The Prefigurative Imagination of John Keats: A Study of the Beauty-Truth Identification and its Implications.* Stanford University Publications in Language and Literature, Vol. IX, no. 2. Stanford and London: Stanford University Press and Oxford University Press, 1951.

Foucault, Michel. *Madness and Civilization: A History of Insanity in the Age of Reason.* Trans. Richard Howard. 1965; rpt. London: Tavistock Publications, 1967, 1971.

——*The Order of Things.* 1966; rpt. New York: Random House, 1973.

——*The Archaelogy of Knowledge.* Trans. A. M. Sheridan Smith. New York: Random House, Pantheon Books, 1972.

——*The Birth of the Clinic: An Archaelogy of Medical Perception.* Trans. A. M. Sheridan Smith. London: Tavistock Publications, 1973.

Frei, Hans W. *The Eclipse of Biblical Narrative: A Study in Eighteenth and Nineteenth Century Hermeneutics.* New Haven and London: Yale University Press, 1974.

Fruman, Norman. *Coleridge, The Damaged Archangel.* London: George Allen & Unwin, 1971.

Frye, Northrop. 'Notes for a Commentary on "Milton"'. *The Divine Vision: Studies in the Poetry and Art of William Blake.* Ed. Vivian de Sola Pinto. London: Victor Gollancz, 1957, pp. 99–137.

——'Poetry and Design in William Blake'. *Blake: A Collection of Critical Essays.* Ed. Northrop Frye. Englewood Cliffs, N.J.: Prentice-Hall, 1966, pp. 119–26.

Gadamer, Hans-Georg. *Truth and Method.* 1960; ed. Garret Barden and John Cumming. London: Sheed & Ward, 1975.

——*Philosophical Hermeneutics.* Trans. David E. Linge. Berkeley, Los Angeles, London: University of California Press, 1976.

Garber, Frederick. *Wordsworth and the Poetry of Encounter.* Urbana, Chicago, London: University of Illinois Press, 1971.

Gardner, Stanley. *Blake.* London: Evans Brothers, 1968.

Garrod, H. W. *Keats.* 2nd ed. Oxford: Clarendon Press, 1939.

Gellner, Ernest. *Legitimation of Belief.* Cambridge: Cambridge University Press, 1974.

George, Scott. 'The Eighteenth-Century Philosophy of Metaphor'. Diss. Vanderbilt. 1943.

Gérard, Albert S. *English Romantic Poetry: Ethos, Structure, and Symbol in Coleridge, Wordworh, Shelley, and Keats.* Berkeley and Los Angeles: University of California Press, 1968.

Gerard, Alexander. *An Essay on Taste.* 2nd Ed. Edinburgh, 1764.

Gibson, Walker. 'Authors, Speakers, and Mock Readers'. *College English,* 11 (1950), 265—9.

Gillham, D. C. *Blake's Contrary States: The 'Songs of Innocence and of Experience' as Dramatic Poems.* Cambridge: Cambridge University Press, 1966.

——*William Blake.* Cambridge: Cambridge University Press, 1973.

Gleckner, Robert F. *The Piper and the Bard: A Study of William Blake.* Detroit: Wayne State University Press, 1959.

——'Most Holy Forms of Thought: Some Observations on Blake and Language'. *ELH,* 41 (1974), 555—77.

——'Romanticism and the Self-Annihilation of Language'. *Criticism,* 18 (1976), 173—89.

Godwin, William. *Enquiry Concerning Political Justice and its Influence on Morals and Happiness.* 3rd ed., 1797. Ed. F. E. L. Priestley. 3 vols. Facsimile rpt. Toronto: University of Toronto Press, 1946.

Goethe, J. W. von. *Goethes Werke.* Hrsg. E. Trunz, W. Kayser, J. Kunz usw. 7th ed. 14 vols. Hamburg: C. Wegner, 1961—5.

Goldsmith, Oliver. *Collected Works of Oliver Goldsmith.* Ed. Arthur Friedman. 5 vols. Oxford: Clarendon Press, 1966.

Grimes, Ronald L. 'Time and Space in Blake's Major Prophecies'. *Blake's Sublime Allegory.* Ed. Curran and Wittreich, 1973, pp. 59—81.

Grow, L. M. *The Prose Style of Samuel Taylor Coleridge.* Salzburg Studies in English Literature, Romantic Reassessment. Salzburg, 1976.

Gurewitch, Morton. *European Romantic Irony.* Diss. Columbia, 1957. Ann Arbor: Uiversity Microfilms, 1957. DA/00–21607.

Hagstrum, Jean H. *William Blake, Poet and Painter: An Introduction to the Illuminated Verse.* Chicago and London: University of Chicago Press, 1964.

Haley, Jay. 'An Interactional Description of Schizophrenia'. *Psychiatry,* 22 (1959), 321–32.

Halle, M. See Jakobson.

Hamann, J. G. *J. G. Hamann, Sämtliche Werke.* Hrsg. J. Nadler. 6 vols. Vienna: T. Moraus, 1949–57.

Hamlin, Cyrus. 'The Temporality of Selfhood: Metaphor and Romantic Poetry'. *New Literary History,* 6 (1974), 169–93.

Harding, Anthony John. *Coleridge and the Idea of Love.* London and New York: Cambridge University Press, 1974.

Harper, George Mills. See Taylor, Thomas.

Harris, James. *Hermes: or, a Philosophical Enquiry Concerning Language and Universal Grammar.* 1751; facsimile rpt. Menston: Scolar Press, 1968.

Hartley, David. *Observations on Man, his Frame, his Duty, and his Expectations.* 1749; facsimile rpt., 2 vols. in 1. Gainesville, Florida: Scholars' Facsimiles and Reprints, 1966.

Hartman, Geoffrey. *The Unmediated Vision: An Interpretation of Wordsworth, Hopkins, Rilke, and Valery.* New Haven and London: Yale University Press and Oxford University Press, 1954.

——*Wordsworth's Poetry, 1787–1814.* New Haven and London: Yale University Press, 1964.

——'Wordsworth, Inscription, and Romantic Nature Poetry'. *From Sensibility to Romanticism.* Ed. Bloom and Hilles, 1965, pp. 389–413.

——Ed., with David Thorburn. *Romanticism: Vistas, Instances, Continuities.* Ithaca and London: Cornell University Press, 1973.

——'The Use and Abuse of Structural Analysis: Riffaterre's Interpretation of Wordsworth's "Yew Trees"'. *New Literary History,* 7 (1975), 165–89.

Hatzfeld. See Darmesteter.

Hayden, John O. Ed. *Romantic Bards and British Reviewers.* London: Routledge & Kegan Paul, 1971.

Hayter, Alethea. *Opium and the Romantic Imagination.* London: Faber & Faber, 1968.

Hazlitt, William. *The Complete Works of William Hazlitt*. 'The Centenary Edition'. Ed. P. P. Howe. 21 vols. London and Toronto: J. M. Dent, 1930–4.

Hegel, G. W. F. *Hegel's Logic*. Trans. William Wallace. 1873; rpt. Oxford: Clarendon Press, 1975.

——*Lectures on the History of Philosophy*. Trans. E. S. Haldane. 3 vols. London: Kegan Paul, Trench, & Trübner, 1892.

——*The Philosophy of History*. Trans. J. Sibree. 1899; rpt. New York: Dover Publications, 1956.

——*The Phenomenology of Mind*. Trans. J. B. Baillie. 1910, rev. 1931; rpt. New York and Evanston: Harper & Row, 1967.

——*Sämtliche Werke*. Hrsg. G. Lasson (– J. Hoffmeister). 30 vols (incomplete). Leipzig: 1928–

——*Hegel's Philosophy of Right*. Trans. T. M. Knox. 1952; rpt. London, Oxford, New York, 1975.

——*Hegel's Science of Logic*. Trans. A. V. Miller. London and New York: George Allen & Unwin and The Humanities Press, 1969.

——*On Christianity: Early Theological Writings*. Trans. T. M. Knox. Gloucester, Mass.: Peter Smith, 1970.

——*Hegel's Philosophy of Mind*. Trans. William Wallace and A. V. Miller. Oxford: Clarendon Press, 1971.

——*Aesthetics: Lectures on Fine Art*. Trans. T. M. Knox. 2 vols., continuously paginated. Oxford: Clarendon Press, 1975.

Herder, J. G. See also Rousseau.

Herders Sämtliche Werke. Hrsg. B. Suphan. 33 vols. Berlin, 1877–1913.

——*J. G. Herder: Sprachphilosophische Schriften*. Hrsg. E. Heintel. Hamburg: Felix Meiner, 1960.

Hilles, F. W. See Bloom.

Hipple, W. J. *The Beautiful, the Sublime, and the Picturesque in Eighteenth Century British Aesthetic Theory*. Carbondale, Ill.: Southern Illinois University Press, 1957.

Hirsch, E. D. Jnr. *Wordsworth and Schelling: A Typological Study of Romanticism*. New Haven: Yale University Press, 1960.

——*Innocence and Experience: An Introduction to Blake*. New Haven and London: Yale University Press, 1964.

——*The Aims of Interpretation*. Chicago and London: University of Chicago Press, 1976.

Holloway, John. *Blake: The Lyric Poetry*. London: Edward Arnold, 1968.

Home, Henry. See Kames.

House, Humphry. *Coleridge: The Clark Lectures, 1951–52*. London: Rupert Hart-Davis, 1953.

Huguet, Edmond. *Dictionnaire du seizième siècle*. Paris: Eduard Champion, 1925.

Hume, David. *A Treatise of Human Nature*. Ed. L. A. Selby-Bigge. 1888; rpt. Oxford: Clarendon Press, 1973.

——*Enquiries Concerning Human Understanding and Concerning the Principles of Morals*. Ed. L. A. Selby-Bigge. 3rd ed. rev. P. H. Nidditch. Oxford: Clarendon Press, 1975.

Hutchens, Eleanor. 'The Identification of Irony'. *ELH*, 27 (1960), 352–63.

Immerwahr, Raymond. 'The Subjectivity or Objectivity of Friedrich Schlegel's Poetic Irony'. *Germanic Review*, 26 (1951), 173–91.

Jack, Ian. *Keats and the Mirror of Art*. Rev. ed. Oxford: Clarendon Press, 1968.

Jackson, J. R. de J. *Method and Imagination in Coleridge's Criticism*. Cambridge, Mass.: Harvard University Press, 1965.

Jakobson, R. 'Two Aspects of Language and Two Types of Aphasic Disturbances'. *Fundamentals of Language*. With M. Halle. The Hague: Mouton, 1956.

Jeffrey, Francis. Review of Archibald Alison. *Edinburgh Review*, 18 no. 35 (May, 1811), 1–46.

——*Contributions to the Edinburgh Review*. 4 vols. Edinburgh, 1844.

Jones, John. *John Keats's Dream of Truth*. London: Chatto & Windus, 1969.

Jones, W. T. *The Romantic Syndrome: Toward a New Method in Cultural Anthropology and History of Ideas*. 2nd ed. The Hague: M. Nijhoff, 1973.

Kames, Henry Home, Lord. *Elements of Criticism*. 6th ed. 2 vols. Edinburgh, 1785.

Kant, I. *The Critique of Judgment*. Trans. James Creed Meredith. 2 vols. in 1. 1928; rpt. Oxford: Clarendon Press, 1952, 1973.

——*Immanuel Kant's Critique of Pure Reason*. Trans. Norman Kemp Smith. 1929, rev. 1933; rpt. London: Macmillan Press, 1973.

——*Prolegomena to any future Metaphysics that will be able to present itself as a Science*. Trans. Peter G. Lucas. 1953; rpt. Manchester: Manchester University Press, 1971.

——*Critique of Practical Reason.* Trans. Lewis White Beck. Indianapolis and New York: Bobbs-Merrill, 1956.

——*Foundations of the Metaphysics of Morals.* Trans. Lewis White Beck. Indianapolis and New York: Bobbs-Merrill, 1959.

——*Religion within the Limits of Reason Alone.* Trans. T. M. Grene and H. H. Hudson, New York: Harper & Row, 1960.

——*Kant: Selected Pre-Critical Writings and Correspondence with Beck.* Trans. G. B. Kerferd and D. E. Walford. Manchester and New York: Manchester University Press and Barnes & Noble, 1968.

Kasanin, J. S. Ed. *Language and Thought in Schizophrenia.* Berkeley and Los Angeles: University of California, 1944.

Keats, John. *The Letters of John Keats.* Ed. H. E. Rollins. 2 vols. Cambridge, Mass.: Harvard University Press, 1958.

——*The Poems of John Keats.* Ed. Miriam Allott. Rev ed. London: Longman Group, 1972.

Kierkegaard, Søren A. *Philosophical Fragments or A Fragment of Philosophy.* Trans. David F. Swenson, rev. Howard V. Hong. 1936; rpt. Princeton: Princeton University Press, 1962.

——*Concluding Unscientific Postscript.* Trans. David F. Swenson and Walter Lowrie. 1941; rpt. Princeton: Princeton University Press, 1968.

——*Either/Or.* Trans. David F. Swenson and Lillian Marvin Swenson. 2 vols. 1944; rpt. Garden City, N.Y.: Doubleday & Co., 1959.

——*The Concept of Irony, With Constant Reference to Socrates.* Trans. Lee M. Capel. 1965; rpt. Bloomington and London: Indiana University Press, 1968.

Kirkham, Michael. 'Innocence and Experience in Wordsworth's "The Thorn"'. *Ariel,* 5, i (1974), 66–80.

Kluge, C. A. F. *Versuch einer Darstellung des animalischen Magnetismus als Heilsmittel.* 2nd ed. Berlin, 1815.

Knight, G. Wilson. *The Starlit Dome: Studies in the Poetry of Vision.* London: Methuen & Co., 1959.

Knight, R. Payne. *An Analytical Enquiry into the Principles of Taste.* 4th ed. 1808; facsimile rpt. Farnborough, England: Gregg International Publishers, 1972.

Knox, Norman. *The Word* IRONY *and its Context, 1500–1755.* Durham, N. C.: Duke University Press, 1961.

Kostelanetz, Anne. 'Wordsworth's "Conversations": A Reading of "The Two April Mornings" and "The Fountain"'. *ELH,* 33 (1966), 43–52. See also Mellor.

Kroeber, Karl. 'Graphic-Poetic Structuring in Blake's "Book of Urizen"'. *Blake Studies*, 3 (1970), 7–18.

Land, Stephen K. 'The Silent Poet: An Aspect of Wordsworth's Semantic Theory'. *University of Toronto Quarterly*, 42 (1973), 157–69.
——*From Signs to Propositions: The Concept of Form in Eighteenth Century Semantic Theory*. London: Longman Group, 1974.
Langbaum, Robert. *The Poetry of Experience: The Dramatic Monologue in Modern Literary Tradition*. Harmondsworth, Middlesex: Penguin Books, 1974.
Lange, Victor. 'Friedrich Schlegel's Literary Criticism'. *Comparative Literature*, 7 (1955), 289–305.
Leavis, F. R. *Revaluation: Tradition and Development in English Poetry*. London: Chatto & Windus, 1936.
Lindenberger, Herbert. *On Wordsworth's 'Prelude'*. Princeton: Princeton University Press, 1963.
Linge, David E. See Gadamer.
Lister, Raymond. *Infernal Methods: A Study of William Blake's Art Techniques*. London: G. Bell & Son, 1975.
Locke, John. *Essay Concerning Human Understanding*. Ed. Peter H. Nidditch. The Clarendon Edition of the Works of John Locke. Oxford: Clarendon Press, 1975.
Lowes, John L. *The Road to Xanadu: A Study in the Ways of the Imagination*. 2nd (rev.) ed. London: Constable, 1951.
Lyon, Harvey T. *Keats' Well-Read Urn: An Introduction to Literary Method*. New York: Henry Holt & Co., 1959.

McConnell, Frank D. *The Confessional Imagination: A Reading of Wordsworth's 'Prelude'*. Baltimore and London: The Johns Hopkins University Press, 1974.
McFarland, Thomas. *Coleridge and the Pantheist Tradition*. Oxford: Clarendon Press, 1969.
Mack, Dorothy. 'Metaphoring as Speech Act: Some Happiness Conditions for Implicit Similes and Simple Metaphors'. *Poetics*, 4 no. 2–3 (1975), 221–56.
McKenzie, Gordon. *Critical Responsiveness: A Study of the Psychological Current in Later Eighteenth Century Criticism*. Berkeley and Los Angeles: University of California Press, 1949.
Marks, Mollyanne. 'Structure and Irony in Blake's "The Book of Urizen"'. *Studies in English Literature*, 15 (1975), 579–90.

Matthey, François. *The Evolution of Keats's Structural Imagery*. Bern: Francke Verlag, 1974.

Mellor, Anne Kostelanetz. *Blake's Human Form Divine*. Berkeley, Los Angeles, London: University of California Press, 1974.

Merleau-Ponty, Maurice. Ed. Claude Lefort. *The Prose of the World*. Trans. John O'Neill. London: Heinemann, 1974.

Metcalf, Francis Wood. 'Reason and "Urizen": The Pronunciation of Blakean Names'. *Blake Newsletter*, 21 (1972), 17–18.

Miller, Bruce E. 'Form and Substance in "Ode on a Grecian Urn"'. *Keats-Shelley Journal* 20 (1971), 62–70.

Mitchell, W. J. T. 'Poetic and Pictorial Imagination in Blake's "The Book of Urizen"'.*Eighteenth-Century Studies*, 3 (1969), 83–107.

——'Blake's Composite Art'. *Blake's Visionary Forms Dramatic*. Ed. David V. Erdman and John E. Grant. Princeton: Princeton University Press, 1970, pp. 57–81.

Monboddo, James Burnett, Lord. *Of the Origin and Progress of Language*. 6 vols. 1773–92; facsimile rpt. Menston: Scolar Press, 1967.

——*Ancient Metaphysics*. 6 vols. London, 1779–99.

Monk, Samuel H. *The Sublime: A Study of Critical Theories in Eighteenth Century England*. 1935; rpt. Ann Arbor: University of Michigan Press, 1960.

Muecke, Douglas C. *The Compass of Irony*. London: Methuen & Co., 1969.

——*Irony*. London: Methuen & Co., 1970.

Muirhead, J. H. 'How Hegel Came to England'. *Mind*, 36 (1927), 423–47.

Murray, Roger N. *Wordsworth's Style: Figures and Themes in the 'Lyrical Ballads' of 1800*. Lincoln, Neb.: University of Nebraska Press, 1967.

Nathan, Norman. *Prince William B.: The Philosophical Conceptions of William Blake*. The Hague and Paris: Mouton, 1975..

Nelson, J. Walter. 'Blake's Diction—An Amendatory Note'. *Blake Studies*, 7, ii (1974), 167–75.

Newsome, David. *Two Classes of Men: Platonism and English Romantic Thought*. London: Murray, 1974.

Novalis (Friedrich von Hardenberg). *Schriften*. Hrsg. R. Samuel and P. Kluckhohn. 4 vols. Leipzig, 1929.

Nurmi, Martin K. *William Blake*. London: Hutchinson & Co., 1975.

Page, Alex. 'Faculty Psychology and Metaphor in Eighteenth-Century Criticism'. *Modern Philology*, 66 (1968–9), 237–47.

Parker, Reeve, *Coleridge's Meditative Art*. Ithaca and London: Cornell University Press, 1975.

Parrish, Stephen Maxfield. *The Art of the 'Lyrical Ballads'*. Cambridge, Mass.: Harvard University Press, 1973.

Peacock, Thomas Love. *The Novels of Thomas Love Peacock*. Ed. David Garnett. London: Rupert Hart-Davis, 1948.

Perkins, David. *Wordsworth and the Poetry of Sincerity*. Cambridge, Mass.: Belknap Press, Harvard University Press, 1964.

Piper, H. W. *The Active Universe: Pantheism and the Concept of Imagination in the English Romantic Poets*. London: University of London, Athlone Press, 1962.

Pottle, F. A. 'Wordsworth in the Present Day'. *Romanticism: Vistas, Instances, Continuities*. Ed. Thorburn and Hartman, 1973, pp. 115–33.

Prang, Helmut. *Die Romantische Ironie*. Erträge der Forschung, Bd. 12. Wissenschaftliche Buchgesellschaft. Darmstadt, 1972.

Prickett, Stephen. *Coleridge and Wordsworth, The Poetry of Growth*. Cambridge: Cambridge University Press, 1970.

Priestley, Joseph. *A Course of Lectures on the Theory of Language and Universal Grammar*. 1762; facsimile rpt. Menston: Scolar Press, 1970.

Quine, W. V. O. *Ontological Relativity and Other Essays*. New York and London: Columbia University Press, 1969.

Ragussis, Michael. 'Narrative Structure and the Problem of the Divided Reader in "The Eve of St. Agnes"'. *ELH*, 42 (1975), 378–94.

Raine, Kathleen. *Blake and Tradition*. 2 vols. Bollingen Series. Princeton: Princeton University Press, 1968.

——Ed., with George Mills Harper. See Taylor, Thomas.

Reed, Mark. 'The Speaker of "The Prelude"'. *Bicentenary Wordsworth Studies*. Ed. J. Wordsworth, 1970, pp. 276–93.

Reid, Thomas. *The Works of Thomas Reid*. Ed. Sir William Hamilton. 6th ed. Edinburgh, 1863.

Reiman, Donald H. 'Editing Shelley'. *Editing Texts of the Romantic Period*. Ed. John D. Baird. Toronto: Hakkert, 1972, pp. 27–45.

Reynolds, Sir Joshua. *Seven Discourses*. 1778; facsimile rpt. Menston: Scolar Press, 1971.

Richards, I. A. *Coleridge on Imagination.* 3rd ed. London: Routledge & Kegan Paul, 1962.

Rickard, Peter. *Chrestomathie de la langue française au quinzième siècle.* Cambridge: Cambridge University Press, 1976.

Ricoeur, Paul. 'Metaphor and the Main Problem of Hermeneutics'. *New Literary History,* 6 (1974), 95–110.

Riffaterre, Michael. 'Interpretation and Descriptive Poetry: A Reading of Wordsworth's "Yew Trees"'. *New Literary History,* 4 (1973), 229–56.

Robinson, Dwight E. 'Ode on a "New Etrurian" Urn: A Reflection of Wedgwood Ware in the Poetic Imagery of John Keats'. *Keats-Shelley Journal,* 12 (1963), 11–35.

Rogers, Neville. *Shelley at Work: A Critical Enquiry.* 2nd ed. Oxford: Clarendon Press, 1967.
See also Shelley.

Rossiter, A. P. Ed. Graham Storey. *Angel With Horns: Fifteen Lectures on Shakespeare.* London: Longman Group, 1961.

Rousseau, J. J. *Émile.* Trans Barbara Foxley. 1911; rpt. London and New York: Dent and Dutton, 1974.

——'Essay on the Origin of Languages'. *Jean Jacques Rousseau, 'Essay on the Origin of Languages', Johann Gottfried Herder, 'Essay on the Origin of Languagae'* Trans. John H. Moran and Alexander Gode. New York: Frederick Ungar, 1966.

Salvesen, Christopher. *The Landscape of Memory: A Study of Wordsworth's Poetry.* London: Edward Arnold, 1965.

Schaerer, René. 'Le Mécanisme de l'Ironie dans ses Rapports avec le Dialectique'. *Revue de Métaphysique et de Morale,* 48 (1941), 181–209.

Schelling, F. W. J. von. *Of Human Freedom.* Trans. James Gutman. Chicago: Open Court, 1936.

——*Schellings Werke.* Münchner Jubiläumsausdruck. Hrsg. Manfred Schröter. 6 vols. and 6 supplementary vols. Munich: Beck & Oldenbourg, 1946–59.

——'Concerning the Relation of the Plastic Arts to Nature'. Trans. Michael Bullock. *The True Voice of Feeling: Studies in English Romantic Poetry.* Ed. Herbert Read. 1947; rpt. London: Faber & Faber, 1968, pp. 323–58.

Schiller, J. C. F. von. *Schillers Werke.* Nationalausgabe. Hrsg. L. Blumenthal and Benno von Wiese. Incomplete. Weimar: H. Bohlaus, 1943–

——'Naive and Sentimental Poetry' and 'On the Sublime'. Trans. Julius A. Elias. New York: Frederick Ungar, 1966.

——On the Aesthetic Education of Man. Trans. Elizabeth M. Wilkinson and L. A. Willoughby. Oxford: Clarendon Press, 1967.

Schlegel, A. W. A Course of Lectures on Dramatic Art and Literature. Trans. John Black. 2 vols. London, 1815.

——Kritische Schriften und Briefe. Hrsg. E. Lohner. 7 vols. Stuttgart etc.: W. Kohlhammer Verlag, 1962–74.

Schlegel, Friedrich. Kritische-Friedrich-Schlegel-Ausgabe. Hrsg. E. Behler, with J. J. Anstett and Hans Eichner. Incomplete. Munich, Paderborn, Vienna: F. Schöningh, 1958–

——Friedrich Schlegel's 'Lucinde' and the Fragments. Trans. Peter Firchow. Minneapolis: University of Minnesota Press, 1971.

Schneider, Elisabeth. Coleridge, Opium, and 'Kubla Khan'. Chicago: University of Chicago Press, 1953.

Schubert, G. H. von. Die Symbolik des Traumes. 1814; facsimile rpt. Heidelberg: Lambert Schneider, 1968.

Shaffer, Elinor S. 'Kubla Khan' and the Fall of Jerusalem. Cambridge: Cambridge University Press, 1975.

Shaftesbury, Anthony Ashley Cooper, 3rd Earl of. Characteristicks of Men, Manners, Opinions, Times. 3 vols. London, 1723.

Sharpe, Ella F. 'An Examination of Metaphor'. The Psycho-Analytic Reader. Ed. Robert Fliess. London: Hogarth Press, 1950, pp. 273–86.

Sheats, Paul D. The Making of Wordsworth's Poetry, 1785–1798. Cambridge, Mass.: Harvard University Press, 1973.

Shelley, Percy Bysshe. The Letters of Percy Bysshe Shelley. Ed. F. L. Jones. 2 vols. Oxford: Clarendon Press, 1964.

——The Complete Works of Shelley. Ed. Roger Ingpen and Walter E. Peck. 10 vols. 1926; rpt. New York and London: Gordian Press and Ernest Benn Ltd., 1965.

——Poetical Works. Ed. Thomas Hutchinson, corrected ed. G. M. Matthews. London, Oxford, New York: Oxford University Press, 1970.

——The Complete Poetical Works of Percy Bysshe Shelley. Ed. Neville Rogers. 2 vols. so far. Oxford: Clarendon Press, 1972–

Simpson, David E. 'Keats's Lady, Metaphor, and the Rhetoric of Neurosis'. Studies in Romanticism, 15 (1976), 265–88.

——'Putting One's House in Order: the Career of the Self in Descartes' Method'. New Literary History, 9 (1977), 83–101.

Sinclair, J. M. 'When is a Poem like a Sunset?' Ballad Studies. Ed. E. B.

Lyle. Publications of the Folklore Society. Cambridge and Totowa: D. S. Brewer Ltd and Rowman & Littlefield, 1976.

Smith, Adam. 'Considerations Concerning the First Formation of Languages'. Appended to *The Theory of Moral Sentiments*. 4th ed. London, 1774.

Smith, Barbara Herrnstein. *The Poetics of Closure: A Study of how Poems End*. Chicago and London: University of Chicago Press, 1968.

Solger, K. W. F. *Solgers Nachgelassene Schriften und Briefwechsel*. Hrsg. L. Tieck and F. von Raumer. 2 vols. Leipzig, 1826.

——*Vorlesungen Über Aesthetik*. Hrsg. K. W. L. Heyse. Leipzig, 1829.

——*Tieck and Solger: The Complete Correspondence*. Ed. Percy Matenko. New York and Berlin: B. Westermann, 1933.

——*Erwin*. Hrsg. W. Henckmann. München: W. Fink, 1971.

Southey, Robert. See Coleridge, *Omniana*.

Sperry, Stuart. *Keats the Poet*. Princeton: Princeton University Press, 1973.

Spitzer, Leo. 'The "Ode on a Grecian Urn", or Content vs. Metagrammar'. *Comparative Literature*, 7 (1955), 203–25.

Spurzheim, J. C. *Observations on the Deranged Manifestations of the Mind, or Insanity*. London, 1817.

Stevenson, Warren. *Divine Analogy: A Study of the Creation Motif in Blake and Coleridge*. Salzburg Studies in English Literature, Romantic Reassessment. Salzburg, 1972.

Stewart, Dugald. *The Collected Works of Dugald Stewart*. Ed. Sir William Hamilton. 11 vols. Edinburgh: Thomas Constable, 1854.

Stillinger, Jack. 'Who Says What to Whom at the end of "Ode on a Grecian Urn"'. *Twentieth Century Interpretation of Keat's Odes*. Ed. Jack Stillinger. Englewood Cliffs, N.J.: Prentice-Hall, 1968, pp. 113–14.

——*The Hoodwinking of Madeline, and Other Essays on Keats's Poems*. Urbana, Chicago, London: University of Illinois Press, 1971.

——*The Texts of Keats's Poems*. Cambridge, Mass.: Harvard University Press, 1974.

Strawson, P. F. *The Bounds of Sense*. London: Methuen, 1966.

Strohschneider-Kohrs, Ingrid. *Die Romantische Ironie im Theorie und Gestaltung*. Tübingen: Max Niemeyer, 1960.

Suther, Marshall. *Visions of Xanadu*. New York and London: Columbia University Press, 1965.

Swetman, Ford T. Jnr. 'The Satiric Voices of "The Prelude"'. *Bicentenary Wordsworth Studies.* Ed. J. Wordsworth, 1970, pp. 92—110.

Tannenbaum, Leslie. 'Blake's Art of Crypsis: "The Book of Urizen" and Genesis'. *Blake Studies,* 5, i (1972), 141—64.
Tarbet, David W. 'The Fabric of Metaphor in Kant's "Critique of Pure Reason"'. *Journal of the History of Philosophy,* 6 (1968), 257—70.
Tayler, Irene. 'Say First! What Mov'd Blake? Blake's "Comus" Designs and "Milton"'. *Blake's Sublime Allegory.* Ed. Curran and Wittreich, 1973, pp. 233—58.
Taylor, Charles H. Jnr. *The Early Collected Editions of Shelley's Poems: A Study in the History and Transmission of the Printed Text.* New Haven: Yale University Press, 1958.
Taylor, Thomas. *Thomas Taylor the Platonist: Selected Writings.* Ed. Kathleen Raine and George Mills Harper. London: Routledge & Kegan Paul, 1969.
Thalmann, Marianne. *The Literary Sign Language of German Romanticism.* Trans. Harold A. Basilius. Detroit: Wayne State University Press, 1972.
Thirlwall, Connop. 'On the Irony of Sophocles'. *The Philological Museum.* Vol. II. Cambridge, 1833, pp. 483—537.
Thomson, J. A. K. *Irony: An Historical Introduction.* London: George Allen & Unwin, 1926.
Thorburn, David. See Hartman.
Thurston, Norman. 'Author, Narrator, and Hero in Shelley's "Alastor"'. *Studies in Romanticism,* 14 (1975), 119—31.
Tieck, Ludwig. *Kritische Schriften.* 3 vols. Leipzig, 1848.
Tooke, John Horne. ΕΠΕΑ ΠΤΕΡΟΕΝΤΑ, *or the Diversions of Purley.* 2nd ed. 2 vols. 1798; facsimile rpt. Menston; Scolar Press, 1968.
Turbayne, Colin M. *The Myth of Metaphor.* Rev. ed. Columbia, S.C.: University of South Carolina Press, 1970.
Tuveson, Ernest Lee. *The Imagination as a Means of Grace: Locke and the Aesthetics of Romanticism.* Berkeley and Los Angeles: University of California Press, 1960.

Warburton, William. *Works.* 7 vols. London, 1788.
Warnock, Mary. *Imagination.* London: Faber & Faber, 1976.
Warren, Robert Penn. 'A Poem of Pure Imagination: An Experi-

ment in Reading'. *Selected Essays*. New York: Random House, 1958, pp. 198–305.

Wasserman, Earl R. *The Finer Tone: Keats' Major Poems*. 1953; rpt. Baltimore: The Johns Hopkins Press, 1967.

—— *The Subtler Language: Critical Readings of Neo-Classic and Romantic Poems*. Baltimore: The Johns Hopkins Press, 1959.

—— 'The English Romantics: The Grounds of Knowledge'. *Studies in Romanticism*, 4 (1964), 17–34.

—— *Shelley: A Critical Reading*. Baltimore and London: The Johns Hopkins Press, 1971.

Watson, George. *Coleridge the Poet*. London: Routledge & Kegan Paul, 1966.

Webb, Timothy. Review of Neville Rogers, *The Complete Poetical Works of Percy Bysshe Shelley*, Vol. II. *Times Literary Supplement*, no. 3867 (23 April 1976), p. 493.

Wellek, René. *Confrontations: Studies in the Intellectual and Literary Relations between Germany, England, and the United States in the Nineteenth Century*. Princeton: Princeton University Press, 1965.

Whalley, George. 'On Reading Coleridge'. *Writers and Their Background: S. T. Coleridge*. Ed. R. L. Brett. London: G. Bell & Sons, 1971, pp. 1–44.

Wheeler, Kathleen M. 'Sources, Processes and Methods of Coleridge's *Biographia Literaria*'. Diss. Univ. of Cambridge, in progress.

Wicksteed, Joseph H. *Blake's Innocence and Experience*. London, Toronto, and New York; Dent & Dutton, 1928.

Wigod, Jacob. 'Keats's Ideal in the "Ode on a Grecian Urn"'. *Twentieth Century Interpretations of Keats's Odes*. Ed. Stillinger, 1968, pp. 58–67.

Wilden, Anthony. *The Language of the Self*. 'The Function of Language in Psycho-analysis', by Jacques Lacan. Trans. A. Wilden. 1968; rpt. Baltimore and London: Johns Hopkins University Press, 1973.

—— *System and Structure: Essays in Communication and Exchange*. London: Tavistock Publications, 1972.

Wilkie, Brian. 'Blake's "Innocence and Experience", An Approach'. *Blake Studies*, 6, ii (1975), 119–37.

Wittreich, Joseph Anthony Jnr. See Curran.

Wlecke, Albert O. *Wordsworth and the Sublime*. Perspectives in Criticism, 23. Berkeley, Los Angeles, London: University of California Press, 1973.

Woodring, Carl. *Wordsworth*. Cambridge, Mass.: Harvard University Press, 1968.

Wordsworth, Jonathan. Ed. *Bicentenary Wordsworth Studies in Memory of John Alban Finch*. Ithaca and London: Cornell University Press, 1970.

Wordsworth, William. *The Poetical Works of William Wordsworth*. Ed. E. de Selincourt. 5 vols. Oxford: Clarendon Press, 1940–9.

——*The Prelude*. Ed. E. de Selincourt. 2nd ed. rev. Helen Darbishire. Oxford: Clarendon Press, 1959.

——*The Letters of William and Dorothy Wordsworth: The Early Years, 1787–1805*. Ed. E. de Selincourt. 2nd ed. rev. Chester L. Shaver. Oxford: Clarendon Press, 1967.

——*The Letters of William and Dorothy Wordsworth: The Middle Years, Part One*, Ed. E. de Selincourt. 2nd ed. rev. Mary Moorman. Oxford: Clarendon Press, 1969.

——*The Prose Works of William Wordsworth*. Ed. W. J. B. Owen and Jane W. Smyser. 3 vols. Oxford: Clarendon Press, 1974.

Wright, John W. *Shelley's Myth of Metaphor*. Athens, Ga.: University of Georgia Press, 1970.

——'Toward Recovering Blake's Relief-Etching Process'. *Blake Newsletter*, 26 (1974), 32–9.

——'Blake's Relief-Etching Method'. *Blake Newsletter*, 36 (1976), 94–114.

Yarlott, Geoffrey. *Coleridge and the Abyssinian Maid*. London: Methuen & Co., 1967.

Young, Calvin E. *A Critical Explication of Irony as a Thematic Structure*. Diss. Indiana, 1969. Ann Arbor: Univ. Microfilms, 1970. DA/70–7522.

Young, Edward. *The Poetical Works of Edward Young*. 2 vols. London: William Pickering, 1852.

Zillman, Lawrence John. *Shelley's 'Prometheus Unbound': A Variorum Edition*. Seattle: University of Washington Press, 1959.

Index